# Law Firm Strategies for the 21st Century

## Strategies for Success

Consulting Editor **Christoph H Vaagt**
on behalf of the International Bar Association

**Consulting editor**
Christoph H Vaagt on behalf of the International Bar Association

**Editorial Board**
Chair: Máximo Bomchil

David Barnes
Harvey Cohen
Nicolas Herrera
Armen Khatchaturyan
Rolandas Valiunas
Caroline Zang

Boris Boyanov
Charles Coward
Moira V Huggard-Caine
Christoph H Vaagt
Tomasz Wardyński

**Managing director**
Sian O'Neill

**Editorial services director**
Carolyn Boyle

**Production manager**
Paul Stoneham

**Group publishing director**
Tony Harriss

*Law Firm Strategies for the 21st Century: Strategies for Success*
**is published by**
Globe Law and Business
Globe Business Publishing Ltd
New Hibernia House
Winchester Walk
London SE1 9AG
United Kingdom
Tel +44 20 7234 0606
Fax +44 20 7234 0808
Web www.globelawandbusiness.com

Printed by CPI Antony Rowe Ltd

ISBN 9781909416161

*Law Firm Strategies for the 21st Century: Strategies for Success*
© 2013 Globe Business Publishing Ltd

DISCLAIMER
This publication is intended as a general guide only. The information and opinions which it contains are not intended to be a comprehensive study, nor to provide legal advice, and should not be treated as a substitute for legal advice concerning particular situations. Legal advice should always be sought before taking any action based on the information provided. The publishers bear no responsibility for any errors or omissions contained herein.

# Table of contents

# Introduction

**Máximo Bomchil**
M&M Bomchil
**Christoph H Vaagt**
Law Firm Change Consultants

---

1.    **Why this book?**
Currently, both scientific research and practice are increasingly aware of the need for law firms to address the changes the legal service market faces in most jurisdictions of the world. These changes make it imperative for law firms to think much more strategically than before if they want to preserve their place in the market and remain competitive.

The IBA Law Firm Management Committee, together with the publisher Globe Law and Business, have taken up the challenge to produce an overview of how these challenges can be met, and provide an intellectual framework for undertaking this process. We thus attempt to be both practical and theoretical, addressing some of the major issues when lawyers discuss 'strategy' in the context of their law firms.

2.    **Some general hypotheses on strategies in law firms**
From the outset, we would like to propose some general considerations about strategy work in law firms in order to provide the intellectual context for this discussion, and to which the discussion about strategy will occasionally revert.

- The primary task of a law firm is to provide its clients with legal advice or representation of the highest quality and ethical standards, for which it receives payment which must be sufficient both to stay profitable and to finance future growth.
- It is considered a duty of each lawyer, or at least of each partner as the case may be, to look at the entrepreneurial challenges facing him as this is the only way to secure the independence of his practice – which is a core value of the profession. Strategy is the starting point for these considerations which centre on the competitiveness of the firm. The larger a firm becomes, the more important it is that it is capable of ensuring that all risks are contained and that the strategic development of the firm is duly carried out.
- Strategy work for law firms centres on the same issues as in any other industry: how can the firm differentiate itself in the marketplace sufficiently in order to become a primary provider of services, allowing it to generate higher fees than its competitors? This includes assessing the offer, the service, the people, the organisation, the reputation and the ability of the marketing to communicate this difference.
- Ethical considerations are not alien, but central to the concept of developing a strategy for a law firm, since ethics provide a framework for high-quality advice. As value-based strategies are more successful than others, high ethical

standards are also likely to generate higher returns for firms.

- Strategies which strive only to increase bottom-line profits fail to address the complex challenges in service industries; but without appropriate economic considerations, law firms are likely to fail.
- Despite increasing costs in the market, any strategy must aim for economic growth, whether qualitative or quantitative. In addition, growing firms are more attractive to young lawyers
- In contrast to other industries, strategy work in law firms is much more a process of consensus-building, than a case of implementing a top-down rational decision. Participation, of the partners in particular, is paramount for law firms. In this respect, providing for all issues to be negotiated by relevant stakeholders is much more important than finding the 'right' decision.
- For a long time, strategy in law firms has been an implicit process, in which the financial success of the firm has been regarded as the hallmark of a successful strategy. Under this approach, the idea of a 'planned' strategy is implicitly rejected. At best, there is a consensus among partners regarding what kind of clients and work the firm should not accept.
- Strategic decisions are therefore much more the result of a learning process from day to day producing incremental developments, rather than bold initial strategies. Such decisions can be made more effective by ongoing reflection and discussion. Radical changes, including mergers, often fail to produce the results for which they were undertaken.
- This consensus-building process is guided by group dynamics and characterised by perception and positioning, as well as a political process of negotiating the interests of all present.
- Strategy work in law firms will be successful in so far as the partners are able to negotiate diverging minority interests in a respectful manner.
- Law firms with a pure lockstep profit-sharing agreement are more likely to discuss and execute strategies than firms with merit-based profit-sharing agreements, as there is an inherent need to discuss strategic questions due to the high degree of profit being shared among partners in the former.
- Today's successful law firms are those which have the right processes in place and which have, more or less consciously, made strong strategic decisions in the past which are delivering good results now.
- As most law firms operate on the same business model (bespoke services for clients) and organisational archetype (professional partnership), the most important differentiator among law firms is the culture of collaboration which they foster (ie, the way the partners work together and produce success). This culture is, to a certain extent, induced by the profit-sharing system in place. Working on these cultural issues is therefore critical to the processes underlying a strategy.
- Strategy in a full service firm is much more difficult than for a specialist law firm, in the same way that in conglomerates, strategies for certain divisions or practice groups will be more useful than for others. Strategy for the whole firm may be limited to maintaining a clear brand and profitability targets.

- Quite often, discussion of 'strategy' in law firms is a substitute for discussion on issues which are difficult to address, such as clarifying corporate identity, resolving economic differences that the profit-sharing agreement fails to bridge, or other sources of conflict among partners. In this sense, if it is to be meaningful, discussion of strategy must also address any underlying sources of conflict within the firm.

## 3. Structure of the contributions

This book is divided into three parts:

Part I: General considerations and trends

Part II: The resources of a law firm and their impact on strategy

Part III: The market side of law firm strategy.

The book, therefore, follows the resource-based view of strategy as taken up by social research into the strategy of professional service firms, of which law firms are part. This structure addresses all the dimensions which form part of a law firm's strategic ability, and thus contribute directly to its competitiveness. We have, however, enlarged this view in three areas:

- the underlying business model, as this is the framework within which law firms operate and which constitutes a barrier to the strategies available to them;
- the profit-sharing agreement, as this provides the incentives for internal cooperation, of primary importance when it comes to learning from client matters;
- the culture, this being an enabler for cooperation and the most distinctive feature when comparing law firms in the same strategic group.

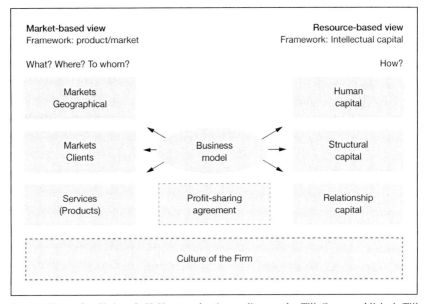

*Source: Picture by Christoph H Vaagt, adapting a diagram by Till Grewe published: Till Grewe, Professional Service Firms in einer globalisierten Welt, Gabler Verlag 2008, p. 53*

Unlike most discussions about strategy, here we focus first on the resource side, since this is usually overlooked by lawyers.

In Part I, Bente Løwendahl takes a look at the definition of law firm strategy from an academic point of view. It is noteworthy that she takes a completely different approach to strategic thinking from most academics and consultants. She sees strategic development as a learning process where professionals learn from each client assignment and thus define the strategy of the firm by the client intake process.

Tomasz Wardyński makes the case that law firms' business is framed by ethical considerations. It is well known in economic science that value-based strategies pay off and thus enable firms to outperform competition. It is therefore not merely an ethical imperative, but an economic one, too. At the same time, it is ethics which constitute the unique selling point of the profession as compared to other less regulated industries, such as chartered accountants, consultants and the like who may also provide legal advice in some form.

Peter Kurer illustrates the contextual difference between corporate strategy and law firm strategy based on his experience in law firms, in-house and as a CEO of several banks.

We also look at the general trends shaping the industry, as illustrated by Miriam Hermann and David Barnard who choose the US market by way of example. Their analysis can easily be adapted to other legal markets which are, nowadays, characterised by the same segmented, buyer-dominated market.

Mats Anderson shares his insights into the changes faced by the law firms for which he has worked during the last 20 years. He has also had experience working as a consultant to others, so he has a broad overview of the challenges law firms face in a more competitive market. He explores the factors he has found to be particularly important during periods of change, namely leadership and finance.

Whether law firms can ignore this discussion and simply 'continue their ways' is called into question by Paul Lippe and Richard Given. They point to assumptions typically made by lawyers which may pose an obstacle when looking at the future of legal services.

Part II of the book analyses the resources side. It is by looking at the human resources, systems, structures and procedures in an organisation that a law firm is able to deliver what clients are looking for. The market in law firms is more often than not the result of an opportunistic process of following clients, rather than an explicit strategic choice made by the owners at the formation of the firm. Dina Gracheva explains why the resource side of law firms is so important, and why this should be made an issue when discussing strategy.

Legal practice is a business serviced by people and staff. The quality of advice depends on the ability of the associates hired, and the manner in which communication and interaction among them is organised. As such, the HR dimension of a firm is crucial.

Jaime Fernandez Madero explores ways in which law firms may develop their business models into a structure better adapted to the current changes occurring in the market, thereby increasingly differentiating lawyers' career paths to find flexible ways to respond to the expectations of a new generation of lawyers.

Peter Oberlechner looks into one of the trickiest issues of law firm management, namely that of performance review for partners. He examines the 'balanced scorecard' system which some firms have recently adopted, and explores the different dimensions of partner contributions and partner remuneration.

Law firms need to monitor their finances at every step. As profit margins come under pressure, financial control becomes a top priority for law firm management. Without key performance indicators and constant supervision of trends, law firms may easily run into difficulties. With new competition from LPOs, continuous in-sourcing of law departments, and new procurement procedures for legal services, law firms need to address this long-neglected area. Ashley Balls looks into this field and specifies the requirements for law firms to survive in a new environment, which some call 'the new normal'.

The literature does not discuss the role of the managing partner in detail, except to highlight the need for firm 'leadership'. This concept, however, is little explored. However, the way a partner who has been elected to this post assumes his roles and responsibilities is crucial for the development of the firm. This is particularly the case for larger firms. The role of the partner elected to this position is a mix between that of a politician, a manager, a hero and an internal consultant, and therefore presents many challenges. Patrick McKenna tackles this area, drawing on his vast experience as a boardroom consultant for law firms.

Reputations and relationships are the two pillars relied upon by most professionals. Many pretend that this is the product of 'good work'. In their chapter, Michael Smets, Tim Morris and William Harvey explain what research tells us about the relationship between reputation and quality, and reveal some surprising results. They outline the definitions of the concept of reputation and show how they derive from different disciplines. They also discuss how definitions are interrelated in the management literature. Reputation is closely linked to an organisation's perceived capacity to produce high-quality goods or services. Yet often quality is difficult to define and measure, particularly in the context of professional service firms. Smets, Morris and Harvey consider the implications of the relationship between quality and reputation, drawing on research conducted among a variety of professional service firms including law and management consulting.

Philip Rodney, a managing partner and noted IP lawyer who has recently managed a merger in Scotland, looks at the issue of reputation. He explores reputation from a practical point of view and demonstrates what is necessary to keep this issue high on the agenda.

Rob Millard looks at structural aspects in the management of the strategic development processes of law firms. He describes how the role of a 'chief strategy officer' (CSO) can help the management of a law firm to stay ahead of all the initiatives on which law firms of a certain level of complexity need to focus.

In Part III, we look at the market-oriented strategies available to law firms.

The very first issue for a law firm to decide is whether it wants to serve its clients only in one jurisdiction, or in more than one. The cross-border needs of certain clients no doubt exist, but it is a major step to establish offices in other countries. Several hurdles stand in the way and firms have suffered as a result of premature attempts to establish themselves abroad. In the course of his professional work, Robert Bata has opened several offices for law firms, and here explains the major pitfalls facing firms setting up overseas.

If a firm is considering merging with another firm in order to improve its competitive position, then the lessons set out in Lisa Smith's chapter will be of interest, as she has advised law firms on this issue for 20 years. Here she advises how not to merge.

The pricing of legal services has become ever more difficult, given the introduction of procurement processes inside client organisations. Such processes also cover legal services, and Silvia Hodges Silverstein provides an overview of how firms can manage these new challenges.

Leigh Dance looks at the individual and organisational capabilities necessary to establish a proper business process approach in the firm, based on her experience of working with both general counsels and law firms.

Firms have typically emphasised to clients that discrete legal issues are equally important, however minor they may be. In this way, firms have been able to bargain for high fees from clients by pointing to work produced, irrespective of the legal difficulty involved in the brief. Nowadays, clients have begun to question the value of an instruction and whether it is truly worth having a lawyer look at all questions. Clients are increasingly negotiating smaller fees for instructions, knowing that there are a range of alternative service providers to do the work. Given this, most law firms need to revise their business offerings and focus on providing services which represent value for money for their clients. This issue is explored by Mark Jones, who is one of the longest-serving managing partners in the United Kingdom and who thus has first-hand experience of this kind of change in the industry. In addition, he explains some of the solutions employed in his own firm.

If you are a law firm partner, you may want to review your strategy. Further to the information provided by our contributors, it will be useful to ask each of the following questions:

- How are we currently approaching these issues?
- Where do I see the biggest differences between what the authors are saying and our practice today?
- What would be a robust first step to changing direction?

We hope this book serves its purpose, namely to help partners of law firms understand the challenges their firms confront and to start a process which may address these to the benefit of each member of the firm and of the legal community at large.

*We would like to thank the authors for their valuable contributions: Máximo Bomchil, Chairman of the Board of Editors, Christoph H Vaagt, Consulting Editor On behalf of the Board of Editors, Buenos Aires and Munich, June 2013*

# Strategy in law firms: what it is and why we should care

Bente R Løwendahl
BI Norwegian Business School

## 1. Introduction

Traditionally, in professional service firms (PSFs) in general, and law firms in particular, strategy has (at best) been implicit in the decisions made by executives (typically partners). Since clients and projects come in unpredictable streams and it is very difficult to know ex ante which of these clients and assignments are likely to be won by our firm, strategy – traditionally seen as formal planning – has often been regarded as impossible for PSFs. In addition to the fluctuating and unpredictable nature of the demand for professional services, most such firms, at least up to a certain size, have traditionally been internally owned, typically in some sort of partnership form. An interesting and not so frequently discussed characteristic of partnerships is that they typically require consensus for any major strategic decision to be made. In many partnerships it is unheard of that some partners (ie, the majority) should make decisions on behalf of the whole collegium, against the will of other partners (ie, the minority). In small firms, this dilemma typically takes one of two possible forms:

- The firm remains fragmented, with each partner taking care of his own practice within the firm, acquiring clients and hiring apprentices according to his local needs. The firm may have common policies, but sanctions reinforcing such policies are unusual, as such sanctions would require the other partners to bring a conflict out into the open, and partners who are already busy with their own portfolio are normally very reluctant to 'rock the boat'.
- The firm remains small, growth (if any) is slow, and the partners pay particular attention to attracting, retaining, and promoting new partners that share the common set of goals and values, such that consensus can more or less be taken for granted. In such firms, client acquisition is based on consensus, and recruiting is a highly prioritised process of very careful selection of people who 'fit in'.

In another chapter in this book (Smets, Morris and Harvey), the importance of building and maintaining a reputation is highlighted. I would argue that partnerships of the type discussed in the second bullet above may relatively easily develop a consistent reputation over time, whereas partnerships of the type under the first bullet are more likely to suffer from a fragmented reputation, where the different aspects of the reputation are highly dependent on the decisions, actions, and reputations of each individual partner or practice manager. As I will argue further in this chapter, strategy is crucial to linking individual partner decisions and developing a consistent reputation over time, both in the client markets and in the markets for legal expertise (new hires). As pointed out by Maister (D Maister (1982) "Balancing the Professional Service Firm", *Sloan Management Review*, 24(1): 15–29), client acquisition and hiring are two sides of the same coin; if you have the best lawyers (in a given area of law), you are also likely to attract the most challenging client assignments. And if you have the most interesting set of client assignments, you are likely to be able to choose among the very best candidates in hiring new professionals into the firm. In this sense, client acquisition (and retention) and hiring (and promotion and retention) are like the chicken and the egg-problem – after the firm has been founded, typically by a few senior lawyers with a particular expertise, reputation, and relationships with (potential) clients, it is hard to know which dimension comes first and which drives the further growth of the firm.

In traditional PSFs, it has been a common view that strategy is 'redundant'. If only you have the right experts and the appropriate list of references to previously successful business with high-prestige clients, an excellent reputation will follow, and clients will more or less queue up at your door. In the past, marketing was paradoxically seen as negative and bad for reputation (see eg RE Sibson (1971) "Managing Professional Services Enterprises – The Neglected Business Frontier", New York, NY: Pitman) – comments were often along the lines of: 'they must be short of business, since they have to advertise for new clients'. An innocent and highly illustrative incident happened to a small IT-consulting partnership in Norway, when they decided to advertise for new partners. They placed an advertisement in Norway's biggest newspaper, in the business section, but the newspaper made a mistake and put the advertisement in a hardly visible spot elsewhere in the paper. They were highly apologetic, and without asking the partners of the consulting firm, they decided to re-run the advertisement the next day, on the front page of the newspaper. Little did they know that compensating their customer through such an expensive spot would be highly negative; the IT partnership received a lot of sceptical comments from colleagues and competitors ('are you desperate for business, since you run such an expensive advertisement?'), as well as clients ('how much profit are you really making on my assignment, when you can afford that kind of advertisement?') (BR Løwendahl (2005) *Strategic Management of Professional Service Firms*, 3rd Edition, Copenhagen: Copenhagen Business School Press, page 78).

Yet telling potential clients that the firm has unique expertise and is doing well in particular practice areas is also important to maintaining a sustainable business, as running short of sufficient 'billable hours' may be a disaster for the firm. It is not just that idle professionals turn from a revenue-generating 'asset' into a cost-generating 'liability'; another danger is, as noted by Johan Sagen, founder and previous CEO of the IKO-group (an Oslo-based management consulting firm, later merged into Cap Gemini):

*"With three or more experts idle in the office for more than a couple of days in a row, you always run the risk of the experts figuring out something else to do with their time. And that 'something' is unlikely to fit well with your own firm's strategic direction! Worst case, you not only get a 'spin-off'. you get a new competitor in the market, who also knows your own business from the inside!"* (See BR Løwendahl (1992) "Global Strategies for Professional Business Service Firms", Unpublished PhD

Dissertation, Philadelphia: University of Pennsylvania (Wharton); BR Løwendahl (2005) *Strategic Management of Professional Service Firms*, 3rd Edition, Copenhagen: Copenhagen Business School Press for an explanation).

Hence, it is important to know what your strategy is, both for client acquisition and retention and to know what professionals to recruit and retain.

## 2.  Value creation in PSFs

As stated above, strategy was often rejected in traditional partnership firms, in the same way as marketing was thought to be unnecessary or even negative. Instead, firms typically advertise promotion of new partners and make large ads for new hires, as this implicitly signals growth and success? The extent to which such hires and promotions are strategic in nature, however, is more questionable.

Strategy in a PSF is not, and cannot be, about planning. As Peter Lorange, professor and former president of IMD in Switzerland, has pointed out in many of his speeches and texts, "Strategy means choice", and choice means not only what to do in the short term or long term, but also what not to do (see Løwendahl, 1992; 2005). If a firm is to achieve consistency over time and thereby build a strong favourable reputation, it needs not only to provide consistently high quality in whatever it delivers; it also needs to have a clear focus in terms of what it does and does not do for and with its clients. Elsewhere I have also argued (T Skjølsvik, BR Løwendahl, R Kvålshaugen, S and Fosstenløkken (2007), "Learning to Choose and Choosing to Learn – Strategies for Client Co-production and Knowledge Development", *California Management Review*, 49(3): 110–28) that PSFs need to have a conscious strategy of target clients and projects in order to maximise potential learning, thereby enhancing the resource base of the firm (see eg Gracheva, in this volume or Løwendahl, 2005 for more elaboration on this). And an improved resource base will again increase the firm's probability of winning the most interesting (and potentially profitable) client assignments in the next period of time.

Lorange and Løwendahl (in Løwendahl, 2005; Figure 3, pages 46 to 47) described this as a three-step value-creation process for PSFs:

- You need to sell a 'credible promise' (ie, convince the client that you are the right firm to solve whatever problem the client might have). Here, reputation clearly plays an important part, and may both enhance and limit the opportunities the firm has in a given market niche. In other words, firms are both supported and hindered by their past performance, as potential clients often check on reputations 'through the grapevine'. It may be very difficult to convince a new client that you are able to solve a particular legal problem that the firm has never faced before, unless the firm has been able to recruit a new senior lawyer with an established reputation in that particular area. Well-established clients who know the firm well, may be more willing to 'experiment' with new service areas, but then frequently at a discounted price and an unusually low leverage (of juniors to seniors) on the project, thereby making such service area expansions expensive (but perhaps still profitable) investments.
- You need to deliver what you promised. That means not only delivering

according to contract (whether formal or 'by handshake'), but managing expectations, managing the interaction with the client's representatives, and delivering on time and on budget (or ideally below budget for within-firm costing purposes). This sounds like the easy part of value creation, but is really at the core of what the law firm is all about. An ability to define, manage and staff client assignments in the most effective (quality assuring) and efficient (cost-minimising) way is crucial to the firm's long-term success, in terms of both profits and reputation. Just as strategy cannot mean plan, the organisation of value creation cannot mean stable and strict formal structure. But somehow the staffing of the assignment needs to be managed for the benefit of both the professionals and the clients, and what we show in our 2007 article (Skjølsvik, *et al*) is that not only should firms manage each assignment as it has been won, but they should also manage the overall portfolio of projects, both for short-term efficiency and effectiveness and for long-term learning and reputational effects that reinforce the position of the firm and help it win the 'most desired' assignments in the next round of competition. The most successful firms succeed at becoming the 'preferred supplier of legal advice' for a given set of clients in a chosen set of legal services, thereby in some sense being able to avoid head-on competition for a number of important assignments. In the 'good old days', such a position was thought to come more or less automatically, if only you had the right people and provided excellent guidance. I would argue that this is less and less true, as clients become more and more sophisticated in their purchasing processes, even for professional services such as legal advice (eg, T Skjølsvik (2012) "Beyond the Trusted Advisor – The Impact of Client–Professional Relationships on the Client's Selection of Professional Service Firms", PhD Dissertation, Oslo: BI Norwegian Business School).

• The third process pointed out by Lorange and Lowendahl (in Løwendahl, 2005), and which I would argue still is under-focused in many PSFs, perhaps particularly in internally owned or partnership firms, is 'learning from the delivery'. All firms have some kind of archival system that allows them to go back to previous cases and build on previous solutions in their legal practice, and most have some kind of electronically based retrieval system which makes it easier for everyone to access previous cases independently of time and place. The quality of such archival systems, however, varies substantially, and the firm typically needs to have very clear incentives in place in order to get very busy lawyers to commit some of today's potentially billable hours to entering previous experience into an archive for further reference. Or the firm may allow juniors to participate on assignments on a non-billable basis, in order to learn from seniors. In the author's experience, most firms, regardless of PSF-industry, struggle with this problem of knowledge retention and transfer, especially in times when business cycles are at their peak. Paradoxically, it is when you have time to take care of archives and knowledge transfer, that you most need access to this information firm-wide, in order to make new sales efforts as target focused as possible.

## 3. What is strategy?

If strategy is not plan, what is it? As mentioned above, the core of strategy is choice. It is choosing what to do, which assignments we should give the highest priority now, what we are not going to do, and what should be our primary targets in the medium to long term. In our model 'The VCPs for PSFs-framework' (BR Løwendahl, Ø Revang, and SM Fosstenløkken (2001) "Knowledge and Value Creation in Professional Service Firms: A Framework for Analysis", *Human Relations*, 54(7): 911–31), we described the value-creating processes (VCPs) by the illustration of 'three bubbles and six arrows', as shown in Figure 1.

**Figure 1: Value creation processes in PSFs**

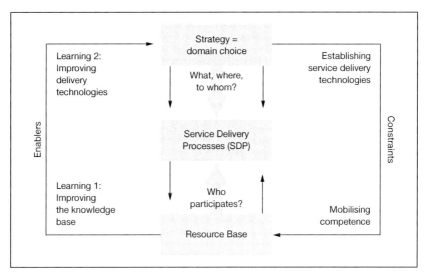

Strategy is the top bubble in Figure 1, and here we define strategy as the same as 'choice of domain', which is a concept from sociology in the early 1960s (Levine and White, 1961). The choice of domain simply means: the choice of what to deliver (ie, the range of services); to whom (ie, the set of (target) clients served); and, if applicable, where (locally, from one office, from multiple offices, nationally, regionally (eg, the European Union), globally, etc?). This may sound simple but in practice often turns out to be difficult, because choosing what to do also implies choosing what not to do; choosing which clients to serve also means choosing what (types of) clients not to serve. And choosing future target practice areas inevitably also means that some seniors will not see their 'pet projects' on the priority list. Again, ownership models requiring consensus on strategic priorities are likely to lead to more difficulty when making such decisions, not less.

Whereas it may be easy to commit to servicing a new client in a new niche, it may be very much more difficult to get consensus on turning down an interesting assignment, or even worse, terminating a long-term relationship with a client that no longer fits within the strategic portfolio of the firm. And if one particular partner has a strong relationship with such a client, substantial resistance is likely to result.

The second bubble of the figure obviously represents the 'how', and is equally important for both profits, quality, and learning/process development. It is not, however, as strategic in nature as the other two bubbles. The bottom bubble represents the resources of the firm, and although these may include both tangible resources (finances, office equipment, etc) and other intangible resources (reputation, client relationships, etc; also called relational resources in the author's book (Løwendahl, 2005)), it is obvious that the most important resources to a PSF in general and a law firm in particular, are its competences – individual as well as collective. Since individuals, especially senior professionals and experts, have not only competences but also strong opinions as to how their own resources may best be deployed, for the benefit of the clients, themselves, and the firm (typically in that order), we have drawn the two strong outer arrows in the above figure. The left-hand arrow, from resources to domain choice, indicates that the stronger your resource base and the more specialised competences you have, the more freedom you have in choosing your strategic domain. It is not, however, a question of some top management deciding on the domain, then ordering the resources into ranks and allocating them to wherever management might see fit. One good reason why so many PSFs in general and law firms in particular are internally owned is precisely that the best professionals do not take orders about domain choices. They want to be listened to and respected in these decisions, and if they fundamentally disagree and they do not expect conditions to improve in the near future, they are likely to leave for a competitor or set up their own business instead. Hence, in many ways the resource base sets the premises for what domain choices are possible (and desirable) to make. The right-hand out arrow has to do with the processes described above as 'selling a credible promise'. As pointed out by Smets, Morris, and Harvey elsewhere in this book, the reputation of the firm rests fundamentally on the perceptions and evaluations of external stakeholders, and these may represent a fundamental constraint on what the PSF is allowed to do, what kind of assignments it is likely to be allowed to undertake and for which clients.

The shorter arrows in the figure pertain to learning processes, and are therefore more operational in nature. The right-hand arrows indicate that the domain choice (ie, the strategic priorities), informs and sometimes largely dictates the composition of the assignment teams and how they work together for and with the clients (the 'technology'). At the same time, the professionals have to be motivated or rather 'mobilised' to put their best effort into this particular client assignment. One important element of the delivery technology of a law firm is how the assignment team is composed and leveraged, in terms of how many senior partners are involved, how they work together, how many juniors are involved and at what stages of the process, etc. Many firms with relatively specialised practice areas have 'templates' that can be put into action very quickly, given a particular type of assignment (eg, should the firm be called in as part of a due diligence team ahead of a potential merger). This organisational template is what we call 'technology' here, in line with traditional organisational theory, and we argue that many PSFs could improve on both quality (effectiveness) and cost (efficiency) by further refining and enhancing such technology, not in terms of rigid structures, but rather in terms of a set of best practices that can be mobilised when the appropriate situation emerges.

The left-hand arrows indicate that learning takes place both within the resource bubble, as individuals learn and collective experience is accumulated, and as resources are combined into task forces or assignment teams for each particular client assignment. Our research has shown (eg, SM Fosstenløkken (2007) "Enhancing Intangible Resources in Professional Service Firms", PhD Dissertation, Oslo: Norwegian School of Management BI (Currently Norwegian Business School)) that the most important competence development factor in PSFs, regardless of industry, is the nature of the assignments undertaken and the role each individual is allowed to play in each assignment. Professionals learn from each other; from the clients; from working on the assignment itself; from working with the 'technology' of the assignment (especially for larger projects) from external sources when information needs to be collected or advice sought, (for example, from a senior professor in that particular legal practice area) and so on (see eg, SM Fosstenløkken, BR Løwendahl and Ø Revang (2003) "Knowledge Development through Client Interaction: A Comparative Study", Organization Studies, 24(6): 859–79 for an elaboration of these learning processes).

## 4.    Strategy in PSFs – an oxymoron?

Is it really possible to develop strategy for a PSF? Is it not always the client who decides what firm to work with, so that the PSF needs to be alert and flexible in order to respond to whatever needs the client might have? From the above discussion it should be clear that the author's view is that strategy is important for PSFs, and maybe even more important than it is for manufacturing firms. The typical (or rather caricatured) manufacturing firm has a set of production machinery and processes that are relatively fixed investments, and will typically strive to maintain and increase its market share based on these already well-established practices. Major strategic investments, especially those leading to diversification, are typically scrutinised in detail before the investment is made. The owners, via the board of directors, are typically involved when investments are of a large magnitude or represent a significant shift from past practices. As discussed above, PSFs very often have internal owners, and these owners – whether partners or not – are typically directly involved, not only in large and long-term financial investments of a strategic nature, but also in the everyday running of the firm. As a result, it may be very difficult to distinguish between an operational and a strategic decision, and this distinction becomes even more blurred if the strategy is not agreed upon by all key decision makers. A strategy, in terms of common goals and priorities, is crucial in order to secure consistency over time; and the more decentralised the decision making and the more autonomy individual partners have, the more important strategy is. This does not mean that every PSF should have a formal strategy document, detailing what, where, when, and with whom the firm should work in the future. Here, even more than in the manufacturing firm, it is the process of coming to an agreement on strategic priorities that is of importance, not the resulting document.

The examples illustrated at the beginning of this chapter talked about the consensus-based, typically small partnership, and the fragmented one. Both of these exist in real life, in all PSF-industries, and further discussion of these will follow in the next section. In addition, there are some large, international firms, that increasingly come to resemble the structures of traditional manufacturing firms (eg, R Greenwood, and R Empson (2003) "The Professional Partnership: Relic or Exemplary Form of Governance?", *Organization Studies*, 24(6): 909–33, 2003; L Empson (2007) *Managing the Modern Law Firm*, Oxford: Oxford University Press). They have a formal hierarchy of authority, defined roles and boundaries between practice areas, clear employment contracts and training and promotion programmes, practice development departments and so on. Some of these also have external owners, who may impose further formal structures and reporting procedures on management, in order to control the return on their (capital) investment. The author's book (Løwendahl, 2005), further describes the challenges faced by these firms. They can grow very large and become global, but they need a substantial set of rules and regulations and formal procedures in order to ensure that every professional, junior as well as senior, performs up to standard and in the best interest of the owners. There is a vast literature on the challenges involved, for example in the area of what is called 'agency theory' (see eg EM Eisenhardt (1989) "Agency Theory: An Assessment and Review", *Academy of Management Review*, 14(1): 57–74, for an overview), but these issues are beyond the scope of this chapter. Without having studied any such law firms in depth, however, the author would expect their strategy work to be highly professionalised, with dedicated staff at the corporate office assessing opportunities for future development, and threats from competitors and stakeholders on a regular basis. Given the formal hierarchy of authority, one might also expect most of the problems of consensus and resistance to top management decisions to be overcome by the natural subordination to common goals set by the owners. That is not to say that such large firms do not have conflicts, especially where financial and professional goals are seen to clash. Conflicts are likely to be substantial, as professional norms of conduct require that the professional puts the client's best interests first (eg, JA Raelin (1991) "The Clash of Cultures: Managers Managing Professionals", Cambridge, Mass: Harvard Business School Press).

In the two types of firms described at the beginning of this chapter, strategy work may be less obvious. In the fragmented type of firm described under the first bullet point in section 1 above, every partner is likely to have his own opinions as to the priority of target clients and assignments, and the two major challenges for such firms will be:

- to achieve the necessary consistency in order to develop a common firm reputation; and
- a very strong tendency towards a myopic focus on current clients and assignments over what may be better for both learning and profits in the long run.

In the most extreme cases, one may ask why these partners have decided to establish a common firm at all, if they are not willing to give up any of their personal autonomy in order to achieve some common goals. And again, the partnership model often exacerbates these problems, especially in small firms, as every common investment, including non-billable hours to manage the common portfolio, is seen to 'come out of each partner's own pockets'. A major paradox in this respect is the fact that in order to gain the necessary respect and legitimate authority to make decisions on behalf of such a fragmented firm, it needs a very strong managing partner, who will also typically be one of the best 'rainmakers' and client advisors of the firm. And the non-billable hours of such partners are the most expensive for both the firm and the managing partner to sustain. As a result, such managing partners typically only manage part-time, and after all client matters have been dealt with. Again, in times of peak demand, setting strategic priorities will be under-prioritised, despite the fact that it is in good times that the firm can easily afford to set aside time and money for longer term investments.

The firms described in the second bullet in section 1 above traditionally operate under an implicit assumption of consensus, and as long as these areas of expertise fit well with client demand, strategy may also be implicit, yet still result in consistency in decisions and actions over time. A major issue for such firms is often how to deal with behaviours that do not conform to the implicit consensus. What should be the sanctions in such circumstances? Who monitors the work of others? What are the consequences of setting personal priorities above those of the common good of the firm? Challenges also typically arise if this firm decides to grow large and incorporate multiple practice areas, and/or if the firm decides to set up offices in multiple geographical locations. In one of the firms studied in the author's early work on PSFs, the firm ended up having more than ten 'divisions' or practice areas, and conflicts soon developed as the practice areas had different activity and profitability levels, and sometimes demand from a client would overlap several business areas, thereby leading to conflicts over billing rates and the distribution of profits. Similarly, conflicts may arise as some practice areas are more likely to require the work of many juniors, thereby resulting in high leverage and a high profit potential, relative to other practice areas where clients prefer to deal with one or two senior partners directly. On the other hand, a large number of juniors means higher fixed costs, and in times when demand is low, partners in other practice areas may be reluctant to finance the non-billable hours of juniors in other practice areas. Again, there is always the danger of the best professionals seeking to take their expertise, reputation, and client relationships elsewhere if they do not feel that their firm adequately compensates them for their efforts.

In all firms, regardless of size and agreement on common goals, the most difficult challenge seems to be to turn down interesting business from attractive clients. Yet it is impossible to develop a consistent strategy, and thereby a strong reputation, without agreeing on and sticking to a clear focus over time.

## 5.    Why strategy is so difficult in PSFs

In addition to the above-mentioned challenges to strategy work, most PSFs face particular challenges in management as a result of their very nature as professional firms – or firms run by professionals, if you will. Most professionals are trained in a particular profession, and they are members of a professional organisation with clear rules and regulations for professional and ethical conduct. The best professionals typically thrive on challenging professional problems, and most of them dislike spending their time on non-billable managerial work. Unfortunately, most firms also struggle to compensate managerial work, not only financially, but even more so in terms of status, respect, and professional development. Many firms therefore prefer some kind of part-time management, either as the managing partner also takes on client work, or as the managing partner role rotates among the senior partners. In both cases, managers reluctantly take on managerial work, and this is work that they have not been trained for. As one of the engineering firm managers in one of the author's early studies put it: 'we have engineers that are jewels in the crown in engineering projects, but they are basket cases in management'. In some cases, firms even run into what one of the author's colleagues termed 'the hostess's dishwashing problem'; if you are asked to assist in washing the dishes, and break one of the most expensive cups or dishes every time, you will soon be taken off dish-washing duty … In other words, there are some perverse incentives here to perform management tasks poorly, in order to make sure you stay as short a time as possible in that unwanted position. The result, in many cases, is that not only does strategy and consistent performance suffer – typically the development of juniors becomes ad hoc, unfocused, and dependent on the goodwill of each individual partner or practice manager taking charge of the training of juniors and keeping them 'billable' and busy with challenging assignments at all times. Again, partners who focus only on their own billable hours and relationships with clients may retain more of the profits, and therefore resist taking on juniors as long as the clients and the market allow them to do so (D Maister (2006a) Strategy Means Saying "No". http://davidmaister.com/articles/4/95/1/).

## 6. Conclusions

Strategy is critically important to PSFs in general and to law firms in particular – perhaps even more so than for manufacturing firms. Its importance has increased over recent decades, and is likely to continue increasing, as both clients and professionals become more sophisticated in choosing the best firm with which to collaborate. Hiring professionals and acquiring client assignments are crucial for the development of a PSF. These two key processes represent a chicken-and-egg problem, in that hiring and retaining the best professionals is a prerequisite for winning the most challenging and interesting (and profitable?) assignments; and winning the most prestigious client assignments over time is a necessary condition for recruiting, developing, and retaining the best professional experts. Developing a strong reputation requires consistency in both hiring and choice of client assignments over time. The courage to turn down business that falls outside of the strategic areas of priority is crucial. Unfortunately, such strategic consistency is unlikely to emerge without a managerial commitment of senior, non-billable time. This is a constraint that may explain – but not justify – why so many firms still hope that strategy will emerge out of high-quality daily operations. That may have been the case in the 1960s and 1970s, but is not likely to be a viable approach in the years to come.

# The role of professional ethics in shaping law firms' strategy

Tomasz Wardyński
Wardyński & Partners

1.      **Introduction**

Among jokes circulated at social events, those about lawyers elicit ripples of laughter. A popular anecdote quoting a client saying, "When I see my lawyer on the street I quickly cross to the other side, because if he greets me, the next day I will be billed 500 dollars", amuses everyone – except lawyers.

Why is it that the legal profession, and especially the vocation of a business lawyer, does not arouse positive feelings, but is often treated with dislike and distrust?

This chapter does not aim at a detailed and exhaustive analysis of society's negative perception of the legal profession. However, it attempts to explain how the commercialisation of legal services poses a challenge to preserving the proper attitude of the public vis-à-vis law firms and consequently the legal profession as a whole, and how this must be taken into account in law firms' strategies. This has a direct bearing not only on the prospects for success of individual law firms, but on the condition of the legal profession as such and its ability to exercise its vested function and role within the system of the rule of law.

2.      **The significance of trust in the legal profession**

The role of the bar was defined by the experiences of the twentieth century which shaped the conception of a democratic society based on the rule of law. The bar, as an institution entrusted with the protection of the rights of citizens against abuses by the authorities and other persons, is an important element of this conception.

The abuse of power or rights, especially by the ruling class, is a natural tendency of human nature against which we should constantly struggle. The rule of law and the state governed by law is the only mechanism which has proved capable of preventing such abuses. The legal profession is one of the fundamental pillars of this mechanism. Effective performance of their function by lawyers and by the bar is impossible unless the particular lawyers and the institution as such enjoy the trust of the public and their respective clients. In social relations, trust constitutes the very fabric, the foundation of a civil society, and enables its proper functioning. This trust takes on a special importance in relations between the legal profession and society. It is an informal 'power of attorney' accorded to the bar by society to represent it in relations with the state and other institutions of power.

Trust means a conviction on the part of clients that the actions of professional institutions and their members (ie, individual advocates and legal advisers), are subordinated first and solely to the justified interests of their clients. Trust in the profession in general, and in each member of the profession in particular, is the fundamental basis for the existence of proper representation and the proper functioning of the relationship under which we are retained to provide legal assistance. It rests on strict compliance with and respect for certain core values, by the institution of the bar as a whole and by individual lawyers as members of the profession.

## 3. The genesis of the law firm as an enterprise and the danger posed by this phenomenon

Preservation of the profession's core values and the trust vested in the institution of the bar by society have posed various challenges throughout the profession's development. This development has been particularly dynamic over recent decades. The worldwide economic boom over the past 30 years has been accompanied by the rapid growth of law firms. This is because law firms play a vital role in the process of economic globalisation. They have assisted their clients in carrying out projects around the world by adapting the forms and methods by which their clients pursue their initiatives to suit the requirements of the relevant local jurisdictions.

The scale and nature of such undertakings has required the formation of teams of specialists working together to implement projects. These teams have evolved into firms which often operate across numerous countries representing various types of legal systems. Law firms are therefore institutions where partners and their associates practise the legal profession collectively and therefore should always be looked at as groups of professionals fulfilling a role vested in the bars and law societies and as an element of the mechanism of the rule of law.

The role of law firms in forging the image of the legal profession cannot be underestimated, even though the bulk of legal assistance is still rendered by sole practitioners and small partnerships, which constitute the basic structure of national bars. Law firms work for big commercial clients on matters often covered by the media. They are attractive to young lawyers because they offer the experience of working on commercial projects which would not be available to them in other segments of the profession. Young lawyers are given this opportunity without having to bear the financial risk related to such work; furthermore, they are offered financial stability. Finally, law firms build up professional goodwill from which coming generations of lawyers can benefit. They transfer this goodwill to younger lawyers, thus securing its sustainability, which ultimately constitutes the law firm's reputation in the eyes of the public.

However, the need to maintain large teams has required, and will continue to require, the assumption of the significant risk of financing them. This risk is tied to the fact that there are no guarantees of a steady flow of an appropriate number of matters generating fees sufficient to cover the costs of the existence of such teams. In assuming this risk, law firms have joined the ranks of numerous other enterprises operating on the market for services. As a result, business plans, budgets, financial targets and efficiency rates influence relations within the firm and with its clients. The pressure to achieve profit targets has become a particularly important driver for law firms' activity. In other words, law firms – apart from being groupings of legal professionals fulfilling their function in civil society – have become enterprises fully dependent on the laws of the marketplace and competition.

4.     **Risks associated with commercialisation**

This dual dimension of law firms' operations poses particular challenges to the need to protect the trust which the bar and individual lawyers should enjoy from their clients and from society as a whole. As stated above, cultivation of this trust depends on the fulfilment of certain core principles. Strict compliance with these principles may, however, appear at first sight to be a burden, impeding the firm's growth in a competitive market and putting it on a worse footing than those who are less scrupulous in respecting them.

The rules of economics require market players to maximise their profits by charging the highest possible prices, subject only to the laws of supply and demand. Those who do not move forward are moving backwards. Competitive pressure forces firms to expand their market share by accepting all possible matters and meeting all existing demand. On a competitive market, a player who refuses to serve a willing client risks not only the loss of the profit which this client could bring, but a deterioration of market share and – consequently – economic extinction. Competitors are required to advertise themselves, demonstrate superiority over other players, and disclose details of their experiences and references from satisfied clients.

This has eroded the lawyer's relationship with the client. Legal assistance, which is primarily based on intellectual and human values, has been reduced to a commodity, and the methods for earning legal fees have come to resemble the manner in which fees are charged on the marketplace by other service industries.

The pressure to achieve profit targets has led firms to charge excessive fees and not pay enough attention to what is most important in the lawyer's profession: a genuine intention to help the client. The need to remain competitive and retain 'market share' pushes firms into accepting as many matters as possible. As a result, the rule prohibiting lawyers from acting for clients with conflicting interests is increasingly compromised. Immediate economic efficiency and the clients' consent become final arguments in favour of accepting such instructions, and the need to preserve a certain image and prevent any suspicions on the part of the public is marginalised. Some law firms are increasingly hesitant to refuse assistance in matters that display the hallmarks of abuses of rights, arguing inconsistent legal positions depending on what a particular client demands. They eagerly help their clients to disguise their abusive conduct as formal legitimate activity. It also happens that in their relations with the media, some law firms reveal without any moderation confidential information relating to their clientele and the cases they handle, with a view to building up the image of celebrities for themselves, their partners and associates. All this is always excused by the argument that the economic interest of the law firm and the rules of competition require such behaviour. In general, an opinion prevails that such are the requirements of the market, and law firms have to proceed with this kind of conduct if they want to survive as economic entities.

As a result, lawyers are perceived as yet another category of service providers who merely by virtue of some incomprehensible tradition enjoy privileges which they exploit to extort high fees from clients. This exposes the legal profession to action by competition authorities, mainly within the European Union, which have conducted research resulting in the Clementi report in the United Kingdom[1] and the Monti report in the European Union.[2] The research analysed legal services purely from an economic viewpoint. As a consequence of this process, there is a shortage of trust in law firms. This deficit deprives the entire profession of the necessary mandate to fulfil its function, thus undermining the rule of law and the foundations of civil society.

**5. Influence of commercialisation on law firms' strategies**

Paradoxically, although commercialisation of the profession can be seen as a reason behind degradation of the lawyer–client relationship and erosion of social trust in the bar, the laws of the market can contribute to the process of regaining the profession's role and position in the system of the rule of law.

Building trust in the law firm among its current and potential clients should be the most urgent business task of every lawyer in the firm and the common denominator for each law firm's entire strategy. This is not only in the interest of the profession as a whole, but in the best economic interest of each individual law firm. There will always be a compelling demand on the market for lawyers who provide honest assistance to their clients and whose trustworthiness in the eyes of the courts, administrative authorities and market participants is uncompromised. If there is a shortage of such law firms today, it can only increase the benefits for those who are the first to fill it.

Therefore, when defining their firm's growth strategy, lawyers must remember that all of their decisions should first and foremost be a function of the principles of professional ethics. To put it provocatively, one can say that the best way to secure a law firm's financial success and stability is not to pay too much attention to its finances. This does not mean that a law firm should neglect to secure the resources necessary for its operations. We must remember that our business costs and investments in the systems in operation at the firm are also our obligation, as alongside our earnest, personal, professional efforts, they also determine the quality of the assistance we are able to provide and will continue to provide for our clients. Nor can we forget about the firm itself, which is the basic instrument that enables us to perform our professional duties. However, the basis for the success of each individual law firm as well as the profession as a whole is the clients' confidence in the firm's brand – that is, the belief that the firm's sole motivation is an authentic concern for the good of the client and the client's interests.

This must have a direct bearing on the firm's pricing strategy. Lawyers cannot forget that in the process of exercising their rights, citizens fully depend on their assistance. The complicated nature of legal systems, which are becoming more and

---

1      Sir David Clementi, "Review of the Regulatory Framework for Legal Services in England and Wales: Final Report", December 2004.

2      Mario Monti, "A New Strategy for the Single Market at the Service of Europe's Economy and Society: Report to the President of the European Commission, José Manuel Barroso", May 9 2010.

more regulated, makes it difficult for the public to comprehend the purpose of legal provisions. In addition, the threat of abuse by the authorities and other players on the market makes clients vulnerable. In this context, the need for legal assistance is perceived as something they simply cannot avoid. Hence, the public perception is that it is not a service but paid help granted to those who cannot do without it. This particular combination of necessity on one hand and the inability of self-assistance on the other provides lawyers with work. This relationship of dependence gives legal fees an ethical dimension; hence the lawyer's need for scrupulous compliance with the ethical obligations which are a condition for the client's trust in the legal profession.

The fee must always correspond to the real intellectual value of the service rendered and may not be excessive. Above all, it cannot be ruthlessly charged to a client when his legitimate rights are being violated and he suffers objective damage from the point of view of a social sense of justice. Very often lawyers and law firms should get engaged in defending clients' interests almost on a pro bono basis, because, in effect, such a defence is not only in the interest of the client but also of society as a whole and the rule of law in particular. In such circumstances, an exacting expectation of a legal fee for every six-minute time unit, as applied in many law firms, makes clients feel blackmailed and abused. Consequently, they have a feeling that the profession is totally commercialised and bereft of moral values. When this feeling is shared by many clients who then exchange their views among themselves and publicly articulate negative opinions about the profession, then it is not only the profession that suffers but the whole of civil society because, as stated above, trust in the profession disappears and the public mandate to the profession ceases to exist. As a result, lawyers cannot expect appropriate respect from society, the public administration and decision makers, and the danger is that they then become an ineffective element of the mechanism of the rule of law.

In gaining a reputation for uncompromising integrity and trustworthiness, a law firm must be prepared to reject potential instructions if so required by ethical norms. In the concrete measures undertaken by a lawyer or a law firm under instructions from individual clients, the aim of legal assistance is to prevent future abuse or to eliminate present abuses. This is so irrespective of whether the lawyer represents the client before a court, during negotiations, or when drawing up measures the client plans to implement. Such representation must always take place within the framework of the existing legal system. It is also vital to understand that for the sake of upholding the values of civil society, lawyers should abstain from collaborating with clients who aim at abusing power or want to act to the detriment of civil society – or the other party – even at the cost of losing the revenue which such a client could generate. It is therefore vital to understand while building a firm's strategy that there are limits to the interest of the law firm as an undertaking and that financial objectives cannot compromise the role of the lawyer within the society.

For the same reasons, a law firm should act with utmost prudence when accepting instructions from clients who may have conflicting interests. 'Chinese walls' can do more to harm a law firm's image than the firm may be able to gain from using them. A reputation for unwillingness to engage in any activities which could cast doubt on the firm's adherence to the principle of eschewing any conflict of interests is hard to overvalue, but very easy to lose.

In its dealings with the media, a law firm must always have in mind that confidentiality is more important than the celebrity image of the firm and its lawyers. The doubtful benefits of disclosing to the public impressive details of cases or transactions handled by the firm cannot outweigh the benefits of a reputation for discretion and absolute respect for the principle of confidentiality of the client's affairs.

## 6. Conclusions

The dual nature of legal services and the legal profession has been clear for many years, and it is no great revelation to state that lawyers perform a service. Given its purpose, however, this service holds a special place defined by the architecture of the system. It is this service that enables implementation of the principles of due process and other fundamental rights. This has to do not only with proceedings seeking to defend or establish rights, but also ordinary advice, which helps a client take decisions that are consistent with the legal order. In consequence, the sum total of all legal services provided by the bar within the global community, and the voice of the bar in the dialogue with authority for the purpose of compelling respect for the rights of a civil society, is one of the most important foundations of a democracy under the rule of law. The tendency towards the abuse of power, by act or omission, is after all a psychological trait of practically every person, and will almost always manifest itself when external conditions allow. Proper performance of legal services has an impact on the decisions taken by clients to act in compliance with the legal order and with respect for the rights of others. Of course, instances do occur in which the profession is misused for purposes inconsistent with its guiding principles. In an age of commercialisation and mercantilisation of life, examples of such abuses are frequent.

While defending the rights of a client, a lawyer also performs a service. That is a truism. Owing to their dependence on cash flows, law firms are subject to the rules of the market. One of them is that an undertaking selling a service on the market should always accept clients and deliver a service the client wants. Thus, it may seem that when a law firm refuses to accommodate a prospective client whose interests conflict with those of another of the firm's clients, and the prospective client must go elsewhere, the firm as a market vehicle will suffer a loss. Or it may seem that the rules of the market require a law firm to spread information about the success it has achieved for clients in other cases, or even reveal certain information which ultimately, under the rules of professional conduct, is confidential. In the same way, building up a celebrity image of a law firm and its lawyers may be considered necessary under the rules of the market. From this point of view, many are of the opinion that professional ethics constitute an unnecessary burden on a law firm which hampers the firm's competitiveness and thus has a negative effect on its financial results. In our view, this is only an apparent contradiction.

A basic rule of the market is that undertakings who survive, especially in times of crisis, are those selling products which are in short supply. In our view, the main shortages on the current legal market, thanks to the commercialisation of the profession, are decency, fairness and honesty. In the view of the authors of this publication, no legal service can be provided to clients unless it carries these three fundamental human values. With a view for the public to be able to make a proper judgment as to whether a law firm secures these values, it will be necessary to know whether the firm fulfils the appropriate ethical standards. With this in mind, we have a strong conviction that even though at first sight ethics may seem to require special effort, ultimately they constitute an essential element of a law firm's strategy.

In developing strategies for their firms, lawyers cannot forget the obligation to provide their firms with the necessary cash flows for their existence. It is also in the best interest of their clients. In drafting financial plans, however, a law firm must not forget that much work that would usually have been charged to clients over the last 30 years will have to be offered either for free or at cost, and also that there may be a lot of work offered to existing and potential clients on a pro bono basis because it will be related to problems of clients fighting for basic justice. This is why lawyers today must be prepared to act often with no regard for their immediate financial interest. That is the only way to secure public trust in a law firm's brand. Moderation and modesty in building up the firm's reputation should always be in mind when it comes to the firm's presence in the media.

Recent publications on the legal profession underline the necessity of investing in upgrading the firm's capabilities and efficiency in delivering legal assistance. All these publications are quite right in pointing out the extent to which technical development, especially in IT and communications, should change lawyers' way of thinking and imagination in inventing new, more effective ways of bringing reasonable value and effective solutions to clients' problems. We could not agree more with the conclusions drawn by Richard Susskind in his books.[3] We think, however, that the basis for effectiveness is not the free market economy and its mechanisms, but first and foremost the honesty and loyalty which lawyers owe to their clients and that the legal profession owes to society. This brings us back to the fundamental truth underlying the nature of legal assistance, which is that it is rendered not for the sake of earning money but with a view to protecting the rule of law and the legitimate interests of our clients. In this sense, this particular philosophy must be implemented and enforced at all levels of a law firm. It should underlie the behaviour not only of partners and associates, but also the entire staff of the firm, through all stages of dealings with existing and potential clients. Everyone in a law firm must always remember that the firm is there to perform the constitutionally defined role of providing legal protection to citizens by complying with the statutory duty to provide legal assistance to those who need it and who are not in a position to protect their rights on their own.

The law firm as an institution is an undertaking and as such is vulnerable to commercialisation. If the commercial side of the law firm is overemphasised, the

---

3      Richard Susskind, *The End of Lawyers? Rethinking the Nature of Legal Services* (Oxford University Press, 2008); *Transforming the Law: Essays on Technology, Justice, and the Legal Marketplace* (Oxford University Press, 2003); *The Future of Law: Facing the Challenges of Information Technology* (Oxford University Press, 1996).

image of the profession suffers, and in consequence the public no longer understands the role of the profession within the mechanism of the rule of law. It may thus be stated that a law firm is a special type of enterprise whose economic interests are always subordinated to the purpose and function of the bar as established by law. When selecting the profession of a lawyer, we must be aware of what this profession is truly about. An awareness of the social role and true nature of the profession enables us to take proper decisions in compliance with our temperament and our internal conviction that the mission of the profession is identical to our own personal mission.

# Easy and difficult at the same time: some general considerations on law firm strategy

**Peter Kurer**
BLR & Partners AG

You thought defining a law firm strategy is a difficult undertaking. It isn't. At least if you compare it with the strategic challenges facing big industrial companies or service providers. Nonetheless, many law firm leaders struggle with the strategic challenge, particularly in today's difficult, post-crisis environment, where so many things have changed and are still changing, and where many law firms have now come under considerable pressure even to the point of finding it difficult to foresee a successful future.

In this chapter, I shall focus on three real-life strategic challenges in industrial and big service companies, with a view to showing how company boards and CEOs analyse difficult situations and then derive the main building blocks for their survival strategy. I shall use these examples as a starting point to describe a model which I call CELESS and which defines the main building blocks for a solid law firm strategy. This is what I call the easy part. The harder side of the story is then to implement the strategy. And here, law firm leaders often face roadblocks and headwinds such as internal dissent and traditions deeply rooted in the history of the legal profession with all its arcane rules and folkways. This may make life difficult for the managing partners of law firms, because unlike CEOs, they cannot rely on their status to say "I lead – you follow" and thus bring a strategic change more easily to fruition. This is what I call the difficult part.

## 1. Beyond law firms: a look at real companies

### 1.1 A paper company in 1996

Put yourself in the shoes of the CEO of a paper company for a moment. (This example is about 20 years old.) He is facing the following predicament: the company produces speciality papers, such as blueprint paper, diazo paper and translucent papers, which are used for technical drawing in classical architectural and engineering offices. The company has been a market leader in this field for many years and made good money, because these papers sold with high profit margins. Recently, however, more and more architects and engineers have started to use computer-aided design (CAD) to produce technical drawings. The demand for the speciality papers decreases rapidly. Obviously, the architects and engineers still need paper for printouts of their CAD drawings, but these are relatively simple papers with only light coating and they sell at relatively low margins. So the CEO decides to build up a new product line of coated papers, which will be used for high-end and large image printing such as billboards and large photo reproduction. He faces three strategic issues. The first is that these new papers and their coating need to be developed, which is quite a challenge in terms of innovation. Secondly, new plants have to be built at the same time. On the other hand, and thirdly, the demand for the classical papers has collapsed so quickly now that one of the plants of the group becomes useless; it cannot be used for other applications and there is no buyer for it. The auditors tell the CEO that the company will soon have to write down this plant. Together with the losses, which have accumulated over the last two years due to the collapse of the classical drawing paper sales, this will wipe out almost all the equity of the company, and it will be hard to pay for the innovation requirements and the construction of the new plant. Finally, it is unclear whether or not the new papers can be developed in time and will pick up sales at a rate and with sufficient margins to balance the ongoing fall of the old papers. No wonder the CEO has sleepless nights.

This CEO had to struggle with issues almost absent in the legal profession: high end innovation as a survival issue, the fast obliteration of products and the whole market for the company, and heavy investment requirements on the one hand, combined with accelerated write-downs of expensive infrastructure on the other hand.

## 1.2 A cement company at the turn of the century

Let us look at another example. This time it is the board of a cement company. This company is a leader in the industry. However, of late, its leading position has been at risk since two other competitors have grown aggressively in the last few years, and the capital markets give a premium to the leader. So the board decides to initiate an aggressive push to re-establish a clear leadership position. This is not easy, however, because the company cannot grow in its established markets, which are mature. The board ponders two alternatives. One is to buy a cement company in a large emerging market country. The other is to build two plants in another, somewhat less developed country. The first option has the disadvantage that in this specific country you can only make such an investment if you enter into a joint venture with a local partner. The company has done this before, but has had consistently bad experiences with such arrangements. The second alternative, the new plant, faces the problem that the country in question is politically unstable and there is the impending risk that the government will change within a short time, which will make a lot of the planning obsolete. On top of this, the new plant would have to be built on difficult ground, which requires a new engineering technique and bears high project risks, a matter which will come to the attention of the analysts and the market if the risk materialises. Finally, the capex in either case is huge, coming close to a billion dollars. The company has always had a relatively high gearing and these investments will bring the leverage up to a level with which the board is uncomfortable.

Again, this board faces very difficult issues which are absent in the case of law firms: huge investments combined with engineering issues and financing problems; the scrutiny of the capital and financial markets and, in particular, geopolitical risks which are hard to control. It goes without saying that this board will apply a very thorough and rigid strategy process before making any decision.

## 1.3     Airlines: a national flag carrier 20 years ago

Let us briefly turn to the airline industry and a typical challenge that might have been faced by a management team of a national flag carrier during the deregulation of the industry in the 1990s. The airline industry is a particularly tough one. It is regulated and at the same time there is cutthroat competition which constantly erodes fares and margins. A well-known consultancy firm once calculated that, since its inception, the airline industry has never really made enough money to pay its real capital cost. This is also the experience of the management of our imaginary airline. These people are experienced, hard-nosed and have a good record. They knew that they are basically in permanent survival mode and they have to reinvent their business model constantly. Their entrepreneurial freedom is, however, quite restricted: there is heavy-handed regulation, they depend on one airport (their hub) which cannot expand since there is political opposition to it, and their flexibility to set fares is limited by the cutthroat competition. Their staff is highly unionised and difficult whenever it comes to collective bargaining. And finally, they are now faced with rapid de-regulation and a string of new competitors – the big global airlines and low-fare carriers.

They can, however, play with a few elements to improve this difficult situation and so they develop a state of the art yield system, a method to make sure that every customer pays neither too much nor too little to fill as many flights as possible at the best margin (and often the margin of one flight is lower than what their leading outside lawyer bills in a half a day). Such a yield system needs complex computing and IT engineering, and it needs years to build up this technical know-how. The second element is to have an optimal feeder and hub system. It is a highly intellectual challenge to strike a balance between the cost of running a feeder system and the additional business it brings to fill the long-distance flights. Then the management has to look at the kind of aircraft they buy: one plane makes less noise (which helps to ease the political environment); another is more comfortable for the passengers; and a third one will fit better into the existing fleet structure and its maintenance base. Finally, the management has to decide which airline alliance it works with. Again this is a complex issue: what brings most feeder business, where does the fleet fit best and what is most attractive from a marketing point of view?

As in our two previous examples, this airline and its management faces strategy challenges which go far beyond those of even the most complex law firm. This management must devise very sophisticated systems, it needs the support of the best system operators and IT engineers money can buy. They have to know how to play a very complicated political game and they have to heed a difficult regulator.

## 1.4    The conclusion

Law firms do not have the innovation challenges, the geopolitical risk, the huge and weighty investment decisions, the balance sheet and leverage hick-ups, the systems, regulatory and political challenges and IT requirements that we have seen as the main elements of a strategy process in our examples of industrial companies or airlines and which may be seen in many other industries such as car manufacturing, oil exploration, high technology, global banks or drug companies in one form or the other. You might object that some law firms, especially some of the big global ones, have built up IT costs and geopolitical risks, and also run into serious regulatory issues in places like India or China. This would be a fair point, but it applies only to a handful of global British firms and even in their cases it is by no means comparable to what a global steel company, a big bank or drug company faces.

This is why I called law firm strategy 'easy'. But I have to qualify this statement: I believe the setting of the proper elements of a law firm strategy – what I call the building blocks – is a relatively trivial thing and should not cause any sleepless nights to its management. By contrast, the execution of this strategy, and the discipline with which it is carried out, is the key. And there the management of a law firm faces some formidable headwinds.

The proper strategy discussion in a law firm should encompass both the elements of the strategy and how to manage the headwinds. Let us look at these in the next two sections.

## 2.    Main building blocks of a law firm strategy

### 2.1    Get the information in

Every strategy discussion should be based on full knowledge of the relevant data and information. No discussion should begin before the information is in. I always wondered at how poorly this almost trivial rule is followed by partners and managers of law firms. Lawyers are trained in rules and norms; they learnt in their professional initiation how the world should be, not how it is. And therefore, many strategy discussions in law firms are exchanges of conceptual dogmas rather than fact-based orientation. An extension of this is that much information about law firms is reduced to oversimplified condensation of facts. A typical example is the profit per partner (PPP) concept, which has caused a lot of misguided strategy discussions. The same applies to rankings and panel memberships. All these are information-reducers, they reduce relevant information to a very simplified view of reality. Take rankings as an example. Most law firms rightly put huge effort into improving their rankings. The problem starts, however, if these law firms think that rankings are the most important or even the sole measure of market recognition. This is not the case. We know that there are many groups of clients who check rankings (eg, smaller and medium-sized companies), but there are others who almost never do (eg, non-legal managers, counsels of large companies or private individuals). And even those who check rankings do it more to confirm and re-confirm what they know from their own sources or trusted contacts.

We all live in information cocoons. But there are many ways to break through these barriers.[1] Our information-oriented and know-how based society has developed so many ways to improve the state of our own information. We know about the value of open deliberations, sophisticated surveys, the internet, internal and external wikis, social media and so on. Very few of these things are used in law firms in a thorough and consistent way to establish a sober and reliable view as to where the firm stands and where it could go. Law firms often know very little about the economics of their markets, the strategy and products of their clients, the job satisfaction and work–life balance of their staff and even the longer-term development of the law. When I worked in a bank, our external law firms developed an interest in the first version of MIFID[2] about two years after our internal people. They were then so kind as to send me memorandums on this challenging new EU financial investment regulation – not without recommending their services in the field. We were so kind as to invite these law firms to come and visit our specialists to learn more on the reality of preparing for MIFID!

There are many ways to go through an orderly information-gathering process. I would normally do it with the CELESS process referred to above:

- *Clients:* What are the strategies, products and real advisory needs of the firm's clients? How do existing and potential clients see our firm? Where are the potential new clients? What are my strategies for certain clusters of clients such as a whole industry or correspondent law firms? Do we really know the business of the clients, their long-term strategic challenges, the beliefs and values of their leadership? Do we have a solid advisory model to cope with this? Do we regularly solicit feedback on our services? Do we fill our brand with content so that clients truly understand what they can and cannot expect? Do we have a sensible business development process? Is it a lifeless marketing and promotion exercise, run by a committee? Or is it, as in all excellent service organisations, a thorough strategic matter and deeply rooted in the execution where the client gets what he asked for?

- *Economy and politics:* Where is the economy heading? Will my home market leave recession or stay stagnant or deflationary for a long time? How will the political system develop? Is it stable and business-friendly? Will capital markets or the banking industry expand, shrink or relocate? Will health and drug research go into an open source paradigm or need more IP protection? Will cloud computing kill software licensing? Will we need more or less renewable energy in the future?

- *Legal developments:* What are the next major legal risks for my clients? Does my client understand these risks? Do I? How do we communicate with clients on this? Like a car dealer just looking for the next sale? Or as grown up business people who invest long term in important business relations and appreciate dialogue with people who might know more about these matters than we do?

---

1    One of the best books on these issues was written by a law professor – Cass R Sunstein, *Infotopia. How Many Minds Produce Knowledge*, Oxford University Press (2006).

2    Markets in Financial Instruments Directive, a directive of the European Union on certain financial services.

- *Staff:* Are my partners happy? And the other fee earners and associates? And what about all the support staff, the receptionist, the secretary and the IT guy who answers emergency calls in the middle of the night? They are often the business card for a firm. But do we treat them as important team members, or are they regularly burnt by the erratic outbursts or arrogance of our great star lawyers? Are all my people up to the challenge? Do I recruit the right people? Do I train them properly? Do they think that they work in a good place? Do they stay or do they easily go to where the grass is greener? Do I understand the many challenges of the work–life balance which have become so important?
- *Shared values:* And where do you stand with these barely visible DNA genes of your organisation, which I call shared values? They are hardly traceable, cannot be reduced to writing and are sometimes riddles even for those who were on the block for many years. But they build up the magnetic field of a firm, define their ultimate nature and like the invisible hand lead all members of the organisation to pull in the right direction.

Once you have made this information analysis you might go through a SWOT review of your law firm:[3]
- Strength: what are the strengths of my firm?
- Weaknesses: what are the weaker parts?
- Opportunities: what opportunities will open for my firm's activity?
- Threats: what will threaten our success?

It is advisable to get a clear view on the SWOT both from within and from without (clients, business community, media and so on). Remember that because we live in information cocoons, we often mistakenly think that our inside view coincides with the outside view.

## 2.2 Tradition

There are law firms that do not have a strategy; they have a tradition. Some of these are amongst the most successful firms. Over generations, these firms have established themselves in the market, are known in, and connected to, the wider business community, have a shiny brand, learnt what they do and do not do, and refined the ways they treat their clients and their staff. As many examples show in New York, Chicago, London, Tokyo, Zurich or Vienna, it is hard to beat these firms whose mantra is 'our tradition is our strategy'.

Tradition has one big advantage over a green field strategy exercise:[4] it embodies the strategic know-how of generations of successful lawyers whilst strategy-building without a tradition relies much more on the snapshot information of one single generation. Tradition, however, also has one substantial drawback: it might make

---

3    The SWOT method was developed by the Harvard Business School as a strategic management tool in the 1960s.
4    See Sunstein, page 122f.

you fat, complacent, arrogant. In their worst form, traditional firms can develop a behavioural pattern which makes them incapable of realising that history is starting to flow against them and that they should change their ways. In the very same cities, New York, Chicago, Tokyo and Zurich, there are many examples of good old traditional law firms that have gone out of business because they did not adjust to the requirements of the day.

Hence, partners of traditional law firms should also do their regular strategy exercise and take a sober view of what should stay and what should change.

## 2.3 Footprint I

The essence of every strategy exercise is to develop products, services and behaviours that distinguish your firm from your competition.[5] This is easy (actually not so easy) for iPhones, Coke, Ferrari, Rolex or in the production of chocolate Easter bunnies, which you wrap into a golden folio. It is not so easy for legal services. After all, law is law, legal advice is legal advice. In a sense, legal services are a homogeneous mass product, which can be delivered by many people with a similar education. Some of the best legal strategists of this world have started with this sobering view. They are much better in the strategy game than those lawyers who think that they are just the most brilliant professionals, unique stars, God's gift to mankind.

There is, however, a big but to the notion that it is hard to differentiate a law firm from the competition. Every law firm can, and should, define, develop and refine a clear, distinguishable footprint, and this is the core of the strategic exercise. The footprint has, in essence, two dimensions: one is the service offerings and the other is geography.

### (a) Service offering

There are three types of distinctive service model:
- The narrowest is the boutique, which is a service model of extreme specialisation. Boutiques offer limited services such as IP law, regulatory law or tax law. They develop very deep institutional know-how on a very limited area of the law. Boutiques are still a very successful and useful business model. In my experience, their knowledge and independent thinking is amazing; they often develop highly efficient global networks amongst themselves; and they are usually much cheaper than the big firms.
- A broader model is that of the specialist expert firm (SEF) such as a litigation/regulatory or a corporate/finance firm. SEFs are broader than boutiques since they have to master a number of legal areas, but they are topically much narrower than the open general service firms. Their real advantage is that they combine a reasonable degree of specialisation (which distinguishes them from full service firms) with an ambition and capacity to hit on the high end. They are after all in the sweet spots of the market such as prestigious litigation or big corporate deals (which distinguishes them

---

5    See Michael E Porter, *Competitive Advantage. Creating and Sustaining Superior Performance*, Free Press (1985).

from the boutiques). No wonder that many, if not most, of the big brands in the legal industry are, one way or another, SEFs. They might develop into multiple SEFs, and combine litigation with corporate/banking, but ultimately most of these firms shy away from the general service firm model even when they add an IP lawyer here and an employment law specialist there. This strategy allows them to keep a distinctive footprint.

- The broadest model is the general service firm. These firms are very much client-oriented in the sense that they go after a specific client sector, such as smaller or mid-size businesses, and where they then offer a one-stop shop for all the client's legal issues. Many clients like this approach, the closeness of these lawyers to their business and the easy and privileged access to them. Hence this is still a very successful model, and even if these firms are normally less profitable (in terms of PPP) than boutiques or SEFs, they employ many more lawyers on a combined basis.

### (b)   Geography

The second dimension of the footprint is geography:

- National firms stick to a single jurisdiction and do not develop any appetite to go into any other territory. Some amongst them do it in such a successful way that they are called 'national champions', which is consistent with the notion that they defend their territory successfully against external competition. Ever since I can remember, the legal magazines and the legal industry pundits have tolled the death knell of these firms. Wrongly so. Many of them still are going strong and do not show any sign of weakening. They have many strengths: they are easier to manage; develop a deep knowledge of and intimacy with the local business community and of the political/regulatory environment; and they do not have to be watchful of conflicts which develop on the other side of the globe. Their biggest disadvantages are that they have to operate in virtual business combinations when it comes to cross-border transactions and that they have clear limits to growth.

- Like national firms, regional firms have a distinct footprint. They go beyond national borders, but expand only to the shores of a clearly defined region. Regional firms have appeared, and make sense, only in certain areas of the world (ie, regions where a number of smaller countries cluster and develop regional characteristics). This is the case for Scandinavia, Eastern Central Europe, the Middle East and South-east Asia. Here, these regional firms can develop the same degree of cultural awareness and intimacy with the business community that we have seen with the national champions; they are much better on these things than bigger organisations which are managed from faraway places.

- Global hub firms are those which are global, but restrict their activities to the big international finance centres such as New York, London, Tokyo and Hong Kong. In a sense, they follow a pattern set by the big global investment banks, which are often their main clients. Most of these firms are topically

SEFs, providing limited specialist services in a limited number of places around the world. If their specialist knowledge is required outside of a hub, they fly in. They are expensive and profitable, but they are also exposed to boom and bust; in times of crisis they are the frontrunners in aggressive de-equitisation exercises.

- Truly global firms are those which strive to be everywhere their clients go. They support their clients in many places and often in all areas of the law. In their business model, they resemble the big international accounting firms (and not the investment banks as the global hub firms do). The advantage of this strategy is that it is easier to break into the domain of global work this way, and you can more easily acquire work opportunistically than with a narrower footprint like that of a global hub SEF. Also, whilst less profitable in boom times, these firms are better protected against the economic down times, a fact which provides more stability and security at the partner level if well managed. This strategy has been followed by Baker McKenzie very successfully for generations, but we now see a more general move in this direction. Many of the newer merger efforts target this model and I foresee a time when even one or more of the magic circle firms readjust their strategy towards it.

## 2.4 Footprint II

The definition of a footprint is rarely a green field exercise. More usually, footprints are developed and refined through decades-long processes of differentiations and adjustments. These processes are pushed by tradition, the preferences of strong individuals within the firm, opportunistic behaviour or pure happenstance. But these are important strategy pointers and many of the best law firm strategies have emerged through such processes. The important thing, however, is that the firm develops a keen understanding of its own footprint, how it originated, how it developed and where it will lead the firm. A good firm will have a proper discussion, and a forum for such a discussion, to discuss, correct and refine its footprint on a continuous basis.

## 2.5 Size and operational leverage

The single most important decision a firm has to take in relation to its strategy after the footprint is probably size and operational leverage. It is also often the most neglected issue. Many firms mushroom into sizes which are neither necessary nor planned, until they have to resort to axing overcapacity; others are unable to increase their size and never achieve the right hitting power. Partners should take the time to discuss how big the firm should be next year, in five years and in 10 years.

Closely related to this discussion is the issue of operational leverage. Operational leverage is the ratio of equity partners to salaried professionals (fee earners). Operational leverage has a number of consequences for the firm's profitability, its potential volatility and its culture. All else being equal, the higher a firm is leveraged the higher will be the equity partners' share in the firm's profits and the higher will be the profit per partner. This, however, comes with a material drawback – higher volatility (as in the case of high financial leverage) as the following simplified example shows:

- Take a firm which makes revenues of 100, has 100 fee earners of which 10 are partners. This firm has to pay a lot of salaries to the 90 employed attorneys and therefore has a high cost–income ratio (let's say 80:20). If revenues go down by 10% in this firm, the equity partners will see their income halved.
- A second firm also makes a revenue of 100 and also has 100 fee earners but this time 50 of them are equity partners. Here the cost–income ratio is, let's say, 50:50. If the revenues of this firm go down by 10% (as in the first example) the profit per partner will reduce by only 20%.

So the partners in the first firm do better when things are good or improve; the partners in the second firm are more secure when things worsen.

The higher volatility in higher leveraged firms has an impact on the culture of the firm. Highly leveraged firms tend to panic in times of economic downturns and start to axe partners, weed them out or de-equitise them. By contrast, firms with low operational leverage, in my experience, tend to take a more relaxed view of economic recessions and accept them as inevitable lows and ebbs of the economy. Also, by the same token, a lower leveraged firm can be more open with its partner positions. If only 10% of your fee earners are partners you can make one additional partner whenever you plan to increase your revenue of 100 by 10%; with the same numbers; if half of your fee earners are partners you can add five new partners.

Obviously, these examples are somewhat theoretical, but in one way or another operational leverage has a tremendous impact on the day-to-day life and culture of a firm. It is my personal experience that lower leveraged firms tend to be more stable and calmer in their strategic reactions, and they also tend to have happier and more relaxed associates because they have better prospects of becoming partners. In a sense, the high leverage firm starts to resemble the corporate model and the low leverage model is closer to the original professional firm idea. I also think that the world is moving in the direction of lower leveraged models after a period where high operational gearing has increased over the years of rapid economic expansion and globalisation. Many sociological factors now pull and push in this direction, such as higher client demands for partner time in an increasingly complex environment, clients also requiring smaller teams for cost reasons, work–life balance moving up the wish list of associates, more democratic values evolving generally within business organisations and, last but not least, the demise of family run businesses in those parts of the world where they have been the standard (especially in emerging markets).

## 2.6 People: recruitment, training, team building, career paths, performance measurement

People fill the footprint and bring the operational model to life. They are the very essence of a business such as law. Thus, a proper HR process is a key building block of a well-run law firm. It is important that the process is not limited only to the salaried staff but extends to the partners too. The process starts with a solid recruitment process including the training of those who conduct the recruitment interviews. Then it moves on to training. Lawyers learn a lot about the law at law school; but they learn little about how the economy and business ticks, what clients want, how one communicates swiftly and precisely and how one manages oneself and others. The third element of a proper HR process is compensation and career path. The fourth is a proper performance measurement system, which goes far beyond just counting billable hours.

Partners, fee earners and staff expect from the leadership of a well-run law firm that it addresses the thorny issues of work–life balance, a proper culture based on solid values and the many facets of non-discriminatory and gender-neutral HR process on all levels.

A key for long-term success is the way law firms select new partners and coach them in their new role. Some of the larger firms have established proper partner selection processes, including outside assessments by specialists. But many law firms are still sloppy about this, or in the worst cases, make it a political exercise with log rolling between different rope teams.

I think that able professionals with a good business sense and a happy client-oriented staff are the key elements of a truly successful law firm and that every firm manager should take a long and hard look at the HR process in its entirety. All law firms want to hire the best and brightest. Once they have done so, they often leave them alone. This is wrong and costly. Many law firm leaders focus too much on short-term success and neglect the many cultural aspects of the HR process, which are so important in creating the environment that allows for long and sustainable success based on the loyalty and shared values of the partners and the staff.

## 2.7    Compensation models

If there is one topic which has taken both the frontline (in the legal magazines) and centre stage (in partners' forums) of law firm strategy, the clear frontrunner is partners' compensation. Just as the fabric of investment banks is spun around variable compensation and high bonuses, the main rule and topic for law firms in many places is the PPP and ongoing debates (sometimes acrimonious) among partners on how to distribute profits.

Over the years, three basic models have developed to distribute profits:
- locksteps, where profits are distributed in line with seniority and where all partners of the same level of seniority receive the same amount of profits and move to the next step together;
- performance formulas, where profit is distributed by hard-wired rules based on own billables, acquisition and management of client portfolios;
- discretionary methods, where a compensation committee awards compensation in line with its judgement as to what extent a partner has achieved or not achieved in relation to targets or otherwise contributed to the general wealth of the firm.

Many things have been written about these matters, which are probably the most exhaustively explored area of law firm strategy. We all know the pros and cons: locksteps encourage people to work for the firm as a whole in a team-oriented approach, but might create an entitlement mentality and complacency; performance-oriented systems are meritocratic and foster entrepreneurship, but often bring the worst out of everybody and lead to uncooperative behaviour; discretionary distributions empower management and allow the firm to be managed on the basis of clear objectives, but they are cumbersome to administer and sometimes lead to disputes over trifling matters and amounts of money.

I have worked in all three models and personally think that a smart mixture works best; but this requires excellent compensation processes as well as good IT and MIS systems. Above all, the management should be able to put the matter into perspective and create an environment where partners accept that there are strategic matters which are much more important than compensation.

### 2.8 Governance, operational model and management

A friend of mine recently told me the secret principle of management in his firm: "In my firm every partner firmly says 'I do not want to be a manager' and every partner also says 'I do not want to be managed'; and if something goes wrong, everybody cries: 'where was the management?'" I think that law firms, by and large, are not the best-run organisations. Some of the larger firms certainly are now well-managed businesses, but a myriad of large and small firms run their operations in ways which prevent them from being more successful, more efficient, more profitable and not least more cost-conscious to the benefit of their clients.

The reason for this is that lawyers, like other professionals, tend to indulge in three mistaken views: they think that management is ultimately not important and only restricts them in their professional life; they think that management is an activity inferior to their own professional activities; and they tend to solve managerial problems by legal methods. Each of these is a fallacy. We need management if we want to have a proper lease arrangement, hiring of the best staff, well run IT, invoices sent out and being paid on time and an MIS which tells me where I stand. It is difficult to get all these things done properly. Real management is much more complicated than being a reasonably good lawyer. All lawyers who have at some point in time been entrusted with a substantial operational task will testify to this. Ask Bob Ayling, Jeff Kindler or Chuck Prince.

Finally, management is something very different from the legal process. The first thing in management is solution and closure of issues; lawyers, by contrast, want to have perfection, balanced adjudication, and they love endless discussions, estoppels, demurrers and so on.[6] Lawyers enjoy their professional independence, and for good reasons, but they often lack the wisdom to see that this professional independence has limits once they join a professional service organisation. Most lawyers are more successful, make more money and have a more interesting life because they are part of a firm. Even the cleverest lawyer would usually be much less successful if they were just on their own out there.

Law firms with a solid strategy think about these matters and will find ways and

---

6    I have expanded on this in Peter Kurer, "Lawyers in the Business Environment: Part of it or Exiles Singing from a Distant Place", GesKR 1/2011.

means to break this counterproductive 'legal' approach to managerial matters. They will entrust their best people with management tasks and, most importantly, give them ample powers to carry out their task in a proper way. It is simply unfair to say that one does not want to be managed and then cry 'where was the management' when things turn sour.

The same applies to governance and operational models. Every firm should give serious thought to how decisions are taken, prepared, documented, executed and risk-managed. Every firm should have a clear idea of how good the flow of relevant information is, what is local, what is centralised, what can and what cannot be delegated to professional managers. Corporate lawyers educate their clients day in day out on these matters and on how important proper governance and a proper operational model is to shield a corporation from liability claims. But they often forget all this when they cross the doors of their own firm.

## 2.9    The invisible hand: culture, shared values and role models

Every firm has a culture. The important thing is to have a good and positive culture. A solid culture is driven by shared values. These shared values will induce people to love working in the firm; and they will induce clients to see the firm as a unique offering, a place where they like to go when they need real help. I believe that all great service organisations, such as McKinsey, Accenture, SpencerStuart, or the Noma restaurant in Copenhagen, are based on a strong culture and shared values.

Creating such a culture is difficult. Values cannot easily be defined or reduced to writing. Even if they are written (in a mission statement or a similar document), they remain empty as long as they are not lived by all members of the firm day in day out. The best service organisations have achieved this through the mediation of exemplary role models who created these shared values and their unique culture by their presence, the way they talked and walked and educated younger colleagues, how they served clients and treated staff.

Leaders of law firms should constantly ask themselves: what are our values; do we love them; do we share them? Who are our role models? Do we support the right ones or allow people to be stars even though they do not contribute to the culture and the sustainable behaviour of the firm in the long term? Do people know that we are in it together and not on our own? That we are stewards of a great firm and not lonely stars in a sky of egomaniacs? Leaders who will have the right answers to this and act as real role models create the proper culture, shared values and a DNA for the firm which will become a magnetic field, and this magnetic field will pull everyone in the right direction as if there were an invisible hand.

## 2.10    A final remark: contrarian strategies

Every firm should know that there are strategic models which break with the standard of the industry. Lawyers are very much alike; they have the same education, the same convoluted ways of expressing themselves, and the same yellow pads. Because it is such a uniform profession, lawyers tend to emulate each other's business models. In all the biggest cities you will find four or five firms that pretty much look like each other. However, you should think from time to time about how you could be different; dream of a world where people say 'these people do things very differently from the others'. Some of the most successful firms in this world are pure contrarians. Just think of Slaughter, Wachtell or QE.

## 3. The headwinds: managing the obstructing factors

### 3.1 Why it is so important

Many strategies fail, although they are based on thorough information and are well defined. The reason is that the acceptance of a strategy and its successful implementation faces a number of obstructing factors, which I call headwinds. Thus, once a law firm management has gone through defining a strategy it should turn its full energy to managing these headwinds and remove the obstructive factors.

### 3.2 Traditions, narrow mindedness and dissent

Traditions have so many good things to tell us (see above). But they might also turn out to be a major break on the implementation of a new strategy. Law firms are professional service firms (ie, firms that are almost entirely composed of professionals who have gone through a very homogeneous education and job initiation and who are subject to sometimes stringent rules of professional ethics). Traditions, as well as bar rules, are often abused to argue against otherwise good strategies. It always needs a thorough analysis to decide where tradition is persuasive and where it stands in the way of a healthy strategic development.

Lawyers are well trained, educated and clever. But their training is not in the vision thing, great strategy or even the basics of sound management. Rather, they know the small print; they are masters in debating trifling matters; they resort to dilatory tactics and take exceptions. They often see problems and issues more clearly than the solution.

This is magnified by the simple fact that strategy discussions within firms almost exclusively take place amongst like-minded lawyers who have never really worked in another environment. I always enjoyed a good strategy discussion in my corporate life: here, you had all faculties around the table, the executive operator, the economist, the marketing specialist, the plant managers, the communication expert and the guy with the bow tie who collected the art for the headquarters. This opened the discussion into spaces which are very difficult to reach in a law firm.

Despite this homogeneous composition, many law firms are rife with internal dissent to a degree that a good CEO would never tolerate in a corporation. Every partner is a major shareholder in the firm and perceives an entitlement to impose his own (narrow) view on the rest of the partners. Thus, it is often painful and time consuming to rally all the open and hidden dissenters behind a strategy. Just talk to any of the managing partners of this world.

### 3.3 Denial of market shifts and unrealistic income expectations of partners

The banking, financial and government debt crisis has had a long-lasting and negative impact on the income of business lawyers. The crisis has reinforced some more structural trends, which have increased the pressures on law firm profits:

- Legal costs have become a major cost item for most clients and these clients develop strategies to keep a lid on them. Fee caps, discounts, panel arrangements, purchase of legal services through procurement departments and competitive bids are now widespread cost strategies among clients.
- Many services which were the product of time-consuming advice in the past are now standardised, and are sometimes available from the world wide web at almost no cost.[7]
- Many services which were traditionally provided by law firms can now be left to cheaper services such as LPO providers or technological platforms.
- Lawyers were among the big winners of the economic expansion and globalisation and have increased their incomes tremendously over the last 30 years. This has attracted a lot of young people to the profession. Law schools now produce many more lawyers than will really be needed in the future. So the legal industry reels in overcapacity.

These economic and structural challenges are here to stay. Like their pet clients, investment bankers, lawyers should realise that the current of history has started to flow against them when it comes to profitability. I always wonder at how this simple and obvious truth is disregarded by many law firm leaders. They do almost everything to keep the PPP up and do not realise that they are destroying the very fabric and competence of their firm. Instead, I believe that a wise law firm leader should stand in front of the partnership and say: "We made lots of money in the past; we will still make good money in the future, more than other professionals such as brain surgeons or auditors; let's accept this simple reality and do not force me to do stupid things which will destroy the sustainability of the firm and the chances of our younger lawyers."

### 3.4    Franchise milking and lack of stewardship and entrepreneurship

Many of the most successful law firms are huge franchises. They have their traditional clients and they attract new clients on the basis of their shiny brand. For these law firms it is true: we all are dwarfs standing on the shoulders of giants. Again, this is an oft-neglected truth, and this takes two forms:

- Lack of stewardship: many very successful lawyers credit their success entirely to their own intelligence and do not appreciate the fact that their achievements also have a lot to do with them being part of a great franchise. This failure to accept stewardship has spoiled many strategy discussions and executions.
- Lack of entrepreneurship: others are more modest and accept that they are part of a franchise. They are so modest that they resort to pure milking of the franchise. They lack the entrepreneurship gene, which is key to cultivating every great franchise. They never realise that they are the shoulders for the next generation.

---

7    See on this and the next point Richard Susskind's seminal book, *The End of Lawyers? Rethinking the Nature of Legal Services*, Oxford University Press (2008).

3.5     **Poor execution and opportunistic behaviour**

But the greatest risk of all in a strategy process is poor execution. Corporate history is littered with good strategies poorly executed, or the other way around: you can be successful with almost everything reasonable as long as you execute it properly.

Lawyers have habits which fly in the face of this truth: they think in small print and not in big visions; they work on what their client puts on their desk in the morning; they are preoccupied with the next closing or filing; they love their timesheets and they are often cynical about the efforts of their management. They also tend to engage in opportunistic behaviour: if they see an opportunity which is good for them but is outside of the strategy, more often than not they take it.

An effective leadership will overcome these attitudes, slowly, gently, over years and with persuasion. The managers of the truly great law firms have done this, sometimes over generations: by being focused, with discipline, patience and persistence, and by acting as shining role models for generations of lawyers. As Alan Lightman has put it: "The passage of time brings increasing order."

*The author would like to thank Heinrich Christen, Daniel Daeniker, Christian Herbst, Christoph Lindinger, Ueli Looser as well as Christian and Tobias Kurer for their helpful comments and valuable input.*

# Drivers of change – driving strategy in law firms

Mats Anderson
Linklaters; clear blue water

## 1.    Introduction

*"In my old firm we waited for the telephone to ring. If the matter in any way could be described as business law, we took it on. In the new firm we decide what kind of work we want and then we go out and try to get it."*

This quote is not from a deeper thinker than myself. It is a simple way of describing change. This chapter deals with the issue of how to manage change and how to drive strategy in a law firm from the perspective of a practitioner. To put it simply, the chapter seeks to describe how to get from the first to the last sentence in the quote.

We have only just seen the start of globalisation. Information technology will develop further. What we have today will look like the Stone Age in just a couple of years. It is easy to say that these will be the major drivers of change for law firms in the future, because this will probably be true for all industries. Sometimes, political decisions affect an industry. Many years ago, there were limits in England on how many partners there could be in a law firm (at least if it was organised as a partnership, which most law firms are). Partners in a firm which now has some 400 partners have told me that they remember times when all the partners in the firm could meet to have lunch in a small dining room. It is ironic that at the time of writing, there are discussions in my home country, Sweden, regarding a proposed amendment to the tax rules, which would mean that law firms will effectively not be able to have more than 25 partners.

We could also look at some other drivers of change. For many years, law firms have heard – to the extent that they have been prepared to listen – that clients want more for less. For a long time nothing happened. When we discussed different ways to compete in an exercise in my old Swedish firm some 20 years ago, I suggested that price was one way to compete. The senior partner who was leading the exercise looked at me as if I was something the cat had dragged into the room. Price competition is here now. The days when you just started working, did the job, looked at how much was on the clock and sent invoices to the client are gone. Now you have to give an estimate or agree on a price before you start working. If you get the job.

Globalisation, development of technology, political decisions and price pressure are of course general factors that can drive change. Then there are other kinds of drivers of change; those that you as a firm can to some extent control. You might want to improve your market position, be a 'market leader'. You might want to have a larger home market (ie, expand into new markets). You might simply be less happy with what you are and try to improve your business.

Diversity – in particular gender aspects – is in my opinion not given the priority it should have in the context discussed here. Regardless of whether you look at larger international law firms, regional firms or national firms, the picture is the same. Less than 20% of partners are women. In Sweden, the larger firms have hired more female lawyers than male lawyers for at least 20 years; but very little has happened. It was true decades ago that women often left the firm after two to four years. And it is the same now. This picture is probably true in most countries in the western world. From my perspective it is not very productive to discuss diversity or gender as a discrimination issue. The better view is that almost half the population is a resource and talent pool and it is time to make better use of it, in order to improve our business.

On to the subject of this chapter, it is not to describe what drivers of change there might be for different firms. They will often be a combination of the above factors. What I am going to address is, as stated above, rather how to drive the strategy of a firm specifically in management of change situations.

I have had the privilege to be involved in this kind of exercise in two different capacities, as a partner in a law firm and as a law firm consultant. I think it will be easier for the reader to relate to the points I will make as regards driving strategy if I very briefly provide some examples of projects in which I have been involved. It should be noted that the type of law firms I have in mind when I share my thoughts and experience in the following are business law firms which are owned in the traditional way (ie, partnerships). The cases discussed in sections 2.1 and 2.2 below are two real projects I have experienced, while the case in section 2.3 is not. It rather describes types of projects I have experienced.

## 2. The cases

### 2.1 The first case

The L firm had for decades been the leading firm in its jurisdiction.

The 1980s saw a string of mergers among law firms in the country. In 1990 three leading firms had been formed. These firms were roughly the same size (whether measured by turnover or headcount). Their geographical coverage was identical; they had offices in the three major cities in the country. And they all had the same strategy – or perhaps, rather they shared the same lack of strategy.

In the 1990s the firms fared differently. One of them was the success story of the decade. Those who had heard about the firm in the late 1980s associated its name with a family law firm. A decade later the firm was a household name, at least among those dealing with business law firms in the region. The third firm saw a steady development of its business and it gradually strengthened its position further among blue chip clients.

The L firm did not fare so well. In 1992, a group of partners left the L firm. In 1997, another group left. In the following year, the firm joined the International Firm & Alliance and in September 2001, the L firm merged into the International Firm.

This project is an exercise where a leading national firm is transformed into an office and a part of a leading international firm.

## 2.2 The second case

Mergers in western Europe and a few other places had taken place. Business was coming back in the beginning of the 2000s. In the different offices of the International Firm referred to above, partners and local managers were busy trying to adapt to the strategy. People were generally happy; but not central management. In their view, the firm should not just be a leading firm; it should be the leading firm.

## 2.3 The third case

This concerns a national business law firm. It is doing alright. It is a top or second-tier firm, but only in its country or region. The firm s partners feel that the firm is losing ground to its competitors and needs to improve its market position, but they are not sure exactly how this should be done.

## 3. Driving a strategy

### 3.1 Perspectives of strategy

My proposition is that as a partner in a modern law firm you should be able to bring in clients and matters, carry out the work and see to it that money comes in, develop your people and develop your business. I appreciate that very few people are star performers in all these areas, but my view is that in a modern law firm you should strive to perform in four areas: acquisition, financials, leadership and business development.

I apply the same perspectives when looking at a firm, an office or a department. It is a simple way of looking at it, but simplicity is a virtue here and it helps you to be consistent when you are looking at the various parts of your business and its people. I apply this perspective, regardless of whether I am hiring young associates, other staff (this is a terrible expression, as it reflects the view that there are two kinds of people in this world, lawyers and non-lawyers), electing new partners or drawing up next year s business plan etc. I believe that this helps me to take a consistent approach (holistic, if you like) when seeking to drive the strategy of the firm. Thus, much of what I say below is influenced by this 'credo' and structured on the basis of: acquisition, financials, leadership and business development. Most of the discussion below is within the fields of leadership and financials. Initially, however, I would like to make some general points and observations.

### 3.2 The experience industry and a clear strategy

Law firms are in the experience industry. It is simply not possible to say that one firm is 'better' than another, because we cannot measure what is 'good' or 'better', even if we have agreed what qualities we should appreciate. But some firms have such standing that clients think they are receiving Rolls Royce service when a matter is handled by a given firm. Or the legal counsel of a corporate thinks that if I retain this firm, nobody will ever criticise me for having done so (except perhaps on grounds of cost). While it is very difficult, perhaps even impossible, to explain why certain firms have achieved such a position in the market, I think that there is one thing such firms have in common. A very clear strategy.

The clearer the strategy, the better. Truly successful firms are those where the partners, associates and other staff share a view with the outside world of what the firm is and what it stands for. When the client thinks that this matter is one where we should go with firm X, and the people of firm X agree that yes, this is really our business, then there is something that perhaps best can be described as trust. The clients trust that this is a matter that is best handled by firm X and the people in firm X trust that clients come to them for this kind of matter.

Another aspect of a clear strategy is guiding your people (ie, partner appraisal, or partner development as I prefer to call it). If the firm does not have a clear strategy, it is doubtful whether you should spend resources on a partner development programme, as such a programme among other things is an instrument to help partners understand what is required of them in order to contribute to what the firm wants to achieve. If the firm cannot clearly express what it wants to achieve, it will be very difficult to provide any guidance to partners about what they should and should not do (eg, what kind of clients and matters they should take on).

### 3.3    User friendliness

This issue applies in many areas – time recording, the structure for contributing to the know-how system, the drafting of business plans and so on. Whatever it is that you want people to do, you must see to it that is as simple and user friendly as possible. If one always seeks to have the things functioning perfectly on day one, not much will happen. It is better to get things started and to adjust later than to seek perfection from the outset. (See, for example, section 4.3 below on partner development programmes.)

### 3.4    Discipline and repetition

It is important to have discipline in the firm, particularly when you are trying to implement a new or revised strategy. Actions should be taken and sessions held within an agreed time frame. People must be held accountable for what they have done or for what they have not done. Too many partners in too many law firms have experienced too many partners' meetings where people have agreed to do various good things and nothing has ever happened.

In a law firm, the clients come first. If the client has an important and urgent matter then your partner should go and see the client rather than attend to internal meetings. (Whether matters are always so urgent is a different discussion, but let us just say that it is the client's privilege to decide on this – see section 3.2 above on the experience industry.) In my view, best practice for handling this is to be very consistent, perhaps to the point of being stubborn. If, for example, the department you are working in has not had weekly meetings before, it is my experience that it will take quite some time to get it into everybody s mind that you actually have these meetings. If you are consistent, and hold the meetings at the same time every week or month, it will eventually be in people's minds and they will show up. If you are flexible and shuffle your meeting times around, this will never happen.

## 4. Leadership

### 4.1 Buy-in from partners

It is fundamentally important that partners buy in to the firm's strategy. The firm's strategy is not what management or a majority at a partners' meeting has decided. Rather, it is what the partners do in the daily struggle in the office. If the management says that the strategy of the firm is to act for large, international clients in cross-border deals, but partners are more preoccupied with acting for closely held companies in local deals, then it is the latter that is the strategy of the firm. Though this is not the main subject of this chapter, it is important to touch upon the issue of how you get buy-in from partners for a strategy, especially if you want to get yourself a new strategy. There are different techniques that one can imagine to achieve buy-in. But in my experience the only way that really works is to convince the really influential partners of the firm that this is the right way to go. The project referred to, as section 2.2 above is a situation where this particular skill of the leaders of the firm was really tested. The reason for this was probably that, as opposed to the normal course of events, this project could not be driven on the back of discontent among people in the firm.

### 4.2 Listen to people

When I am involved in projects as a consultant, I seek at an early stage to carry out one-to-one interviews with partners and other people who carry the values of the firm. There are a number of reasons for this. One is, of course, that I as an outsider will get a better understanding of the firm and its people. Moreover, it is a way of opening up channels of communication. In my experience, people find it hard to resist the temptation to speak their mind for an hour or two, when confronted by somebody who is sitting there taking notes. A few common themes will always emerge from these interviews. Such themes can be good things, such as what it is that I appreciate and am proud of in my firm. But in the context of a strategy exercise, it is more the issues in the firm that need to be addressed that are of interest. I have carried out this kind of exercise in different countries and cultures. In each and every one of these cases, three to five issues have emerged as common themes. When I say common, I really mean common. Practically 100% of interviewees observe these common themes and describe them as issues that need to be addressed.

Interviews of this kind are very useful, particularly in an exercise such as section 2.3 above. They help you articulate what the issues really are and what it is that needs to be done. I have often found that what you can bring to the table as an outside counsel is the ability to identify an issue and describe how it can be addressed and handled.

So listen to people. But do not fool yourself and think that they will do as you say, just because you can present some good arguments. If you are in the business of managing change, you will find that people will only change and do things that they really believe in. It is, of course, better still if they think it was their idea in the first place!

## 4.3 Follow up what individuals do

I strongly believe in partner assessment programmes. They have been around in UK firms for many years now, but are still a relatively new feature in many other countries. In order to make it clear that it is not just a one-way exercise where the firm tells the partner what to do, but a process of two-way communication, I refer to this kind of tool as a partner development programme.

From the perspective of the individual partner, the programme will help him to understand what is expected by the firm on a detailed and concrete level. Being a partner in today's law firm is a much more complex challenge than in the past. It is no longer sufficient to bring in work and execute it well. In addition, a partner is expected to bring in the right kind of work, manage people and actively take part in the development of the firm. The programme should focus on areas where the individual partner could or should improve. As noted above, this is not a one-way process of communication. While feedback is given to the partner in the programme, it also provides an opportunity for the partner to express his opinions and expectations.

From the firm's perspective, it is a tool designed to ensure that the individual partner is actually doing what can reasonably be expected in order to assure the success of the firm. What can be expected varies with the strategy and culture of the firm.

The partner development programme also eases tension between partners or groups of partners. It seems almost inevitable that there are built-in tensions in partnerships. Junior partners often take the view that older partners do not work as hard as they should (lockstep firms), or that they watch their contacts jealously (performance-based firms). A properly conducted partner development programme makes partners more confident that such issues are handled by the firm. The partner development programme should be straightforward. The procedure, therefore, should be so framed that it takes a minimum of partners' time to prepare; questionnaires should be uncomplicated and easy to fill in, input data from the financial system must be presented in such a way that it is easy to understand etc.

The parameters (ie, the areas covered in the partner development programme) should also be easy to understand. This will not usually be a problem as far as 'hard factors' such as acquisition and financials are concerned (see section 3.1 above). 'Soft factors', such as business development and leadership are typically dealt with in a 360-degree feedback. But you cannot run before you walk. If you have not previously run programmes of this type, there is a risk with going directly into a fully fledged 360-degree exercise. It may take up too much of people's time and energy, so that they will feel limited enthusiasm for repeating the exercise. One alternative is to carry out this part of the programme in a simplified way the first time it is carried out. Instead of sending questionnaires around, the appraiser and appraisee sit down and go through the questions that you would typically have in a 360-degree questionnaire. It is important that the questions are straightforward and do not allow much room for individual interpretation. If you go to a 360-degree feedback, it is important to remember that all those taking part will need some introduction and education on how to handle this tool.

In summary, a partner development programme, typically serves the following purposes:
- It helps the partner understand what it is the firm expects from him.
- It is a tool to let the individual partner know what he is doing well and what areas should be improved.
- It helps the partner articulate his wishes and expectations.
- It is a forum for the partner and the firm to agree on necessary actions.
- It is a part of the profit-sharing system. In performance-based firms it helps the firm to come to a fair decision on profit sharing. In a lockstep firm it serves the purpose of checking that the partner is pulling his weight.

## 4.4    Appointing the leadership

I shall not elaborate further here on how the management or governance of the firm should best be structured, or what the partnership agreement should say on, for instance, the balance of powers between the firm and the individual partner. However, it is worth making just one observation on how the leadership of the firm is appointed. If you want to bring about change in a firm which traditionally is not very managed (if I can use that expression), one thing you should consider is how you appoint the central management of the firm, and typically the managing partner. You will get a stronger management if you do it through elections, and particularly where you have two candidates standing against each other. The drawback of elections of this type is that it is often the most successful partners who throw their hats in the ring and someone inevitably has to lose. You run the risk that the loser will then leave the firm.

## 5.    Financials

## 5.1    Figures make people tick

I often do benchmarking studies. I compare a firm s performance measured as turnover and profitability (using the 'classical' profit per equity partner as profitability measure) over time compared to its peer firms or other comparable players. This is a very powerful instrument. It is a guaranteed trigger for discussion and can often serve as an effective tool to make people take action.

There might be various reasons for this. One is that some markets are more transparent than others. In the United Kingdom and the United States, for instance, markets are very transparent in this field. For many years, it has been easy to follow how UK and US firms develop in terms of turnover and profitability. That is not the case in many countries in continental Europe. Moreover, it can differ a lot within a region. If you look at the Nordic region, Finland, Norway and Sweden are transparent in the sense that firms in these countries publish their turnover; but this is not the case in Denmark. However, this openness relates only to turnover, and profitability has to be figured out. So, often people simply do not have a clue as to how their firm is doing compared to their peers. But I think that to a large extent it is the comparison in itself that triggers people.

## 5.2    Figures when driving change

My experience is that figures are equally effective as a tool when you are working on the integration of businesses and offices. The projects referred to in sections 2.1 and 2.2 above were largely about integration. We had numerous management group meetings and exchanged information regarding best practice in the areas of marketing, know-how and recruiting etc. However, it was not until we started to look at figures that things really started to happen. It was when you understood how much another office billed its major clients, what the utilisation of another group or its average turnover per fee earner were, that you could relate to your own group or office and understand the synergies from which you could benefit.

Looking at figures can, however, also be counter-productive. In my practice as a law firm consultant, the kind of assignment that has come up most frequently has been looking at and attempting to improve profit-sharing systems. This is a topic you could probably spend a lifetime discussing. (Although there are only a few basic profit-sharing concepts such as lockstep, total contribution and eat what you kill, the variations seem endless.) Profit sharing is something you must handle with extra care, especially when you are in the business of managing change. When you are doing a merger (see section 2.1), you often simply have to introduce a new profit-sharing system for parts of the new firm. Normally, it is the smaller firm and its partners that have to accept the system of the larger firm (which is usually the surviving firm in the merger). But if you are not forced to change the profit-sharing system, for instance when you seek to improve the business of a 'standalone' firm (see section 2.3 above) and are not involved in a merger, my experience is that you should consider waiting before changing the profit-sharing system, and look at other things first.

I appreciate that the suggestion to hold back on the issue of profit sharing when you are trying to achieve change might sound like nonsense. Nowadays, people like me emphasise that the law firm must be more effective as a business organisation and one ingredient of this is that the partners should strive for a common goal. It then seems logical that if the firm has an 'old fashioned' eat what you kill system – which induces people to work hard as individuals but typically does not reward them for contributing to the firm – then you start your change management exercise by looking at the profit-sharing system. This sounds logical, but my experience is the opposite. If you want things done, do not start with the profit-sharing system unless you have to.

Key performance indicators (KPIs) are tools that you cannot do without if you try to run a law firm. A senior partner in my firm once said that running law a law firm is a high income, high-cost business. While people nowadays (after Lehman) pay much more attention to the cost side, I believe that this is still true. Naturally, you must control your costs; but the really material costs are salary, rent and (to a lesser but growing extent) IT. It is also true that you must see to it that you send out your invoices and ensure that they are paid. But I still think that it is the KPIs on the income side that are of interest.

I am happy to admit that I am almost obsessed when it comes to figures and law firms. I have mentioned traditional benchmarking above. But I have also spent many hours looking at other things, such as gearing (financial), where in the world a firm has its offices (if it is an international firm), the average value of corporate deals the firm is involved in, turnover per fee earner, the firm's ranking in certain league tables etc. And I have tried to cross-compare these parameters with each other. Before going into the KPIs that are more closely linked to the daily life of the firm, I would therefore like to touch upon some more general measurements.

We have already mentioned profit per equity partner (PEP). This is of course the classical measure of a law firm's profitability and it has been much criticised, especially in recent years. It is true that you can manipulate the PEP figure without really improving your business, for example simply by removing partners. But PEP has been around for many years, it is easy to understand and in most markets firms that have the highest reputation (in leagues tables etc) also show a high PEP relative to their competitors. I think it is here to stay for the foreseeable future.

The more I have looked at different indicators, the more convinced I am that the best measure of the quality of the work of a law firm (at least an international firm) is the income per fee earner figure.

Let us go back to the KPIs in the context of the daily struggle. One has to appreciate that one places more focus on different indicators in different firms and at different times. In a downturn for instance, it is critical that you invoice your work in a timely fashion and get the cash in. I would like to limit myself to what I think are the most important aspects to look at for most firms. In order to serve as efficient tools, your KPIs must be simple (ie, simple to understand and simple to apply). In one firm we had an interesting KPI – the gross margin per partner hour (GMPPH). I think that the idea behind it was that the only resource in the firm which was not endless was partners' time. So the more work the firm could carry out and get paid for, for each time unit spent by the partner, the better. I can understand that. I think. So if you as a partner have a number of matters in which you have recorded only a few minutes and other fee earners hundreds of hours, your GMPPH will look great. The problem was that no one really understood what we should do with the GMPPH figures.

The indicators that I think are 'must haves' if you try to run a law firm, are utilisation, notional billing rate and average billing rate.

Utilisation is often expressed in relative terms and seeks to describe what you get out of your people in terms of billable hours. If you choose to assume that eight billable hours per day equals 100% and associate X has produced eight billable hours one day, then the utilisation figure for associate X that day was 100%. The utilisation figure is useful because it provides you with adequate information on how you make use of your workforce. It is easy for everybody to understand and it prompts you to take action quickly when it is going the wrong way. It is also relevant to apply on all levels, be it at firm, office, group or individual level. As firms compute utilisation differently (eg, in the above example an eight-hour basis was used, whilst another firm might perhaps use a 10-hour basis), one should think twice before using this measurement in benchmarking exercises.

The notional billing rate (NBR) is an important tool especially when you are trying to change your business, because it is through this tool you can clearly express internally what kind of business it is that you really want. If you manage to push the NBR up in your business plans and budgets, then this is a signal to your partners that they must go after better-paid work. The average billing rate then serves as a reality check.

## 6.     Conclusion

At the outset, the working title of this chapter was "Driving strategy in changing market conditions". Initially, I mentioned some factors that I believe will be significant drivers of change in the future. Looking at historical, changing market conditions, I have in my professional life experienced the booming 1980s, financial crisis and recession in the early 1990s, the dot-com boom which saw the bubble burst in 2000, the years from around 2004 to 2008 – which was probably a golden age for business law firms – and now since 2008, the post-Lehman era where market conditions can at best be described as uncertain. It is, of course, true that when driving strategy and change you put emphasis on different aspects depending on whether times are booming or you are in a downturn. In the golden age, the credo was that partners should sell and look after relationships with the clients; and senior associates would manage projects. In the aftermath of Lehman, the emphasis is on bringing cash in, with partners having to dig into files rather than do client entertaining. But I believe that what works and what does not work when you are driving a strategy in a law firm is much the same, regardless of whether you are in a bear or bull market; and this is what I have tried to address in this chapter.

# Trends in the legal industry: a US perspective

David Barnard
Miriam Herman
Blaqwell

## 1. The US legal market

The US legal market is the largest in the world. Generating about $270 billion in revenue, the US legal industry accounts for 40% of the global legal market, and has continued to grow over the last few years, albeit at a lower rate than in the past (a compound annual growth rate of about 1.5% between 2008 and 2011, compared to more than 6% between 2002 and 2008).[1] Moreover, despite recent job losses, the US legal industry is expected to add about 75,000 jobs by 2020.[2]

About 60% of the country's more than 750,000 lawyers work in law firms with fewer than 160 attorneys (outside the *National Law Journal 250*), or in solo practice. These lawyers primarily serve individuals and small to medium-sized private companies. About another 25% of US lawyers work in government, business or other non-law firm settings.[3]

This chapter focuses on the upper end of law firm practices in the United States – namely, the 100 largest firms by revenue, or the *American Lawyer 100* (AmLaw 100).[4] These law firms primarily serve medium to large public and private companies, and collectively, they generated over $73 billion in revenue in 2012 and employed about 8.5% of the lawyers in the United States (over 65,000 lawyers) and roughly another 20,000 lawyers outside the United States.

As a group, the AmLaw 100 law firms have enjoyed tremendous success over the last 20 years. The total AmLaw 100 revenue and attorney population have grown in every year of the last two decades except 2009, and the compound annual revenue growth rate for the AmLaw 100 has been 8.5%.[5] Total profits for the AmLaw 100 have grown at a slightly higher compound annual growth rate (CAGR) of 8.8%. However, behind these collective numbers lie significant changes in the complexion of the

---

1    Datamonitor, *Legal Services: Global Industry Guide* (Datamonitor, November 2011), 113.
2    Mark Koba, "Courtroom Drama: Too Many Lawyers, Too Few Jobs", CNBC: Economy, June 9, 2013.
3    Harvard Law School, "Harvard Law School, Program on the Legal Profession", *Analysis of the Legal Profession and Law Firms (as of 2007)*, 2007, www.law.harvard.edu/programs/plp/pages/statistics.php. See also US Bureau of Labor Statistics: Occupational Outlook Handbook: Lawyers (citing 728,000 legal jobs in United States in 2010 and projecting 10% increase over 10 years). The ABA, however, reports a larger number (about 1.2 million) of licensed lawyers (as distinct from lawyers earning a living through the practice of law) in the United States in 2011 with a "significant but unknown number maintaining their licenses but working in other fields" according to ALM's "US Legal Industry Facts and Figures: How many lawyers are in the US?"
4    ALM, AmLaw 100 (ALM Legal Intelligence, 2012). All financial data for the AmLaw 100 used in this chapter is drawn from ALM Legal Intelligence's AmLaw 100 publication.
5    CAGR for the AmLaw 100 attorney population between 1992 and 2012 was 4%.

average AmLaw 100 firm and the competitive landscape, as well as a widening gap in the performance of individual firms.

Life in the highest echelons of the US legal industry has changed dramatically over the last 20 years, and we expect the next 20 years to be even more transformational.

## 1.1 The AM 100 from 1992 to 2012

We start with a comparison between the average AmLaw 100 law firm of 1992 and the average AmLaw 100 law firm of 2012. The comparison reveals significant increases in the scale, value creation, non-equity partner population and number of foreign offices and attorneys at the average AmLaw 100 firm. Moreover, looking at the AmLaw 100 as a whole, we see a reasonable amount of change in the composition of this elite competitive set.

A closer look at the last 10 years reveals two distinct periods, a high growth era (2002 to 2008) and the more recent slow growth era (2008 to 2012). The latter period was characterised by overcapacity among the AmLaw 100, a shift in the balance of power from the sellers of legal services to the buyers, and unprecedented price competition. As we look to the future, we find the AmLaw 100 is an increasingly differentiated group. We identify eight distinct categories of firms based on the nature of their geographic footprint and practice portfolio.

Each of these categories of AmLaw 100 firms offers a different value proposition to clients and talent. And yet fundamentally, these firms are all facing the same core challenge: how to survive and thrive in a low-growth US legal environment, and how to profit from international opportunities. In today's environment, there is not a single AmLaw 100 firm that can take for granted its ability to raise rates, add heads, or hold on to clients and talent.

Competitive firms have accepted key premises that characterise the new landscape and are quickly abandoning old models and mindsets. The defining features of the new legal landscape include the following:

- Clients are doing more in-house and via low-cost service providers, and are more discerning and hard-driving in their outside counsel relationships.
- Law firms have become multi-business enterprises and must be managed as such.
- The scale required for success is higher in most practices and markets.
- Profitability increases will depend heavily on driving greater value from each attorney.
- Law firms must master the three Ps: profitability analysis, pricing and project management.
- Exclusive reliance on the industry's historic and relatively monolithic talent and service delivery model is no longer an option.
- Effective lateral hiring and integration is an essential, but insufficient, growth engine.

These changes have strained traditional law firm models and intensified the competition for clients and talent. While the NY elite (and the magic circle) retain significant advantages, their pre-eminence is no longer assured. We see no single

model for success in the future and expect the leading firms to come from several
different corners of the legal industry.

2.     **Then and now: 1992 versus 2012**
The top 100 law firms in the United States look quite different today than they did
20 years ago in terms of their scale, profitability, and structure.

2.1    **Scale**
Law firms are operating on an entirely different scale than they were in 1992. Today
the average AmLaw 100 law firm has approximately five times the revenue ($730
million vs $140 million) and more than twice as many lawyers as the average AmLaw
100 law firm in 1992 (870 vs 370). Viscerally, the change is most dramatic among the
largest firms. Averaging nearly $1.4 billion in revenue (the largest have now broken
the $2 billion mark) and 1,600 attorneys, the 25 largest firms in the AmLaw 100 are
behemoths compared to the top 25 in 1992 which averaged $250 million in revenue
and 570 attorneys.

2.2    **Value creation**
The value created by (and expected from) an AmLaw 100 equity partner has also
soared. Twenty years ago, a $1 million book of business was the norm for an AmLaw
100 equity partner. Today it is the mark of an underperformer, with the average
revenue per equity partner at over $3.8 million. Average profit per equity partner
(PPEP) among the AmLaw 100 has also more than tripled (almost quadrupled),
jumping from $400,000 to nearly $1.5 million.

2.3    **Leverage**
One of the key changes underlying these figures is the evolution of the law firm leverage
model. Even post the recession era attorney cuts, the equity partner leverage of the
average AmLaw 100 firm stands at 3.5 compared to 1.9 in 1992 – and reflects a markedly
different pyramid. The increase in equity partner leverage has not been driven by a
sharp increase in the ratio of non-partner attorneys to partners (this ratio has increased,
but modestly), but by substantial growth in the income partner population. In the mid-
1990s, fewer than half of the AmLaw 100 firms reported having income (or non-equity)
partners, and those that reported income partners averaged fewer than 50. Income
partners accounted for about 5% of the AmLaw 100 attorney population. Today more
than 80 of the AmLaw 100 law firms report income partners, and these firms average
over 150 income partners. The income partner population has jumped to nearly 13,000,
or 15% of the AmLaw 100 attorney population. Meanwhile equity partners, once 35%
of the AmLaw 100 attorney population, now account for just over 20%.

2.4    **Internationalisation**
Another significant change in the AmLaw 100 has been internationalisation. While
today's AmLaw 100 firms range from the regional to the global, internationalisation
has been an industry-wide phenomenon.[6] In 1992, about half of the AmLaw 100 had
one or more offices outside the United States and these firms averaged approximately

38 foreign attorneys.[7] Today, virtually every AmLaw 100 firm (91 of the AmLaw 100) has at least one overseas office, and these firms average eight foreign offices and 219 foreign lawyers.[8] Moreover, a number of AmLaw 100 firms completed at least one merger or acquisition with a foreign law firm, including a handful of large-scale combinations under the verein structure (Norton Rose Fulbright, Dentons, Hogan Lovells, Squire Sanders, and DLA Piper).[9] For most of this period, the focus of internationalisation was on London and the European continent, but with the onset of the recession, that focus shifted abruptly to China.[10] Between 2008 and 2012, the AmLaw 100 added more lawyers in China than in any other country outside the United States, giving China the second largest AmLaw 100 attorney population outside the United States (just behind the United Kingdom).[11]

## 2.5    Winners, losers, and mergers

There has been a reasonable amount of change in the composition of the AmLaw 100 over the last two decades. Only 59 of the firms that were in the AmLaw 100 in 1992 were still in the AmLaw 100 in 2012 under the same (or similar) name. Eleven AmLaw 100 firms have dissolved since 1992, and another 19 firms have been acquired or merged into a new firm of a different name. Movement between the AmLaw 100 and the AmLaw 200 has also been substantial, with 29 firms moving up from the AmLaw 200 into the AmLaw 100 and 11 firms dropping from the AmLaw 100 to the AmLaw 200. Nonetheless, the difficulty of gaining access to the AmLaw 100 remains considerable: only two notable 'start-ups' (both litigation-focused) have made their way into the AmLaw 100 over the last 30 years: Boies Schiller, founded in 1997, and Quinn Emanuel, founded in 1986.

We have also seen the emergence of an increasingly powerful class of apparent 'winners' among the AmLaw 100. In 2012, the 25 AmLaw 100 firms with the largest total profit pools controlled 51% of the total profits in the AmLaw 100. In 2002, this

---

6    Georgina Stanley, "New World Orders: The 2012 Global 100", www.legalweek.com, October 19 2012, www.legalweek.com/legal-week/analysis/2218042/new-world-orders-the-2012-global-100.

7    ALM, AmLaw 100 (ALM Legal Intelligence, 1992); The National Law Journal, *NLJ 250* (ALM Legal Intelligence, 1992). 1992 figures are calculated based on the 80 AmLaw 100 firms appearing in the 1992 *NLJ 250*.

8    The National Law Journal, *NLJ 350* (ALM Legal Intelligence, 2012); ALM, *AmLaw 100*, 2012. Select firm websites. Six of the 91 firms do not list foreign attorneys in the *NLJ 350*, but list foreign office(s) on their website. 2012 figures are calculated based on the 85 firms with foreign attorney data in the *NLJ 350*.

9    A *verein* is a structure under Swiss law that enables businesses to associate while maintaining separate profit pools and remaining distinct for tax and liability purposes. The *verein* structure has been used extensively by accounting firms and other commercial and non-profit organisations operating in multiple jurisdictions. Baker McKenzie has long used the *verein* structure, and other law firms seeking to forge a global network and brand and share certain costs without the challenges of full integration have followed. Other similar structures or contractual relationships among firms can accomplish the same objectives. *Verein*-type structures are, however, not without their critics and challenges. For a discussion of the extent of integration under a *verein* and other issues, see, Chris Johnson, "Vereins: The New Structure for Global Firms", *The American Lawyer*, March 7 2013, www.americanlawyer.com/PubArticleTAL.jsp?id=1202591158156&slreturn=20130803121637.

10    "China Sees Global Law-Firm Growth as Jobs Fall in US", UK, Bloomberg, February 23 2009. Elizabeth Broomhall, "Top Firms Relocate More Senior Lawyers to Asia as East's Rise Continues", www.legalweek.com, March 28 2013, www.legalweek.com/legal-week/news/2257762/top-firms-relocate-more-senior-lawyers-to-asia-as-easts-rise-continues; Jessica Seah, "Singapore's Wall Street Problem", *The American Lawyer*, April 15 2013, www.americanlawyer.com/PubArticleTAL.jsp?id=1202596010795.

11    The National Law Journal, *NLJ 350*.

same group of 25 firms accounted for only 43% of total AmLaw 100 profits. We believe profit pool is a particularly important measure of a law firm's success as it is the best proxy for a law firm's ability to invest and for its resilience in the face of market downturns.[12] Moreover, more than half of the top 25 by total profits were also among the top 25 by PPEP.

## 3. The last 10 years – a tale of two eras

The last 10 years have been a bit of a roller coaster ride for US law firms.[13] The decade can be divided into two eras – the high growth era (2002 to 2008) and the more recent, slow growth era (2008 to 2012).

### 3.1 The high growth era (2002 to 2008)

In 2002, law firms were feeling the effects of the tech bubble burst. And a handful of firms built around tech (eg, Brobeck, Testa, Venture Law Group)[14] ended up dissolving or merging into other firms.

However, the survivors had a lot to celebrate in the next six years, as the AmLaw 100 enjoyed tremendous growth in revenue and profitability. Combined revenue for the AmLaw 100 nearly doubled from 2002 to 2008, fuelled by a combination of headcount growth (the AmLaw 100 attorney population grew at a CAGR of 4% during this period) and consistent annual rate increases, averaging over 5% per year.[15] Driven by this steady annual growth in revenue, average profit per partner for the AmLaw 100 grew by almost 60% during this period. This was a heady time for the AmLaw 100, characterised by growing summer associate and first-year associate classes, steep increases in associate compensation, lavish retreats and holiday parties, and eye-popping bonuses.[16]

In many respects, the 'rising tide' lifted most ships in the AmLaw 100. But the stratification of the AmLaw 100 was well underway. We saw a widening gap between profitability per equity partner at the most profitable firms in the AmLaw 100 and the rest. The gap between the average PPEP for the 25 most profitable firms in the AmLaw 100 and the next quartile grew from $500,000 to $800,000 between 2002 and 2008. And while there was an abundance of transactional work, the highest

12 Wendy Becker et al, "Lawyers Get Down to Business", McKinsey Quarterly (2001): 50–52.
13 Precipitating a great deal of commentary and analysis, see, for example, Richard Susskind, Tomorrow's Lawyers: An Introduction to Your Future (Oxford University Press, 2013); Richard Susskind, The End of Lawyers: Rethinking the Nature of Legal Services (Oxford University Press, 2008); Bruce MacEwan, Growth is Dead: Now What? Law Firms on the Brink (New York: Adam Smith Esq, 2012); Stephen Harper, The Lawyer Bubble: A Profession in Crisis (Basic Books, 2013); Brian Tamanaha, Failing Law Schools (Chicago: The University of Chicago Press, 2012).
14 Ellen Rosen, "The Complicated End of an Ex-Law Firm", The New York Times, February 9 2007, www.nytimes.com/2007/02/09/business/09legal.html. John Cook, "Venture Law Group Agrees to Merger", SeattlePi, September 2 2003, www.seattlepi.com/business/article/Venture-Law-Group-agrees-to-merger-1123185.php. "Brobeck Falls", The Recorder, January 31 2003. "Testa, Hurwitz and Thibeault Votes to Dissolve", Boston Business Journal, January 14 2005.
15 Citi and Hildebrandt Consulting, 2013 Client Advisory (Citi, 2013), 4 (citing average partner rate increases of 6.7% per year between 2004 and 2008); Jennifer Smith, "Law Firms Regain Some Pricing Power", WSJ.com, June 23 2013 (citing average rate increase of 8.2% between 2007 and 2008).
16 NALP – The Association for Legal Career Professionals, Salaries for New Lawyers: An Update on Where We Are and How We Got Here, June 25 2013. For a satirical piece on the impact of the recession on law firm largesse see: The Snark, "Big Law's Small-Budget Holidays", Law.com, December 17 2009, www.law.com/jsp/article.jsp?id=1202436387433.

value transactions were consolidating in a relatively small group of primarily New York firms (plus a few 'out-of-town' stand-outs, such as Latham and Kirkland).

By 2008, there were also clear signs of stress in the wake of the financial crisis. Firms heavily invested in structured finance were hit hardest (Thacher dissolved in late 2008; Cadwalader laid off about 130 lawyers in 2008; McKee Nelson was acquired by Bingham in 2009).[17] Others were not immune. Heller Ehrman dissolved in 2008, and the legal industry saw the beginning of what would be an unprecedented number of lawyer lay-offs.

### 3.2    The slow growth era (2008 to 2012)

The recession and post-recession era have been sobering times for the legal industry. Collective revenue for the AmLaw 100 dropped for the first time in 2009 on a year-to-year basis. And between 2008 and 2012, compound annual revenue growth for the AmLaw 100 decelerated to just over 2%. The AmLaw 100 attorney population also dropped in 2009, and has grown more modestly since then. Two more once high-flying AmLaw 100 firms, Dewey LeBoeuf and Howrey, went out of business, and more may follow.[18] Profitability has been under pressure industry-wide, but by aggressively managing equity partner ranks, and improving margins via attorney and staff lay-offs and expense reductions, the AmLaw 100 managed to keep average PPEP climbing albeit at a much lower rate (AmLaw 100 average PPEP grew at a CAGR of under 4% between 2008 and 2012, down from nearly 8% between 2002 and 2008).

With growth no longer a given, the competitive intensity within the AmLaw 100 rose dramatically.

### (a)    Overcapacity

Significant overcapacity emerged within the AmLaw 100, reflected in lower average billable hours per attorney since 2008.[19] Many firms took aggressive action in 2008 and 2009, laying off associates, exiting or de-equitising partners, rescinding or delaying offers to first-year associates (and in some cases paying them to pursue public interest work), cancelling or abbreviating summer programmes, and significantly reducing summer associate and first-year class sizes.[20] Entry-level hiring

---

17    "With 96 More Layoffs, Cadwalader Faces its 'Cataclysmic Event'", *New York Law Journal*, July 31 2008; "How Thacher Proffitt Came to an End", *The AmLaw Daily*, December 22 2008; Bingham McCutchen Acquires McKee Nelson, *The American Lawyer*, June 7 2009.
18    "Why more law firms will go the way of Dewey LeBoeuf", *Forbes*, 5 August 2012.
19    *2013 Report on the State of the Legal Market* (Georgetown Law, 2013), 4, 16–17. Citi and Hildebrandt Consulting, *2013 Client Advisory* (Citi, 2013), 2.
20    "Law Firms Feel Strain of Layoffs and Cutbacks" *New York Times*", November 11 2008; "Top Layoff List Led by Orrick and Latham", *ABA Journal*, March 5 2009; Getting paid not to work, CNN Money, May 1 2009. Zack Needles, "Law Firms Predict More Layoffs Among Non-Equity Partners, Support Staff", *Law.com*, June 23 2010, www.law.com/jsp/article.jsp?id=1202462916505; Tamara Loomis, "Don't Look Back; The Recession Has Helped Usher in a New Era. Better to Embrace It Than Yearn for the Good Old Days", *The American Lawyer*, October 1 2009. Robin Sparkman, "Back in Black", *The American Lawyer*, May 1 2011; NALP, "Law School Grads Face Worst Job Market Yet – Less Than Half Find Jobs in Private Practice", *NALP The Association for Legal Career Professionals*, June 7 2012, www.nalp.org/2011selectedfindingsrelease. Entry level hiring has improved from lows in 2008 to 2009, and is now largely flat, see NALP, "Perspectives on Fall 2012 Law Student Recruiting", *NALP The Association for Legal Career Professionals*, 2012, www.nalp.org/uploads/PerspectivesonFall2012Law StudentRecruiting.pdf.

among large US law firms was up in 2012 relative to 2011, but nowhere near peak levels;[21] and overcapacity persists in the AmLaw 100. Citibank estimates that law firms continue to have between 6.5% and 8.5% excess lawyer capacity.[22] Associate lay-offs are making news again in 2013, as are partner compensation cuts and exits, and more are expected.[23] However, some firms are holding onto excess capacity because of the premium they place on traditional professional service values. Others are holding onto expertise they need, but cannot fully utilise. Some are driven by seniors with short time horizons and little motivation for a paradigm change; and others by partners who lack a full understanding of the changing environment and the economics of their firms.[24]

(b)    *Clients in the driver's seat*

The client–law firm dynamic changed markedly during this period, as clients, under intense economic pressure themselves, now had both the imperative and the opportunity to demand more for less.[25] Increasingly sophisticated general counsel and the equivalent, generally drawn from the ranks of law firm partners, were armed with an intimate knowledge of law firm economics, staffing models, talent, and practice strengths and weaknesses in part due to the increased access to information about law firm performance, pricing, and costs, and the performance of individual law firm practices and lawyers.

Clients, especially the largest ones, adopted a commercial approach to their outside counsel needs, bundling and unbundling the work to secure the best deals,[26] grading outside counsel on everything from their expertise to their collaboration,[27] demanding detailed project plans and budgets, and inserting themselves in law firm decisions on staffing to demand fewer partner hours, fewer associate hours (and in some cases, no first-year associates at all), or both.

(c)    *Price competition*

With cost control as their top management priority, most clients, especially the largest financial institutions and multinationals, reacted by aggressively negotiating

---

21    Karen Sloan, "Large Firms in a Hiring Mood Again", *The National Law Journal*, June 24 2013; Karen Sloan, "Demand for Associate Help Remains Flat in NLJ 350", *The National Law Journal*, June 10 2013.
22    Julie Triedman, "Weil Slashes 60 Associates, 110 Staffers", *The Am Law Daily*, June 24 2013 (citing Dan DiPietro of Citibank).
23    Ashby Jones and Joe Palazzolo, "Law-Firm Slowdown Fuels Cuts at Weil Gotshal", *The Wall Street Journal*, June 24 2013; "17 Partners Plan to Leave Patton Boggs", *Legal Times*, June 24 2013.
24    For a discussion of the extent of overcapacity and some of its causes see, Bruce MacEwan, "Excess Capacity", in *Growth Is Dead: Now What? Law Firms on the Brink* (New York: Adam Smith Esq, 2012).
25    Alex Newman, "Feeling the Squeeze – GCs Are Trying to Get as Much as They Can from Their External Advisers", www.legalweek.com, April 19 2013, www.legalweek.com/legal-week/analysis/2261410/feeling-the-squeeze-gcs-under-pressure-to-cut-costs-are-pushing-for-more-value-from-their-external-lawyers; Shannon Green, "The Big Squeeze", *Corporate Counsel*, December 1 2012, www.law.com/corporatecounsel/PubArticleCC.jsp?id=1202578084293; Susskind, *Tomorrow's Lawyers*, 4.
26    For an example of how corporations are restructuring their relationships with law firms see, Alex Newman, "Shell to Scrap Single Global Panel in International Shake-up of Advisers", *www.legalweek.com*, March 22 2013, www.legalweek.com/legal-week/news/2256491/shell-to-scrap-single-global-panel-in-international-shakeup-of-advisers.
27    Aric Press, "The Pfizer Model, One Year Later", *The AmLaw Daily*, January 10 2011.
28    Altman Weil "2012 Chief Legal Officer Survey" (71% of General Counsel respondents negotiated price reductions from outside counsel in last 12 months and 41% shifted work to lower-priced law firms).

price discounts.[28] And with growth no longer a given and underutilisation a pervasive reality, law firms, even the most elite, began to compete more aggressively on price. Increased price transparency flowing from growth in the number of RFPs, panels, and bidding wars has further intensified the competition.[29] The result has been deeper discounts, lower realisation rates, and more extensive use of alternative fee arrangements.[30]

## 4.     Different firms playing the game differently

From a strategic standpoint, the AmLaw 100 law firms of 2013 fall into eight high-level categories based on their geographic focus, their position on the value spectrum, and their breadth of practice: global high-value, global broad-value, national high-value, national broad-value, NY elite, regional high-value, regional broad-value, and specialists.[31]

These categories of firms are by dint of their origins, evolution, and strategies, competing on very different bases and facing different challenges and opportunity sets:

- *Geographic focus.* Today's AmLaw 100 law firms have vastly different geographic footprints, ranging from global to national to NY-focused to regional. The extent and focus of a firm's geographic footprint is, of course, central to its market position.

- *Position on the value spectrum.* Another defining feature is a law firm's position on the value spectrum. While there is no perfect measure of value, average revenue per lawyer (RPL) is a reasonable proxy, as it reflects the average revenue generated by each lawyer (and, unlike profit per lawyer, is not directly affected by the firm's partnership structure/classifications).[32] A high RPL can be achieved in multiple ways, including premium work (high hourly rates, success fees), collection of contingencies, efficient deployment/management of resources (eg, high billable hours, effective deployment of alternative staffing, effective pricing and matter/project management in the context of fixed fee arrangement). A low RPL does not necessarily reflect an exclusive focus on low-value work, but instead is often associated with firms that compete across a broad span of the value spectrum.

- *Breadth of practice.* As a general matter, high-value firms tend to have more focused practice portfolios than broad-value firms. There also continues to be a small number of specialist firms that compete based on distinctiveness in a

---

29      Patrick G Lee, "Pricing Tactic Spooks Lawyers", *Wall Street Journal*, August 2 2011, sec Business Technology, http://online.wsj.com/article/SB10001424053111904292504576482243557793536.html. LexisNexis® RFP Activity Summary Report, www.lexisnexis.com/pdf/intelligence/rfpsurveyreport.pdf.

30      Citi and Hildebrandt Consulting, 2013 Client Advisory (Citi, 2013), page 7; Altman Weil "2012 Chief Legal Officer Survey;" *2013 Report on the State of the Legal Market*, 5–6. Relying on a recent survey ALM concludes that while the billable hour is still dominant, "[a]lternative fee arrangements are of growing importance to both law firms and legal departments because they currently represent one of the periodic shifts in how legal business is conducted". ALM, *Speaking Different Languages: Alternative Fee Arrangements for Law Firms and Legal Departments* (ALM Legal Intelligence, April 2012), 9.

31      Generally, law firms were classified based on several metrics (RPL, percentage of attorneys outside the United States, percentage of attorneys outside home state) with some adjustments based on qualitative factors.

32      We note that all other things being equal, firms and practices with lower leverage will tend to have higher RPL; and thus RPL is not an effective proxy for profitability.

narrow practice portfolio, focused in one or two legal disciplines, typically litigation and/or IP.

## 4.1 Global firms

We have classified as global those firms with more than 25% of their attorneys outside the United States. These firms were strong performers between 2002 and 2008 with annual growth in revenue and total profits of over 11%, but performance since 2008 has been constrained by the slower recovery overseas. This is particularly true for the global broad-value firms which collectively have seen compound annual growth rates of less than 1% in revenue, total profits, and PPEP.

### (a) Global high-value

High-value global firms have RPL over $850,000. Generally, their focus internationally is on capturing a large share of high-value cross-border transactions, regulatory matters, and disputes, as opposed to local foreign opportunities. Examples of global high-value firms include: Latham & Watkins, Cleary Gottlieb, and Weil Gotschal. These firms are focused on a portfolio of high-value practices and their overseas footprints tend to be tightly crafted around these practices.

### (b) Global broad-value

Broad-value global firms generally have RPL under $850,000. Global broad-value firms tend to operate in a wider and more diverse set of locations and to have broader-based domestic practices in the countries in which they operate. A number are the product of significant mergers, and several are operating under Swiss vereins. When successful, their overseas offices serve as portals for inbound US work and for a share of high-value cross-border work. For these firms, the key to success is integrating and capitalising on their networks to capture a growing share of high-value work, while effectively marshalling different service delivery and pricing models to achieve profitability on their broad base of mid-tier and lower value national and multi-jurisdictional work. Examples of global broad-value firms include DLA Piper, Baker & McKenzie, Dentons, Jones Day, Mayer Brown and Hogan Lovells.

## 4.2 National firms

We have classified national firms as those with more than 50% of their attorneys outside their home state and under 25% of their attorneys outside the United States. Judged by their economic trajectory, the national high-value firms have, as a class, been the strongest performers over the last decade.

### (a) National high-value

High-value national firms have RPL over $850,000. They tend to drive growth and stature through a portfolio of high-value franchise practices that are heavily rooted in the United States (eg, private equity, litigation, and IP among others). They have more limited overseas presence than their global peers, and their foreign capability is generally focused on cross-border opportunities in a subset of their core practices. On the whole, the national high-value firms have been especially successful in achieving continued growth in revenue (3% CAGR), total profits (over 8% CAGR), and PPEP (over 6% CAGR) between 2008 and 2012, outpacing all other segments of the AmLaw 100. Their success in this tough market environment bodes well for them in the coming decade. Examples of national high-value firms include Gibson Dunn, Kirkland & Ellis, King & Spalding, and Ropes & Gray.

### (b)    *National broad-value*

These national firms have RPL below $850,000. Many have grown by acquisitions and mergers. On the whole, they tend to have a broad geographic footprint in the United States and a broad practice portfolio, but the firms range significantly in terms of size, geographic spread, and practice focus. The challenge for these firms is to distinguish themselves on the basis of their cost-effectiveness, attractive pricing, and disciplined and flexible staffing, project/matter management, and firm management. Some like Greenberg Traurig and K&L Gates are among the largest in the AmLaw 100 and have relatively broad geographic footprints; while others, like Drinker Biddle & Reath and Troutman Sanders, are well outside the AmLaw50 and retain a regional character. Similarly, some retain access to a share of high-value work, either in their area of regional strength or in one or more practices of strength, while others do not, resulting in a broad range of PPEP levels.

## 4.3    NY elite

The NY elite have long dominated high-value work with a nexus to New York. While most now have one or more offices outside NY, generally, these NY-originated firms remain NY-centric in their strategy, attitude, and management. Collectively, their share of total AmLaw 100 profits has dropped over the last 10 years, but their average RPL and profit per equity partner remain at the top-end of the AmLaw 100. Their average RPL is more than $1.2 million, and their average PPEP is $2.7 million. Generally, they compete based on their distinctive brands (which typically have global reach), talent, and track records in a set of practices associated with New York capital markets and financial institutions, both of which were hit hard by the recession. While these practices are primarily transactional, they can include transaction-related litigation and regulatory specialties (eg, securities litigation, M&A-related litigation, antitrust, tax). No longer sheltered from pricing pressure or the competition from global and national firms,[33] the challenge for NY elite firms is to adapt to the new legal landscape while maintaining their distinctiveness. Examples of NY elite firms include Sullivan & Cromwell, Simpson Thacher, and Cravath.

## 4.4    Regional firms

Regional firms continue to have 50% or more of their attorneys based in their home states. They can, and often do, have significant presence and practice reach in other domestic and foreign locations and many have nationally prominent brands, but their home-state concentration gives them a regional character and focus. Regional

---

33    "The view from 9th Avenue – the emerging challenges facing New York's elite", *Legalweek*, November 30 2012.

high-value firms have done particularly well at sustaining profit pool and PPEP growth in the post-recession period.

(a)     *Regional high-value*
Regional high-value firms have RPL over $850,000. While their attorney populations are concentrated in their home state, many have distinctive national (and international) practices, attractive profitability levels (average PPEP for the group is nearly $1.6 million), and stand-out brands based on their regional and practice strengths. Collectively, these firms have managed to grow total profits and PPEP at a healthy, compound annual rate of about 5% between 2008 and 2012. Examples of regional high value firms include Arnold & Porter, Vinson & Elkins, Wilson Sonsini, Jenner & Block, Steptoe & Johnson, and Hughes Hubbard.

(b)     *Regional broad-value*
Regional broad-value firms have RPL below $850,000. These firms find themselves at a lower value point for a variety of reasons. Some are constrained by the nature of work and price points available in their home states. Others miss out on the high-value work in their home state because they lack a leadership position in key home state practices. And many have a strong base in their home state, but relatively limited higher value, national and international pieces to their practices. Examples of regional broad-value firms include Faegre Baker Daniels, Pepper Hamilton, Dorsey & Whitney, and Haynes & Boone.

4.5     **Specialists**
The specialists are defined by their focus on one or two legal disciplines, typically litigation and/or IP. Specialists can be national or global in character, and their RPL varies depending on their specialty. Their focus benefits them in terms of branding, talent and expertise development, management, and execution. However, they lack the benefits of diversification, and thus are vulnerable to a downturn in their area of focus. Their primary challenge is to maintain, in their area of specialty, a wide enough lead (in terms of expertise, brand and talent) over broader practice firms and a sufficiently distinctive value proposition to clients and talent to outweigh the attractions of a broader platform (eg, a client's ability to access a broader set of services in an integrated fashion, partners' ability to cross-sell and be cross-sold). Examples of specialists include Boies, Schiller (litigation), Quinn Emanuel (IP litigation/ litigation), Finnegan Henderson (IP), and Fragomen (immigration).

5.      **The future of the AmLaw 100**
We offer views on the future of the legal industry with an appropriate degree of caution and humility. Looking back, there were certain legal industry trends of the last decade that were already evident in the 1990s (eg, consolidation, stratification, differentiation). At the same time, there were others that seemed significant but proved fleeting (eg, the threat from accounting firms and the proliferation of tech-sector/new economy-focused law firms). Moreover, we recognise that the pace of change has increased across all sectors, including the legal industry.

## 5.1    The US market

The US legal market remains the largest and most lucrative in the world.[34] We expect this to continue to be true over the next decade; and as a result, defending and growing US market share will be the primary focus for most AmLaw 100 firms. However, we do not expect a return to the buoyant, law firm-led US legal market we saw from 2002 to 2008.[35] Demand growth in the US legal industry was estimated at 0.5% in 2012, and we believe it will continue to be slow.[36] This is in part due to the growth in in-house legal capacity as large companies internalise substantial amounts of work to reduce their total costs.[37] With reduced entry-level hiring and continued lay-offs, fewer students will choose law school,[38] and the overcapacity will eventually dissipate, but it could take quite a while.[39] Moreover, with clients having recognised their power and asserted themselves in their relationships with outside counsel, there is no going back.

## 5.2    The international opportunity

Although most AmLaw 100 firms are now international in character, relatively few have succeeded in wringing sizeable profits from international opportunities. We see two types of international opportunities for US law firms – both of which present significant challenges. The high-value opportunity is narrowly focused on significant cross-border transactions, disputes, and regulatory concerns and centred primarily on a defined set of global economic hubs. The competition for these high stakes, cross-border matters (primarily among NY elite, global high-value, magic circle, and global broad-value firms) is exceptionally intense. The broader opportunity lies in important, but more routine cross-border work, and also in a growing number of local markets overseas (generally, these opportunities are targets for the global broad-value firms, able to leverage expansive geographic platforms and local capabilities). We expect most local markets overseas to generate lower profitability levels for the foreseeable future with the European market still suffering from the economic

---

34    Datamonitor, *Legal Services: Global Industry Guide*, 113. See also *The Economist*, "Law Firms: A Less Gilded Future", *The Economist*, May 5 2011, www.economist.com/node/18651114.

35    Susskind, *Tomorrow's Lawyers*, 55–57; Report: The Boom Years Are Not Coming Back, Get Used to It, *The AmLaw Daily*, January 13 2013; Tom Huddleston, "Survey: Firm Leaders Admit Downturn's Permanent Impact", *The Am Law Daily*, May 21 2013, www.americanlawyer.com/PubArticleALD.jsp?id=1202601129609&slreturn=20130424103533.

36    Leigh Jones, "The Old Rules No Longer Apply in The NLJ 350", The National Law Journal, June 10 2013 citing 2013 Report on the State of the Legal Market (Georgetown University Law Center and Thomson Reuters Corp., 2013). Aric Press, "Study Shows Drop in Demand for Legal Services", *The American Lawyer*, August 31 2013 (citing study by TyMetrix Legal Analytics showing drop in legal services hours purchased and legal services fees paid by 70 large corporate clients in first half of 2013 compared to first half of 2012). "Big Firm Salaries Drop: What it Means", *The National Jurist*, September 21 2012.

37    Law Firm 360, "Law Firms Lose Out On Billions As GCs Take Work In-House", June 20 2013.

38    "Law Firms Keep Squeezing Associates", *The Wall Street Journal*, January 30 2012. We are already witnessing a reduction in law school applicants, see Ethan Bronner, "Law Schools' Applications Fall as Costs Rise and Jobs Are Cut", *The New York Times*, January 30, 2013, sec Education, www.nytimes.com/2013/01/31/education/law-schools-applications-fall-as-costs-rise-and-jobs-are-cut.html.

39    Mark Koba, "Courtroom Drama: Too Many Lawyers, Too Few Jobs", CNBC: Economy, June 9 2013 ("the Bureau of Labor Statistics projects nearly 74,000 new lawyer jobs created in the United States over the next 7 years … [but] American law schools will graduate about 44,000 students each year during that time.").

40    IMF, *World Economic Outlook: April 2013 – Hopes, Realities, Risks*, World Economic and Financial Surveys (Washington DC: International Monetary Fund, April 1 2013), 46–49.

downturn[40] and Asian and other emerging markets still offering a relatively low return compared to the US legal market. Longer term, it is not clear whether the US/UK style of legal practice will be the dominant paradigm in Asia, whether a new Australasian model will emerge (ie, led by King & Wood Mallesons), or whether national champion firms will emerge and succeed in protecting their markets. For now, we expect most international expansion will come through focused, relatively small offices in growth markets (eg, Singapore and Korea),[41] formal and more meaningful alliances among independent national market leaders,[42] and large-scale acquisitions and mergers (primarily the purview of the global broad-value firms and increasingly executed via a verein or verein-like structure).

## 5.3    The oligopoly

High-value work and top talent will continue to consolidate in a smaller number of firms. Much more numerous than a traditional oligopoly, this collection of firms is amassing an increasing share of high-value US and cross-border work and top talent, as reflected in their growing share of total AmLaw 100 profits, and their increasing stature and brand power. The challenging, slow-growth legal market has accelerated this trend. The number of firms with the financial resources to sustain expensive networks, high-end talent acquisitions and essential investments in technology is shrinking; and only a few have the brand power and platinum home-grown talent models to continue to draw a growing share of high-value work absent these investments. While it is impossible to predict with certainty, we estimate that of the AmLaw 100, 20 to 25 firms may make it into the oligopoly (another five to eight will likely originate in the United Kingdom based on their dominance in that market and their share in the oligopoly for cross-border work). We do not expect all of these US oligopoly firms to emerge from the same strategic segment. In fact, we expect the oligopoly to include a mix of NY elite, national high-value, global high-value, and global broad-value firms. This is consistent with a recent BTI survey in which corporate counsel identified a list of firms most likely to survive and thrive over the long-term that included firms as diverse as Skadden, Jones Day, Baker McKenzie, Cravath, Kirkland, Latham, Sidley, Sullivan & Cromwell, and DLA Piper – all of which we view as good bets to end up in the oligopoly.[43]

## 5.4    The performance imperatives

Many law firms in the AmLaw 100 have the opportunity to thrive over the next decade whether they end up in the oligopoly or not. The key to success lies in a handful of performance imperatives which sound deceptively simple.

---

41    Anthony Lin, "Korea: How much is too much", Asian Lawyer, January 2013 ("Some 17 US and UK firms have either applied to open an office in Korea or publicly stated their intention to do so ..."); Julia Love, "Firms Beef Up Singapore Offices as a Launching Pad for Other Markets", The Recorder, January 7 2013.
42    Martha Neil, "UK Megafirm Linklaters Forms Alliance with Australia's Allens Arthur Robinson", ABA Journal, April 23 2012; Alex Newman, "Linklaters and Simpson Thacher forge close relationship for key deals", Legalweek, June 21 2013.
43    BTI Consulting Group, 2013 BTI Brand Elite: Client Perceptions of the Best-Branded Law Firms (Wellesley, Massachusetts: BTI Consulting Group, 2013).

(a)     *Meet important client needs in a way that sets your firm apart*

Client needs are constantly changing. The law firms with longevity will be those that consistently meet an important set of client needs in a distinctive fashion. Some will win on the basis of their distinctive legal expertise (the traditional basis of competition), others on preeminence in one or more client sectors, their global platforms, or their value for money. There is no single formula. But to be fungible is to be vulnerable. And the bar is rising continuously. Clients are creating larger, more capable and more efficient in-house legal departments; and they have a growing number of options for outsourcing low to moderate-value work that is not expertise-intensive.[44] In-house counsel are also increasingly adept at unbundling portions of individual matters to different law firms to achieve greater cost-effectiveness. Moreover, with the surfeit of AmLaw 100 lawyers courting their business, clients are looking for the perfect fit for their highest stakes matters; this means a combination of a stand-out lawyer, stand-out team, stand-out practice, and stand-out firm for the particular type of work in question. Typically, this translates into choosing the law firm and lawyers that have a long and successful track record handling the particular type of matter in question for others in the same industry (or sub-industry) and in the same geographies. Clients are also amassing and analysing an increasing amount of comparative law firm expense data, not just on hourly rates by type of lawyer, but also on the full cost of different types of matters and phases of work. This information advantage is further enhancing client leverage in fee negotiations,[45] and clients are switching firms more readily in search of greater value. Although selection to a client's panel of preferred providers remains a source of advantage, it is no guarantee of high-value work, a large share of wallet, or a profitable relationship. That said, clients are more prepared to invest in broad-based relationships where they see significant upside. The implication for law firms is that mutually advantageous institutional client relationships are harder to build, but more valuable than ever before.

(b)     *Manage your firm as a multi-business enterprise*

Professional and disciplined management is no longer optional – or a price to be paid by only the largest or most global AmLaw 100 firms. Even at a modest annual growth rate (ie, roughly 3%), revenue at the average AmLaw 100 law firm will approach $1 billion over the next 10 years. Businesses of this size demand more and better management than most AmLaw 100 firms have today. This includes more effective attorney leadership and management at the firm and practice levels and more effective professional management in key functions including finance, marketing and business development, talent management, client relationship management, and information technology. Moreover, today's AmLaw 100 firms consist of multiple

---

44      Corporate Counsel, "2012 Law Department Metrics Benchmarking Survey", *Corporate Counsel*, 2012, www.law.com/corporatecounsel/PubArticleCC.jsp?id=1202578197775. Altman Weil "2012 Chief Legal Officer Survey". Alex Newman, "Shell to Scrap Single Global Panel in International Shake-up of Advisers", www.legalweek.com, March 22 2013, www.legalweek.com/legal-week/news/2256491/shell-to-scrap-single-global-panel-in-international-shakeup-of-advisers.
45      Citi and Hildebrandt Consulting, 2013 Client Advisory (Citi, 2013).

businesses and need to be managed that way. The primary axis along which a firm's businesses are defined will vary depending on the firm's portfolio, its strategy, and its basis of differentiation in the market. For some firms, the businesses will be best defined along traditional practice lines (around legal disciplines or competencies such as M&A, capital markets, securities litigation, tax). For others, industry-focused businesses (eg, life sciences, technology, private equity) or geographically focused businesses will be most effective, and for some law firms, a hybrid model will prove optimal. The overarching imperatives are to recognise the real businesses in which your firm is competing; organise around these businesses; put effective leaders in place (leaders who are credible business generators distinguished by their ability to motivate and facilitate collective initiatives and success); set revenue, profitability, and market-focused performance objectives; empower each business to adopt the talent, service delivery, and pricing models best suited to their business; and measure and reward business performance in a meaningful and consistent fashion. Moreover, successful firms will also generate substantially greater value from cross-business and cross-office opportunities and from the 'corporate centre' (eg, via brand management, risk management, training, systems, knowledge management); and will find ways to strengthen the 'glue' that holds their firm together in the face of the heightened strains created by increases in firm size, geographic dispersion, and competitive imperatives.

(c)   *Achieve competitive scale in your core practices/geographies*
The competitive scale required for success has risen significantly in most practices and geographies. In every practice and geography, clients are looking for greater depth and breadth of expertise, a longer and more directly relevant track record, the headline talent and bench strength to take on multiple large matters, and a brand that represents a 'safe harbour', all of which correlate with greater scale – not scale for its own sake, but the right scale. While a practice or office's sheer number of attorneys is, of course, an imperfect measure of competitive scale as we have defined it, it is nonetheless instructive. For example, a look at leaders in the IP litigation arena reveals that many of the leading national firms in the field now have 250 to 300 IP litigators; and a look at top 'out-of-town' firms in the NY market suggests that the minimum scale required for success in NY is 250 attorneys.

(d)   *Drive greater value from every attorney*
The next 10 years in the legal industry are more likely to resemble the last five years than the earlier high-growth era. Thus, most AmLaw 100 firms will not be able to rely on brisk growth in the number of attorneys and partners or annual, across-the-board, increases in hourly rates to fuel further increases in profitability. Instead, they will need to drive greater value from every attorney. There are a range of paths for achieving this goal, including a greater share of premium work, more effective attorney utilisation and performance management (including systematically shedding excess capacity and unsustainable businesses, and exiting underperforming attorneys), better success in contingency work, more disciplined client and matter intake, improved pricing policies and execution (including effective use of

alternative fee arrangements), efficient use of alternative resources (non-lawyers, contract lawyers, outsourcing), and effective matter/project management in the context of fixed fee arrangements.

*(e)* ***Build institutional muscle in profitability analysis, pricing, and project management***
All paths to driving greater value from every attorney depend on three core competencies which remain highly underdeveloped at most AmLaw 100 firms:
- analysing client and matter profitability;
- pricing; and
- project planning and management.

Law firms that do not build these capabilities on an institutional basis and ground them in a deeper understanding of the economics of different types of client relationships, matters, pricing arrangements, and staffing models will be flying blind in a turbulent environment.

**Analysing client and matter profitability:** Although many in the AmLaw 100 have the analytical tools to analyse client and matter profitability systematically, few are doing it. And even fewer firms have made client and matter profitability important performance metrics for their partners and integrated this analysis into their ongoing matter intake, planning, pricing models and negotiations, staffing, matter management, and performance assessment processes. Many are using realisation as a proxy for profitability even though a lower realisation matter can, of course, be quite profitable depending on the staffing model. To the extent AmLaw 100 firms are conducting client and matter profitability analyses on more than an ad hoc basis, it remains largely the province of the finance department with few in firm leadership and the broader partnership having internalised the relevant metrics and data, and their implications.

**Pricing:** For decades, pricing was a relatively simple exercise in the legal industry. Despite the acknowledged problems and widespread complaints associated with hourly billing, the hourly rate system went largely unchallenged until the recession. Firms set their rates primarily based on associate tenure and partner tenure or tier with some variations based on geography (eg, a New York rate and a national rate) and practice; and generally increased rates by well over 5% each year.[46] With the onset of the recession, many froze rates temporarily, and while average rates have started to increase again, this growth is muted.[47] Rate increases continue to be hard-fought, while deep discounts and declining realisation rates are increasingly the norm.[48] Despite underutilisation, few firms have managed to deploy marginal cost

46   Citi and Hildebrandt Consulting, 2013 Client Advisory (Citi, 2013).
47   Jennifer Smith, "Law Firms Regain Some Pricing Power", WSJ.com, June 23 2013 (average rate increase in 2012 did not approach the average increase of 8.2% between 2007 and 2008).
48   *2013 Report on the State of the Legal Market*, 5–6. Citi and Hildebrandt Consulting, 2013 Client Advisory (Citi, 2013).

pricing effectively. Moreover, the talk about alternative fee arrangements has finally turned into action, but most law firms are ill-prepared to price and manage on this basis. In the last few years, many firms have hired full-time pricing professionals, some of whom also have project management responsibilities, but few firms have a well-developed pricing function equipped with appropriate historical firm data on costs, staffing and profitability by matter and activity type, timely market data, and the right metrics; and integrated with law firm practices and client service teams.[49] Moreover, even fewer firms have established lawyer accountability for effective pricing.

**Project planning and management:** While many law firms have been bastions of excellence, few historically would claim to be bastions of efficiency. With clients demanding transparency, predictability, more sophisticated cost–benefit analysis, and substantially greater cost-effectiveness, disciplined and systematic project planning and management are now essential to a law firm's market and economic success. If pricing is on an hourly basis, clients are inserting aggressively themselves into decisions on firm activities and resource deployment, looking for assurance that hours are being wisely spent and pressing for write-downs where they see 'uneccessary hours'. And if pricing is on a fixed-fee basis, law firms must manage to a budget or see their margins eaten away and face the prospect of significant cost over-runs. Most law firms recognise the importance of project planning and management, and many have hired project managers, purchased and implemented supporting systems, and conducted training programmes.[50] However, few have made project planning and management a way of life among their partners and associates. Making project planning and management a way of life requires a new paradigm for matter management (including more rigorous, informed decision analysis),[51] robust data sets, insight-producing analysis, lawyer accountability, and a commitment to continuous learning and improvement. Law firms need to collect and analyse data on the time, resource deployment, costs, and outcomes for different types of matters, phases of work, and individual tasks; derive insights from this data; and apply those insights in a way that improves decisions on the optimal approach and service delivery model for individual matters, and enhances the law firm's overall efficiency and effectiveness. Moreover, the frontline behavioural change required will only happen if partners and associates are fully engaged in and accountable for effective project planning and management.

- *Rethink your talent model and service delivery.* For decades, the law firm talent and service delivery model was relatively static and homogenous. And

---

49    "Firms Hire Price Watchdogs As Clients Up Cost Pressure", Law360, 5-14-13. Susan Hackett, "Reconnecting Law Firm Pricing to Cost, Profit, and Value", Corporate Counsel, September 25 2012, www.law.com/corporatecounsel/PubArticleCC.jsp?id=1202572446358; Susan Hackett, "6 Critical Strategies Used By Law Firm Pricing Directors", Corporate Counsel, September 27 2012, www.law.com/corporatecounsel/PubArticleCC.jsp?id=1202572601682.
50    Alan Cohen, "The Eureka Moment – the Implementation of Legal Project Management", www.legalweek.com, September 14 2012, www.legalweek.com/legal-week/feature/2204722/the-eureka-moment-the-implementation-of-legal-project-management.
51    Leonid Kravets, "Lex Machina Raises $4.8M First Round Led By Cue Ball Capital As IP Litigation Reaches New Highs", TechCrunch, May 1 2013.

despite its shortcomings, it might have lived on for many more decades if not for the recession. Overcapacity, the low growth environment, non-law firm options for routinised work, and more demanding clients mean the status quo is no longer an option. The challenge is to seize the opportunity to innovate instead of keeping the old model on life support. Leading firms will develop multiple new talent and service delivery models, aligned to meet the needs of different types of clients and matters. Moreover, they will take a more disciplined approach to talent and service management. Consistent with these trends, we expect to see further declines in first-year associate class size and in the ratio of total associates to partners;[52] an end to ballooning income partner populations; growth in the number of staff (or non-partner track) attorneys (increasingly co-located in lower cost locations following the trend in support staff centralisation and relocation); and more extensive use of outsourcing, temporary/contract attorneys, and technology-driven solutions for routine legal functions. We also expect to see more effective ongoing performance management in the associate, income partner, and equity partner ranks – with underperformers at all levels exited more systematically. Moreover, there will be increasing differentiation in associate compensation levels based on geographic market, practice and individual associate performance. At the same time, we expect to see greater investment in attorney development at all career stages, focused on a crisply articulated and agreed set of core competencies consistent with each individual firm's strategy and value proposition to clients and talent; and a return to real partner–associate mentoring relationships.

- *Make your lateral hiring accretive, but do not count on it to be your core engine of growth.* Virtually all AmLaw 100 law firms have jumped on the lateral partner hiring bandwagon, but most are not getting a good return on their investment (many are not even measuring it).[53] We expect partner mobility to ramp up over the next decade, creating real opportunities for firms that know what kind of talent they want, are good at finding it and quick at jumping on opportunities created by dissolving firms and dissatisfied groups (we expect more of both), know how much the talent is worth to them and resist the temptation to overpay, invest as much or more in integrating their

---

52    "Recession ripples through large firm associate ranks", *Chicago Lawyer Magazine*, June 1 2012. "Law Firms Keep Squeezing Associates", *The Wall Street Journal*, January 30 2012. "Big Firm Salaries Drop: What it Means", *The National Jurist*, September 21 2012 ("The legal industry is going through exactly what so many other industries have gone through", said James Leipold, NALP's executive director. "Globalization and advances in technology are eroding jobs. Some jobs have gone overseas; some are better done by software and computers. Even if the market picks up, that's still not necessarily going to increase head count [at law firms].")

53    William Henderson and Christopher Zorn, "Playing Not to Lose", *The American Lawyer*, March 1 2013, www.americanlawyer.com/PubArticleTAL.jsp?id=1202585323924. For further reading and analysis on lateral hiring trends see Marc Galanter and William D Henderson, *The Elastic Tournament: The Second Transformation of the Big Law Firm*, SSRN Scholarly Paper (Rochester, NY: Social Science Research Network), accessed May 23 2013, http://papers.ssrn.com/abstract=1104711; William D Henderson and Leonard Bierman, *An Empirical Analysis of Lateral Lawyer Trends from 2000 to 2007: The Emerging Equilibrium for Corporate Law Firms*, SSRN Scholarly Paper (Rochester, NY: Social Science Research Network, May 19 2009), http://papers.ssrn.com/abstract=1407051. See also Citi and Hildebrandt Consulting, 2013 Client Advisory (Citi, 2013).

laterals as they do in finding and hiring them, and know when to cut their losses. That said, even the best at hiring and getting value from lateral partners should not assume that lateral hiring will achieve the kind of growth to which they aspire. Internally driven growth strategies, effectively executed, are a far more certain path to consistent, high-value growth in the current and anticipated, market environment.

- *Learn from the failures of the past.* There are some important lessons to be drawn from the law firm failures of the last decade.[54] While they may seem obvious, many firms are not heeding them. Over reliance on an individual sector or practice leaves the broader firm highly vulnerable to a downturn in that business. Fast-paced growth via high-paid laterals can strain a firm's economics, compensation system, and sense of partnership beyond repair. Use of debt financing should be conservative. Failed merger negotiations can put a firm in an irreversible, downward spiral. The abrupt departure of a group of partners or end of one or more large matters can be a life-threatening event for even a reasonably large, well-regarded firm with a stable of loyal attorneys and clients.

## 6. The trends to watch

### 6.1 Alternative legal service providers

The legal process outsourcing industry generates over $2 billion in revenue globally, and has expanded from document management to a broader range of legal services.[55] Moreover, firms like Axiom are going head-to-head with the country's largest law firms by providing leading corporations and financial institutions with expert lawyers at a substantially lower cost. If Axiom were a law firm, it would already rank among the AmLaw 200.[56] Axiom's success and, in particular, the growth of its managed services division (offering permanent outsourcing solutions to Fortune 500 clients and the equivalent) suggests that alternative legal service providers may be a threat to certain tranches of work performed by the AmLaw 100 that are not expertise-intensive and can be performed more efficiently through a scale operation leveraging strong process management and technology.[57]

### 6.2 Technology

Technology has already produced dramatic changes in the way lawyers practice law in areas ranging from e-discovery to legal research to knowledge management to

---

54 Mark Harris, "Why More Law Firms Will Go the Way of Dewey & LeBoeuf", Forbes, May 8 2012; Victoria Pynchon, "Why Billion Dollar Law Firms Fail and How to Avoid Their Fate", Forbes, May 21 2012. Heidi Moore, "Ambitious Corporate Law Firm Collapses", *Marketplace Business*, May 29 2012.
55 Leigh Jones, "The Old Rules No Longer Apply in The NLJ 350", NLJ June 10 2013 citing a 2012 study by Mary Lacity, a professor at University of Missouri-St Louis, and Leslie Willcocks, a London School of Economics professor, estimating the LPO market at $2.4 billion globally with annual growth of 28%.
56 Drew Combs, "Axiom Global is Trying to Beat Firms at Their Own Game", *Corporate Counsel*, July 17 2012, www.law.com/corporatecounsel/PubArticleCC.jsp?id=1342343127168.
57 Benjamin H Barton, *A Glass Half Full Look at the Changes in the American Legal Market*, SSRN Scholarly Paper (Rochester, NY: Social Science Research Network, January 30 2013), http://papers.ssrn.com/abstract=2054857.

client interface and data sharing. We take for granted the impact of video conferencing, and blackberry and smart phone technology. And yet, technology has not to date been a 'disruptor' in the legal industry.[58] Linklaters Blue Flag[59] dates to 1996 and provides online legal services in areas including compliance and e-learning among others, though its industry impact has been limited. But consistent with the premise that disruptive technologies tend to come from 'below',[60] our attention should be focused on players like LegalZoom.[61] Named one of the world's 50 most innovative companies by Fast Company in 2012,[62] LegalZoom's 2011 revenue was over $150 million and the company has recently added online consulting services to its business line, and built a network of law firms and attorneys across 40 states in the United States.[63] The possible applications of artificial intelligence to the legal industry are also worth considering. We note that the winning idea at the March 2013 IBM Watson Case Competition was a business plan for using Watson to predict the probability of success in legal disputes.[64]

## 6.3    Third-party financing of litigation

Litigation finance is a small but growing industry that has sprung up over the last five years.[65] Pioneered by firms including Burford and Juridica Capital Management, this burgeoning industry initially focused on financing plaintiff class actions in exchange for a share of the award if the suit is successful. However, there is increasing interest and investment in financing litigation by big business interested in capping their legal costs.[66] The future of third-party litigation financing and its implications are unclear. Many have expressed concern over the risks to clients and the profession with some calling for regulation of the litigation finance industry.[67] Others see it as a source of value for plaintiffs, defendants, and the legal system with the potential to

---

58      *Ibid*, 10–21.
59      BlueFlag, "Online Legal Services from Linklaters", *Linklaters BlueFlag*, 2013, https://blueflag.linklaters. com/Pages/BlueFlagHome.aspx.
60      See www.claytonchristensen.com/key-concepts/ ("Disruptive innovation, a term of art coined by Clayton Christensen, describes a process by which a product or service takes root initially in simple applications at the bottom of a market and then relentlessly moves up market, eventually displacing established competitors."); Clayton M Christensen, *The Innovator's Dilemma: The Revolutionary Book That Will Change the Way You Do Business*, (HarperBusiness, 2011).
61      Benjamin H Barton, "A Glass Half Full Look at the Changes in the American Legal Market", SSRN Scholarly Paper (Rochester, NY: Social Science Research Network, January 30 2013), http://papers.ssrn.com/abstract=2054857.
62      David Lidsky, "LegalZoom", *Fast Company*, 2012, www.fastcompany.com/most-innovative-companies/2012/legalzoom.
63      *Ibid*; Joe Palazzolo, "The IPO That Everyone Is Talking About ...", *WSJ Blogs – Law Blog*, May 18 2012, http://blogs.wsj.com/law/2012/05/18/the-ipo-that-everyone-is-talking-about/.
64      Disruptive Legal Innovators, "How long before IBM enters legal services industry? ... It Already Has", March 14 2013. See also Leonid Kravets, "Lex Machina Raises $4.8M First Round Led By Cue Ball Capital As IP Litigation Reaches New Highs", TechCrunch, May 1 2013.
65      For a good introduction to this new area see, Maya Steinitz, *Whose Claim Is This Anyway? Third Party Litigation Funding*, SSRN Scholarly Paper (Rochester, NY: Social Science Research Network, August 2 2010), http://papers.ssrn.com/abstract=1586053. See also Roger Parloff, "Have You Got a Piece of This Lawsuit? – Fortune Features", *CNNMoney*, June 28 2011, http://features.blogs.fortune.cnn.com/ 2011/06/28/have-you-got-a-piece-of-this-lawsuit-2/. And Jason Lyon, "Revolution in Progress: Third-Party Funding of American Litigation", *UCLA Law Revue* no 58 (2010): 572–608.
66      David Lat, "Litigation Finance: The Next Hot Trend?", *Above the Law*, April 8 2013, http://abovethelaw.com/2013/04/litigation-finance-the-next-hot-trend/.
67      Nate Raymond, "Businesses Call for Controls on Litigation Funding Firms", October 26 2012, www.insurancejournal.com/news/national/2012/10/26/268092.htm.

fuel a substantial increase in the demand for legal services.[68] Although we think it is unlikely that third-party litigation financing will have a transformative effect on the US legal industry over the next decade, given its highly pedigreed talent base (culled from the ranks of elite law firms, hedge funds, and investment banks),[69] it would be imprudent to discount this new industry's potential impact.

### 6.4    Non-lawyer investment in law firms

Both Australia and the United Kingdom now allow non-lawyer investment in law firms.[70] However, activity and interest to date has been limited and concentrated among smaller firms, particularly in the personal injury arena (the most prominent exception is Australia's Slater & Gordon which listed on the Australian Stock Exchange in 2007).[71] In the United States, non-lawyers are generally prohibited from owning a stake in a law firm (the District of Columbia, where lawyers are allowed to share profits with non-lawyers, is an exception). That said, there is active debate in progress at the state and national levels on the merits of opening up law firms to public and private investors with prominent advocates on both sides of the argument.[72] Proponents of non-lawyer investment in law firms argue that outside investment would provide the funds and incentives for enhanced law firm efficiency and client value, as well as enhancing US competitiveness against other jurisdictions; while opponents cite the risks to lawyer independence, professional ethics, and the lawyer–client relationship.[73] It seems unlikely that the US legal establishment will be a change leader on this issue; and the limited interest and pace of change in the United Kingdom and Australia are instructive. Nonetheless, its potential impact makes this another trend worth watching.

### 7.    Conclusion

Today's law firms are facing multiple challenges, including a slow growth environment, powerful and increasingly capable and informed clients, more aggressive and differentiated law firm competitors (many of which are operating on

---

68    Bradley T Borden, "Third-Party Litigation Financing and the Impending Resurgence of the Legal Profession", huffingtonpost, May 4 2013.

69    Leigh Jones, "Another Litigation Finance Firm Opens Its Doors", *The American Lawyer*, April 8 2013, www.americanlawyer.com/PubArticleTAL.jsp?id=1202595169879&Another_Litigation_Finance_Firm_Opens_Its_Doors&slreturn=20130507123513.

70    John Eligon, "Selling Pieces of Law Firms to Investors", *The New York Times*, October 28 2011, sec Business Day, www.nytimes.com/2011/10/29/business/selling-pieces-of-law-firms-to-investors.html.

71    *Ibid*; Thomson Reuters, "UK Law Firms Shun Private Equity Investment", Reuters, October 21 2012, www.reuters.com/article/2012/10/21/britain-law-privatequity-idUSL5E8LJFTC20121021.

72    ABA Commission on Ethics 20/20 Working Group on Alternative and Business Structures, *Issues Paper Concerning Alternative Business Structures* (ABA Commission on Ethics, April 5 2011), www.americanbar.org/content/dam/aba/administrative/ethics_2020/abs_issues_paper.authcheckdam.pdf. See also, William Henderson, "What Would Happen If Nonlawyers Invested in Law Firms? Soon We Will Have Data", *The Legal Whiteboard*, November 1 2012, http://lawprofessors.typepad.com/legalwhiteboard/2012/11/what-would-happen-if-nonlawyers-invested-in-law-firms-soon-we-will-have-data.html.

73    A recent case brought by firm *Jacoby & Myers* has brought to the fore the arguments for and against alternative business structures for law firms in the United States, see *The Economist*, "The Case Against Clones: A Lawsuit Could Lead to More Competition and More Choice", *The Economist*, February 2 2013, www.economist.com/news/business/21571132-lawsuit-could-lead-more-competition-and-more-choice-case-against-clones.

an unprecedented and global scale), a host of non-law firm competitors invading previously uncontested spaces in the legal market, partnerships accustomed to high and growing levels of profitability, a frothy market for top lateral talent, and a greater investment imperative. And yet legal and regulatory complexity and risk are on the rise, generating myriad opportunities for AmLaw 100 firms to create real and substantial value for their clients and to prosper as a result. In this context, we expect to see disproportionate returns going to a defined set of 'winners', that further distance themselves from the pack. We also expect to see continued opportunities for a broader set of firms able to meet the challenges of the new legal environment with greater strategic focus and more disciplined and innovative business models.

# Emerging market response to trends shaping the legal market

Irina Paliashvili
RULG – Ukrainian Legal Group, PA; CIS Local Counsel Forum

---

## 1. Introduction

This chapter summarises the results of collective brainstorming by legal market leaders of the countries of the CIS economic region on most of the aspects of law firm strategy covered in other chapters of this book.

First, a few words on the CIS economic region, its legal community and its place in the global economy and global legal market. The abbreviation 'CIS' is taken from the name of the international organisation which emerged after the dissolution of the Soviet Union – the Commonwealth of Independent States. In the economic context, however, the 'CIS' abbreviation has long lost its political connotations, and in the absence of a better term, is used in the global market to define an emerging economic region which covers most of the post-Soviet space. One of the countries of this region, Russia, is also a part of the group of emerging economies known as BRIC that also includes Brazil, India and China. Globally BRIC is treated as one group, but when it comes to Russia within BRIC, not only Russia is implied, but a much broader CIS economic region. Global CIS-centred transactions and projects always cover more than one country of the CIS region (eg, Russia, Kazakhstan, Ukraine, Moldova, Belarus and so on). In addition there is also an active market within the CIS region with direct business and investment activity among its constituent countries.

It is therefore only natural that, in response to this global and regional activity, national law firms of the CIS countries saw it as vital to become involved in the process of globalisation and also to form their own CIS legal community. To strengthen their current position and to enhance their future prospects, many CIS law firms are looking for international capabilities and to take their place within the global legal market. Understanding that globalisation is inevitable and irreversible and that it is up to us to decide whether we want to be active participants or stay behind and be outsiders watching the rest of the business and legal community adapt to the changes, business-minded CIS lawyers got organised in order to join the process instead of just staying on the sidelines and watching globalisation pass by.

## 2. The CIS Local Counsel Forum

The key platform of the CIS Legal community for the past eight years has been the CIS Local Counsel Forum (www.rulg.com/cisforum/), an informal network of managing and senior partners of national law firms from the CIS economic region, who gather every year in different countries of the region and invite partners from international law firms from around the world to join these meetings. The members of the CIS Forum understand the significance of globalisation and are actively and enthusiastically involved in it. In particular, at every meeting they eagerly discuss law firm management strategy, what Christoph H Vaagt summarises as "how to manage a firm in an emerging country, how to make it more 'resilient' and how to make sure that the firm prospers".

In terms of internationalisation of CIS law firms, and their contribution to the global legal market, the CIS Forum has demonstrated very interesting and important dynamics over the past eight years. The Forum covers the firm-to-firm segment of the legal market, and over the years a huge number of referrals were made at the Forum or through the contacts made there. When the first Forum was held in 2006, however, the majority of the referrals, if not all of them, came from international law firms to CIS law firms. This was basically one-way traffic and hence the name 'CIS *Local Counsel* Forum'. Then, gradually, CIS law firms developed and strengthened, CIS clients went global, and more and more CIS law firms started giving referrals to their international counterparts. Today it has come to the point where the referral traffic is definitely a two-way street, with referrals from CIS law firms to international law firms sometimes outweighing the referrals they receive, and each of us becoming local counsel to one another.

Although there are various topics discussed at the CIS Forum, the topic of law firm management and law firm strategy, which is the subject of this book, is discussed each year. The different aspects of this topic are dictated by the current challenges of today's life, which is moving with phenomenal speed. For example, some of the more recent aspects of this topic have been:

- How global trends reflect on CIS economic region law firms.
- Unique aspects of managing a local law firm in an emerging market.
- Meeting the challenges of growth and cross-border capabilities.
- Going from competing for clients, to competing for talent and back to competing for clients.
- Merge or not to merge? And if the latter – then internationally, regionally or locally?
- The role of the legal infrastructure industry (professional media, consulting, legal directories, HR, marketing) for a local law firm.
- Marketing: when and how to say 'no'?

3.    **Formats for discussion at the CIS Forum**

There are several formats for this discussion at the CIS Forum. One has been there from the beginning and is called 'management hour'. This is an internal meeting of CIS law firms (also open to international delegates), conducted in an informal manner in the afternoon before the main conference opens. Very often the topics raised at this meeting set the tone for the rest of the particular Forum.

The other format, which was introduced at the seventh CIS Forum in Yerevan in 2012, and continued at the eighth CIS Forum in Kiev in 2013, is an interactive audience panel on the most current and critical topic of the year, moderated by the leaders of the international and CIS legal communities. There are no speakers at this panel, only moderators, who outline the issues and then engage the audience in the discussion. This panel is followed by instant voting on several provocative questions on the main topic, with the results, sometimes unexpected and controversial, being instantly displayed.

The first audience panel in June 2012 focused on globalisation and its impact on law practice. The second in June 2013 continued with the topic of globalisation, but focused on a new aspect, basically discussing how we can adjust to the 'new normal' of the current economic environment. This idea had been in the air for several months, but seemed to be best expressed in a CNN interview in the winter of 2013 by the founder of the World Economic Forum, Klaus Schwab. He commented that the economic crisis has continued since 2008, with all of us suffering from it for years, but that the moment has finally come to accept the new realities and adjust to these new circumstances with optimism, which he termed 'resilient dynamism'. This idea also works perfectly for the legal community, both global and in the CIS, so we discussed how to transform the shock, which we have been experiencing all these years, into a positive.

## 4. Weathering the economic crisis: 'resilient dynamism'

First, we have to accept that a new reality, new conditions and new business environment, including for the law practice, have emerged; and instead of complaining about the crisis and waiting for the 'good old days' to return, we need to understand that we have reached 'the point of no return' and learn to accept this new environment. This also turns out to be a topic championed by the IBA, and thoroughly discussed in this book: how to shift the focus from the conditions that prevailed before and during the crisis, and to press the 'reset' button to carry on perestroika within each law firm, and within the legal community.

The questions posed and the results of instant voting deserve some analysis. First, it should be mentioned that the entire CIS Forum audience votes. This audience comprises roughly 40% of delegates who are partners of CIS law firms, 40% who are partners of international firms, 15% who are in-house counsel from major multinational and CIS companies and 5% from the legal industry (professional media, legal market consultants, law firm directories, etc). During voting we do not distinguish between these categories of delegates, so the voting results are not representative of just the CIS legal community, but of all the delegates of the Forum.

The first group of questions both in 2012 and 2013 was related to the place of CIS law firms in the global legal market. In 2012, 57% of the delegates believed that we will see new global law firms emerging from the CIS region. In 2013, 57% of delegates concluded that international clients acknowledge that the leaders of local markets can provide advice at the top international standard level, but only 27% thought that international clients are prepared to pay the leaders of local markets rates equal to, or exceeding those of, international law firms.

Keeping in mind this competitive disadvantage in their own market, the delegates were asked whether the CIS countries should introduce protectionist measures, restricting the access of foreign law firms to practice in their jurisdictions. In 2012, there was a majority of votes in favour of protection measures (50.1% for and 47% against, with the rest undecided). In 2013, this changed to a majority voting against (42% for and 52% against, with the rest undecided). This represents quite a liberal approach, which is also followed in practice in many CIS jurisdictions, especially considering how tough, complicated and restrictive admission to law practice is in many countries of the world (not only in most western countries, but also in the BRIC countries – Brazil, India and China).

The next series of questions related to how the delegates view strategies for globalisation and enhancing the international capabilities of their law firms. In 2012, 67.5% of delegates confirmed that they are members of international legal networks; and in 2013 70% acknowledged that they benefit from globalisation (from the work international law firms bring to the region).

When it comes to closer ties, however, the delegates were not so sure. In 2013, 53% rejected the argument that merger with an international law firm would present a cost-saving resulting from shared administrative and marketing functions as not persuasive for the CIS region. Moreover, only 38% expressed an intention to merge with an international law firm; only 23% expressed a wish to merge with a local law firm in their jurisdiction; and a significant 30% declared that they will never merge (the rest being undecided).

Finally on the topic of economic crisis and 'resilient dynamism', in 2013 the most surprising results came in response to the question: 'Has the economic situation in general and in the legal market improved?' Some 49% of delegates demonstrated 'resilient dynamism', stating that although the crisis had been chronic, they had managed to adjust. This result might have been expected. The unexpected result though was that some delegates took extreme positions: 5% believed the crisis to be over and are back to pre-crisis scope of work and revenues, and sadly 8% had lost hope and decided to close their practice.

Delegates also shared their experiences as to how exactly they had overcome the crisis: 18% had reduced their office and rental costs; 29% had reduced personnel; only 2% had reduced salaries and some 36% had reduced all of the above costs. Paradoxically as many as 16% had increased hourly rates.

The 'resilient dynamism' strategy is not based on an illusion. CIS law firms understand very well that the tendencies the crisis provoked are still here. The buyer's market is still the buyer's market. Our clients still dictate. This phenomenon takes new forms; there is a new balance in relations between the client and a law firm. This process is taking place in the CIS economic region and all over the world, particularly in the United States. It has become evident how clients are getting used to doing business without external lawyers. Before the crisis, in the United States, for example, clients literally did not take a step without seeking advice from their external lawyers in any matter, however small. During the crisis, legal services budgets disappeared and clients somehow handled things on their own, believing that they would function without much assistance. Budgets were saved and in-house legal departments expanded. Many issues that would otherwise be referred to law firms are now handled internally by clients and they are satisfied with the results.

In March 2012, I attended an excellent conference in New York, the Best Lawyers Advisory Board Meeting, where leading law firms from the United States and other countries were represented by their managing partners. During a client session three general counsel of major international companies spoke about their vision regarding the role of external counsel. After they had shared their ideas I turned to the person sitting next to me, the managing partner of an Australian firm, and said, "you know, it looks like we just need to commit collective suicide after this session". He seemed to be of the same opinion. What we heard from the corporate lawyers could be summarised as follows: "Generally we don't need you any more, and when we need you, it will be on our terms".

Heads of in-house legal departments first expanded their staff, secondly limited the scope of the issues they refer to law firms, and thirdly have come to like these changes and are developing them further. The scope of the issues referred for external legal advice is being limited and narrowed, and this tendency has increased both in the CIS economic region and internationally.

## 5.    The changed business environment

What we discussed at the post-2008 CIS Forums is that we need to learn the lesson, to identify the steps we have to take, to discuss how we can show our value to the clients and what products of value we can offer. We brainstormed together on most important issues for the survival of our profession. The questions about value of external counsel were also addressed by the corporate lawyers participating in the Forum, who eagerly and frankly shared their vision of our place in servicing them, in terms of what we need to develop in our practice in order to remain of value.

Part of the problem for the CIS legal community is to accept that private legal practice is a business and that there is a legal services market. This is not a very easy task, considering where we come from.

As a brief historical background, our current private practice has its origins in the advocate's profession. It was considered to be a liberal arts occupation, somewhat artistic, intellectual and so on. Advocates have always perceived themselves to be above business and identified their occupation as something more inspirational. Of course, fees and incomes did matter, but the cornerstones of the highest value have always been professional activity, client representation and services. They also did not have a tradition of law partnerships, working mostly as individuals, sometimes only sharing the office costs.

Today, we can probably no longer pretend that we have a special profession that has nothing to do with business; that 'legal business' is an incorrect definition; that legal profession and business are *a priori* incompatible. One cannot fail to see that the legal market and legal business have developed in the CIS region and in every country of the region. Certainly, the basic sense of consulting is not doing business for the sake of doing business; it means offering legal services, providing legal support, value to the clients and so on, but the consulting format today is indeed a business with all its attributes – processes, marketing, management and so on.

Lawyers and especially partners in law firms involved in this business must master marketing and other aspects that require soft skills, such as personnel management, PR and business development. CIS lawyers have acquired these skills with varying degrees of success, but most of them are still far behind in terms of mastering the numbers. I will risk stating that the aspects that are the least interesting or appealing to CIS lawyers are numbers, accounting, financial indices, costs and expenses, profit margins and so on. And, of course, we need to learn. If we were good at numbers, we would not be lawyers. We would be accountants, mathematicians, auditors. As we are basically not on friendly terms with numbers and earning money has historically not been the primary purpose of our profession, this in my opinion is a painful area for most law firms. And somehow we need to overcome those barriers and we need to pay particularly close attention to the financial and business aspects of our practice. Those who do not will lose their positions. You cannot operate a private practice today without earning enough money to cover costs, pay salaries to lawyers and earn some profit. Our profession has become more pragmatic and business oriented and probably tougher, with competition being another driver.

In many ways, recent developments in western countries and in the CIS region have been very similar. In the western world, however, the modern understanding of the profession evolved 150 to 200 years ago, while in our part of the world such an understanding began to emerge as recently as 25 years ago. This means that lawyers in the CIS, especially lawyers who work in business areas and in private practice, have covered this path in a substantially shorter period of time to reach today's understanding.

Moreover, we have to do our business today in a tougher environment than before, while firms in our region face this challenge in a time of upcoming generational shift. One of the peculiarities of the CIS legal market, as with any other emerging region, is that most established law firms are still run by their founders, who are still at an active stage of their careers. Those law firms, which were founded in the early 1990s, have matured to the extent that the next generation feels ready to take leading positions. There have been many examples where this evolutionary process has taken the shape of a revolution, resulting either in their collapse or in losing their positions because of generational changes which have gone wrong. We highlight this aspect at the CIS Forum's 'management hour', and discuss how the generational change can be handled smoothly and without such negative impacts.

Various other ideas have been discussed at the 'management hour'. In particular, we discuss every year the IT and social media revolution and its effect on the legal market. It is interesting that there is a clear division in the views of CIS and international delegates, with CIS delegates taking a far more conservative position and not accepting the cost-saving and other advantages of IT as championed by international delegates. Again, as with numbers, perhaps partners of CIS law firms do not feel as comfortable with IT and social media, and implement only such measures as are absolutely necessary. The idea of having a paperless office, in the less prestigious part of town, with many lawyers not having their own desk and telecommuting, and the managing partner sharing space with other lawyers at the table in the conference room, does not appeal at all to partners of CIS law firms, who still value prestige, hierarchy and subordination at their law firms. However, they understand that this global trend is coming to our region, and pay serious attention to international delegates sharing their experiences.

Among other global trends that might potentially reach the CIS region are outsourcing (sending the bulk of legal work to law firms in the regions, for example regions of Russia or Ukraine, which can perform them at much cheaper cost), re-focusing from existing practices (eg, M&A, the volume of which has dramatically decreased, especially in our region), to developing new practices that are in demand with the clients (eg, compliance, mediation) and offering new formats for services. To this end, the author's firm has developed and shared two innovations at the CIS Forum – a client appreciation programme (available to our priority clients) and 'virtual secondment', which is a collective work of several lawyers of different specialties at a fixed cost without the need for them to be physically present at the client's office.

## 6.    Conclusion

To sum up, we believe that the CIS legal community and the international legal community mutually benefit from each other: from sharing ideas and experiences; from adopting and implementing global and regional trends; from exchanging referrals and cooperating with each other, either directly or within legal networks; and from actively participating in international conferences and organisations, such as the IBA and CIS Forum. All of these have played a part in one emerging legal community's story of successfully joining the global market.

# Resource-based approach to strategy

Dina Gracheva
Dow Chemical

## 1. Introduction

Legal business has always been seen as a special case. With strict restrictions allowing only lawyers to own law firms and regulations that to a certain extent limited competition, partners managed their law firms in a very traditional way. There were only slight differences in the organisational structures of firms and in the ways of managing and allocating resources. The legal profession has been slow to innovate and there was a widely held opinion that law firms do not 'do' strategy. Even before the economic crisis, however, law firms recognised the need to change their business model, structure and operations. The crisis made it even more urgent for lawyers to respond to the challenges of the new economic environment; to start to think and act more like corporate business leaders, and to bring strategic thinking to the management of their resources.

At this crossroads, with the rapidly changing environment, managing partners should look at their firms and ask themselves: what were the core competences that made our business successful? Are these resources still in demand? How can we modify them to serve emerging clients' needs? What new capabilities should we develop? Here the resource-based approach to strategy comes into play and helps management to disaggregate resources and pick up and develop those that will help to achieve competitive superiority and win in the long run.

The resource-based approach to strategy is deeply grounded in economics and it explains how a firm's resources drive its performance. The approach combines internal and external perspectives and views strategy as an effective organisation of the firm's resources with profitable market opportunities. This statement reflects two elements: external market needs and internal firm capabilities. The external element includes the firm's decisions about its target clients, markets, practice areas and geographies. The internal element embraces all the resources the firm has (or develops) to be able to deliver value to the chosen market. The decision on allocation of resources will determine the mix of professional services offered (or deliberately not offered), service delivery, price and so on – all that will make up a firm's value proposition to its clients. As a simple definition, strategy is a choice as to how to use a firm's resources to serve chosen markets. A strategic analysis of the nature of the market, resources and economic aspirations of the firm is required to understand how to produce the best possible output with the existing resources for input.

## 2.    The need to differentiate

An important angle from which to look at the firm's resources is the necessity to differentiate in a highly competitive and shrinking market. Competing with equally strong law firms is a challenge. Quality of services, quality of relations and track record of deals is equally strong for all top market competitors. Increasing the firm's attractiveness for a global client is therefore about finding a differentiator – unique and demanded capabilities that can be appropriated by the firm. Finding capabilities that can become a competitive advantage for the firm and then managing and developing these capabilities become vitally important strategic tasks that can assure firm stakeholders of the firm's ability to manage its resources more efficiently than competitors, and therefore to sustain profits and growth. In a professional service environment, where most resources are rented rather than owned by firms, this task becomes even more important.

It is hard for clients clearly to differentiate between top-tier law firms, but this does not mean that differentiation in the legal market does not exist. The differentiator for a top law firm is a function of its unique capabilities, which will be a basis for the firm's competitive advantage. Prahalad and Hamel, who originally developed the concept of the resource-based approach, compare a corporation to a large tree, where (putting it into legal business environment) the services and expertise are the leaves, flowers and fruits, but the root system that provides nourishment, sustenance and stability is the core competence. The main benefit of the resources is their long-term nature and a high degree of plasticity when they can be adopted to changing markets. Hence, a law firm should be seen and managed as a bundle of competences – its key resources – not as a portfolio of practices. And a differentiator of the firm should lie in its sources and be embedded in the whole organisation, its structure, its decisions – that is, embedded in the law firm strategy. So the core of the strategy in the resource-based approach lies more in the ability to identify and effectively deploy and develop the right resources than in the ability to appear different.

## 3.    Classifications of resources

There are various classifications of resources among strategy experts, but the basic distinction is between tangible and intangible resources. In the professional services environment, the most important intangible resources are relational resources such as brand, reputation, client relations etc, and competences (also defined as a third type of resource – organisational capabilities). Intangible resources often play a critical role in competitive advantage, they cannot be 'consumed' and they can serve as a valuable platform for diversified expansion.

Not all resources qualify as creating competitive advantage. The value of resources is determined in the interplay with market forces, and researches on strategy suggest several 'tests' for evaluating resources and their ability to serve to create core competences. The real value is created in the intersection of the following resource qualities:

- market demand (clients see value in a resource);
- scarcity (a resource is hard to copy); and
- appropriability (value created by a resource is captured by the organisation).

While market demand is quite an obvious test for all resources, the other two qualities require more detailed analysis. Resource scarcity means that the resource is unique or rare. It is not available to other players in the market. Uniqueness of resource gives companies the opportunity to sell value generated by it at a price higher than that of the competition. In the legal services market, one of the most common reasons for a valuable resource to be inimitable is physical uniqueness (eg, resources such as firms' partners with their individual mix of knowledge, skills, talents and connections). Path dependency is another reason: such resources as track record of deals, past experience with client or brand awareness require significant time to copy and thus give firms competitive advantage. Casual ambiguity is another origin of the resource scarcity. Casual ambiguity is about how the firm can generate value for the customers. It usually lies in the organisational capabilities and presents the complex combination of people and processes used to produce the output. Ability to innovate is a vivid example of such competence and can act as a key differentiator in highly competitive and changing markets. While competitors may develop the same technologies and skills, the combination of relevant organisational learning and coordination processes cannot easily be replicated.

## 4.    Resource ownership and control

Appropriability determines who captures the value that the resource creates. This seems to be one of the most problematic areas for professional services firms, where individual capabilities of firm partners play an essential role not only in production and delivery of the services, but also in managing the business. Appropriability of a resource is largely determined by who owns and controls it. Both relational resources and capabilities can be controlled by an organisation or by individuals. Using Bente R Løwendahl's framework[1] for classifying resources by the degree of a firm's ownership and control, all the specific firm's intangible resources can be presented by the scheme set out in Figure 1 overleaf.

Managing partners of the top-tier firms usually mention brand/reputation, individuals and track record of major deals as the most important key success factors. Leading law firms operate on two levels of competition for global clients. On the first level, they compete to be included in the panels of preferred legal advisors. Being included, they enter the second level of competition where they struggle to win the best possible share for the available work. These two levels require different core capabilities from the market players. On the first level, the key success factors include the ability to deliver the legal advice globally; brand (overall credibility), quality and project management capabilities. On the second level – understanding of the client's business, competitive pricing, partners' credibility and individual relations with clients come into play. If one plots these capabilities on the above map of resources (highlighted in bold text), it can be seen that the majority are either partly controlled by the firm or are completely out of control. Therefore, it makes it hard for law firms to capture profits when their key resources are not inextricably bound to the organisation.

---

1    *Strategic Management of Professional Service Firms*, Bente R Løwendahl.

**Figure 1: Ownership and control of resources**

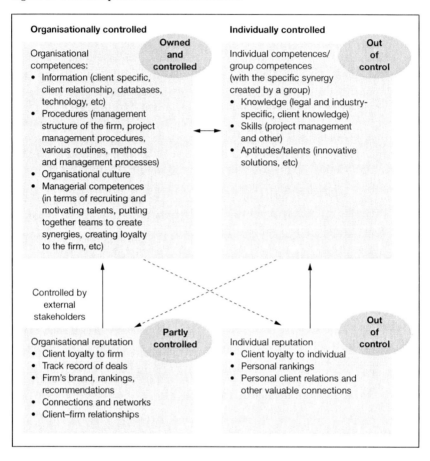

The role of individuals (ie, law firm partners) is undoubtedly important for all kinds of firms – from an advocate cabinet to 1,000-lawyer international firms. But in my interviews with the firms, global and local, I always try to understand what is the role of their strong brand compared with the role of partners. With more and more clients establishing the panel of preferred consultants as a part of their selection process, the role of individuals should became less important through the attempt to institutionalise relations. Indeed, brand and firm's reputation is a capability 'needed to win' on the first level of competition. To get on the panel of Fortune 500 companies, a firm must have its name on the market (ie, be known for the good quality of its advice, enjoy high professional rankings etc). But the role of brand alone seems to be questionable among the managing partners and the role of individuals, even in widely known firms, is vital. In the majority of top firms the role of brand is strong only in connection with their individuals (partners). Through interaction with clients, partners reinforce the power of brand; at the same time brand will be the key factor in attracting leading individuals to the firm. The winning factor for many top-tier firms is a combination of partners and brand, where it is difficult to break down the role of each element, because it is partners who provide clients with the high-quality advice, acting as a point of delivery, as an ambassador of the brand and thus reinforcing it.

This insight helps us to understand that all the key winning resources (individual reputation, client relations, brand and track record of deals) are to a large extent controlled by firms' partners. Partners 'deliver' the brand, they 'own' client relations and can also 'hold' the track record of deals. But partners themselves are not controlled by law firms, and this makes law firms extremely vulnerable: they can easily lose the resource and they need to share a significant portion of profits with partners. While this model is widely accepted in the legal market, its attractiveness may be questionable from the investor's perspective: first, it is inefficient in terms of cost structure, and secondly, its sustainability is not controlled by the firm. Both external investors and business-minded managing partners should also look for the resources within the firm, which will not only be unique and valuable, but also appropriable (ie, will be fully controlled by the firm). Such resources lie in organisational capabilities: it is information management, project management, internal organisation of the firm, its unique corporate culture and managerial competences (in talent management, marketing, strategy, finance, etc). After the crisis of 2008 many firms looked for the internal resources that would enable them to optimise their cost structure, but the value of these resources is in fact much higher. They may present a real opportunity for firms to differentiate and to ensure sustainable returns for the shareholders. The nature of the legal business will always allow room for a 'personalised' element, so the role of partners will always be strong. But by developing organisational capabilities firms will be able to shift the power of control from individual level to firm level, and therefore to create a more sustainable basis for the future.

## 5.    Individual versus organisational controlled resources

One of the 'winning' approaches for the future is increasing the control over valuable and unique organisational competences without reducing the absolute value of individually controlled resources. A successful example of this approach is McKinsey & Company: while having strong individuals (consultants and partners), the firm developed an array of internal processes and frameworks that on the one hand ensure the delivery of the highest quality results, but at the same time protect the firm from losing the appropriability of the resources. If all consultants and partners leave a firm's office, it will be able to redeploy resources from other offices, who will deliver the same quality results without delays. This is possible because McKinsey constantly transforms individual knowledge and skills into organisational capabilities and distributes this organisational knowledge throughout the firm. It is therefore the primary task of law firm leaders to strengthen the organisational capabilities of their firms in both transforming individual knowledge into organisational capability and developing the resources that the organisation owns and controls.[2]

---

2    All information about McKinsey is taken from the publicly available sources.

Joseph Ryan, professor of management at Wharton, cites three levels to build strategic thinking into a law firm. The first is defining a process for allocating resources which could result in more efficient operations. The second level is clearly articulating the firm's competitive advantage and value proposition. The third is developing an honest assessment of talent within the firm and making the most of that talent.[3] In my view, the third level is in essence the implementation phase of formulated strategy, and it cannot be narrowed only to talent management. Competitive advantage should lie not only in the individual resources (lawyers), and the firm should consider and evaluate the role and the competitive dynamics of all its resources. Moreover, firms' capabilities other than talents can become a real competitive advantage to help them to increase their efficiency. Understanding the sources of competitive advantage in firms' capabilities and nurturing and growing these competencies across organisational boundaries becomes the most important management objective.

## 6.   Alignment issues

Alignment of resources/competencies to the external environment is a critical strategic task for the achievement of success, but it is also vital to protect and nurture the resources that may deteriorate with neglect. Key questions that a law firm's strategists should always answer are:[4]

- Do we have the necessary resources? What kind of resources do we need to develop?
- Will the particular project or client contribute to efficient resource use?
- Will the project or client contribute to efficient and effective resource accumulation?
- Will the project or client increase, decrease, or stabilise the firm's degree of control over the resources accumulated?

Investing in core competences alongside the development of organisational capabilities out of individual ones becomes the key area of focus for law firms. Returning to the resource ownership and control map, this task can be summarised as 'shifting the control', as shown in Figure 2.

Formulating strategy (ie, finding the resources that will bring competitive advantage to the firm) is very important; but implementation of the strategy (ie, leveraging, upgrading and investing in these capabilities) is even more important. Proactive building of organisational capabilities, rather than relying on existing individual resources, can ensure superior returns and growth. This becomes an important strategic task for all law firms in order to win markets in context of the new demands for efficiency and sustainability and of the mindset of investors in law firm management.

---

3       Legal Strategy 101: "It's Time for Law Firms to Re-think Their Business Model". Published: April 29, 2009 in Knowledge@Wharton.
4       Bente R Løwendahl.

## Figure 2: Shifting the control of resources

| Individual competences | Shifting the control through: | Organisational competences |
|---|---|---|
| Knowledge | Knowledge management, CRM, etc | Information (client-specific, client relationship, databases, technology, etc) |
| Skills | Project management procedures and training | Procedures (management structure of the firm, project management procedures, various routines, methods, etc) |
| Aptitudes/ talents | Creating an environment to support innovation | Innovation culture |

**Strengthening organisational competences:**

- Organisational culture
- Managerial competences (in terms of recruiting and motivating talents, putting together teams to create synergies, creating loyalty to the firm, etc)

# Introducing a balanced scorecard in a multi-jurisdictional partnership

Peter Oberlechner
Wolf Theiss

## 1. The firm

Wolf Theiss is Austria's largest law firm, and is considered to be a leading regional international firm in the Central Eastern Europe/Southeast Europe (CEE/SEE) region. As of May 2013, the firm had 309 lawyers, and has 14 offices in 13 countries. It is a fully integrated partnership and has undergone strong growth over the last decade. In 2000, besides its main office in Vienna, the firm had only one office outside of Austria. Since then, the number of equity partners has grown from 10 to 29, and a new category of 'contract partners' (ie, salaried partners with a certain share in the firm's profits), has been created. Currently, there are 33 contract partners in the firm.

Wolf Theiss enjoys a reputation as a dynamic and entrepreneurial law firm, and is considered to have been a regional 'first mover' in various areas.

In 2002, the firm gave itself a new legal framework. A hybrid lockstep was introduced, with a fixed annual point progression over a certain period of time. This lockstep is, however, combined with certain 'gates' that require a partner vote for a partner to pass and to further climb up the lockstep ladder. There is also the possibility to 'freeze' partners in their point progression, or to reduce the number of points they receive, and – in a worst-case scenario – to expel partners from the partnership.

## 2. Partner evaluation

It is obvious that the type of managed lockstep system described above requires an evaluation of partners. A systematic evaluation process is also needed for preparing the decision as to which lawyers should be elevated to a partner position within the firm, and to prepare decisions regarding the income progression of salaried partners.

For all these tasks, the firm decided to establish an evaluation committee (EC). This committee cooperates closely with the management of the firm, its role being to prepare decisions of the partnership relating to the above-mentioned evaluation matters.

Currently, all of the firm's partners (ie, both equity partners and the contract partners) undergo a process of an annual evaluation. In the early years of this evaluation process, the EC evaluated partners along the lines of a rather general and broad catalogue of criteria, that can in a comparable form be found in the various partner guidelines and partner criteria of all reputable law firms – so-called 'guidelines for partners': partners need to be financially successful; they have to have a certain standing on the legal market and need to be renowned legal experts in their field; they should be prepared to undertake managerial and administrative tasks within the firm; they need to be role models in dealing with the firm's staff and lawyers; they also need to behave responsibly and follow the firm's policies; they need to attract good people and so on. In addition, and more specifically, partners were evaluated against the achievement of the goals of 'target agreements' that the firm started to prepare with respect to each partner on an annual basis. These were initially rather long documents, often stating sweeping targets in a broad number of different categories.

This combination of a broad and quite general catalogue of principles for partners and rather general, not too specific target agreements made an 'objective' evaluation of partners increasingly difficult, the larger the number of partners grew and the more jurisdictions the firm spanned, leading to results that were sometimes deemed to be arbitrary and lacking in transparency. In recent years, the partnership has increasingly called for a more transparent and objective system, and there were also strong voices advocating that evaluation criteria and consequences should be applied more rigorously.

This caused a shift of paradigm and a change of method. Assisted by an experienced external business consultancy expert, the EC developed a new methodology and approach and, following discussion with the firm's management, presented it to the partnership for approval.

3.    **Balanced scorecard in general**

The new approach the EC presented to the firm at the end of 2011 was based on implementing balanced scorecard. This tool was developed in the 1990s by Robert Kaplan and David Norton and described in their book The Balanced Scorecard, under which title the new concept was presented to the general public. Balanced scorecard had originally been developed to overcome the traditional orientation of (then primarily US) enterprises solely towards financial goals, figures, and parameters. This one-sided orientation needed to be broadened by a balanced set of both financial and non-financial measures. The system was based on the convincing sounding idea that for the correct measurement of performance (ie, performance measurement), all relevant business factors, including financials, but also customers and processes, need to be considered.

It soon showed that balanced scorecard can do much more than measuring performance within the framework of a given set of performance measures. The insight that balanced scorecard can influence behaviour within organisations in the direction of implementation of strategy had significant impact on the concept itself. When targets and their measures are appropriately chosen, a balanced scorecard shows the strategic targets of an organisation, and simultaneously opens them up for measurement. Also, when the targets are correctly chosen and made operational, members of an organisation are aligned with the strategic requirements of the organisation. Thus, balanced scorecard is also an instrument of leadership that is aimed at orienting organisations towards strategic goals.

Kaplan/Norton had stated that balanced scorecard serves four essential purposes that are as important for any managed law firm as they are for any other managed business:

- clarify and translate vision and strategy;
- communicate and link strategic objectives and measures;
- plan, set targets and align strategic initiatives;
- enhance strategic feedback and learning.[1]

Thus, strategic targets are central to balanced scorecard. They derive from the vision and the strategy of an enterprise – accordingly, they are the goals of an enterprise that are decisive for success. But how can the achievement of strategic targets be planned and monitored? What sounds so easy in theory is quite challenging in practice: the targets need to be broken down into concrete, monetary and non-monetary measures, and certain actual and target values of these measures. Concrete actions related to the individual targets safeguard the achievement of the targets. Kaplan/Norton consequently subtitled balanced scorecard with the quite illustrative line "Translating Strategy into Action".

## 4.    The Wolf Theiss balanced scorecard system for target setting

Whereas balanced scorecard has long been adopted by many business enterprises, it is an approach that is still relatively new to law firms, as relatively recent publications have shown.[2] This is not completely surprising. Strategic target setting and performance measurement in general is still a difficult topic for professional service providers, and for law firms in particular. First, lawyers are generally individualists; and secondly, partners of law firms in particular want to have their own way and are often convinced that only they are competent to set their targets and to measure their achievements. However, competition on the one hand, and the need for greater responsiveness to client demands on the other mean there is increasing pressure on professional service providers to proceed more strategically in the provision of their services, and to monitor the achievements of important targets with more scrutiny than in the past.

It is also only in the relatively recent past that articles in legal publications have started to deal with the topic of balanced scorecard in connection with law firms.[3] It has, therefore, been pointed out that thus far there has not been a fully satisfactory implementation of a balanced scorecard system in a law firm.[4] This is to a certain extent contradicted by a list published by the Austrian consultant Bruno Jahn, which details several reputable law firms that allegedly apply balanced scorecard,[5] and includes a list of publications where this has been mentioned.

---

1    Kaplan/Norton, *Balanced Scorecard*, page 10.
2    Eg, Sterling, *Balanced Scorecards for Law Firms*, Ark Group. Furthermore, an article, that essentially describes the balanced scorecard approach but without explicitly referring to the concept, was published by Bruno Jahn in *Strategieumsetzung in Rechtsanwaltskanzleien*, öAnwBl 2009, pages 108 *et seq*.
3    Such as Heussen, *Managementwerkzeuge für die Anwaltskanzlei – Die Balanced Scorecard*, Schweizer Anwaltsrevue 5/2005, 211 *et seq*; Seiter/Marquard, *Die Balanced Scorecard als Instrument der Strategieumsetzung*, dAnwBl 10/2012, pages 808 *et seq*.
4    *Heussen*, Gewinnverteilung-Strategien-Unternehmenskultur, www.ag-kanzleimanagement.de/informationen/finanzen/gewinnverteilung-strategien-unternehmenskultur.html.
5    For example, Allen & Overy, Berwin Leighton, DLA Piper, Freshfields, Linklaters and Herbert Smith.

Be this as it may, Wolf Theiss decided not to spend too much time on what others did and how precisely they did it, but to go its own way, and to develop a new system, geared towards the specific needs of the firm. Not to be able to build on somebody else's experience was both a disadvantage and an advantage. Whereas the process for developing the specific Wolf Theiss approach was long and is in part (and remains) based on trial and error, and whereas the firm was not able to rely on proven concepts developed by other firms in the past, it was deemed that the process of developing a tailor-made new system would help to ensure that the firm's specific needs and requirements were fully reflected.

The balanced scorecard concept is generally characterised by the fact that targets, measures, and strategic actions are each viewed from a certain point of view (ie, a so-called 'perspective'). On grounds of empirical experience, four key perspectives have been suggested by the architects of the system: financials, clients, internal business processes and learning and growth. Naturally, these perspectives can be changed and modified in accordance with the needs of the relevant organisation.

This is also what Wolf Theiss did. The individual points and criteria outlined in the firm's partner guidelines were, as a first step, categorised into only four key criteria that in the world of Wolf Theiss are perceived to be the core elements of partner performance, and thus also have to serve as the key criteria for both partner selection and for the continued evaluation of performance and career progression.

The firm gave them the headings 'Financials', 'Clients', 'People', and 'Firm and Process'. These factors make up the matrix of the criteria in which the firm sets targets for partners and expects them to perform – the 'partner criteria matrix' (see Figure 1). Each of these core criteria was broken down into certain sub-criteria, so as to make the top-level criteria concrete and operational, and enable the firm to set specific targets for its partners.

Essentially, the matrix is self-explanatory. In addition, the EC published brief guidance notes to explain the individual sub-criteria and what precisely is measured under them, and to detail the measurement yardstick.

## 5. How target setting and partner evaluation are carried out

At the beginning of each calendar year, the firm – represented by its management board, and the EC – draws up target agreements for each partner that follow the structure of the above-mentioned matrix. These target agreements are aligned with the heads of the firm's practice groups and then discussed with each partner, and are further refined in this process of joint discussion.

The target agreements are based on the specific role and responsibility that a partner has within the firm (eg, heading an office or a practice or industry group of the firm etc). They also take into account the partner's involvement in certain client relationship teams, and are to a certain extent also based on the results of previous evaluations (eg, the feedback that a partner has received in the course of the annual 360-degree feedback process that each partner has to undergo), and on specific strengths and weaknesses of a given partner.

The goals set in the target agreements focus on areas where specific efforts and specific input are expected and needed. They are made in bullet point form, and are

**Figure 1: The Wolf Theiss partner performance matrix**

| Financials | Clients |
|---|---|
| • Use of human resources<br>  ○ Individual turnover<br>  ○ Team turnover<br>  ○ Ratio of team turnover to personal cost (exclusive partner drawings)<br>• Management of clients<br>  ○ Managed work and turnover<br>  ○ 'Attorney in charge' – turnover<br>• Cash management<br>  ○ Unbilled work in progress<br>  ○ write-offs<br>  ○ Fees outstanding | Acquisitions<br>• Turnover acquired for oneself<br>• Turnover acquired for others<br>Business development<br>• Client identification and pitches<br>• Development of industry expertise<br><br>Client satisfaction<br>• Client feedback<br>• Client retention rate<br><br>Market standing<br>• Publications/lectures<br>• Listings/rankings/media reports |
| **People** | **Firm and process** |
| • Team development<br>  ○ Recruitment<br>  ○ Retention<br>  ○ Promotions<br>• Training<br>• Interpersonal skills<br>  ○ Feedback within team<br>  ○ Feedback outside team | • Management and functions held within the firm<br>• Innovation and improvement<br>• Support of partnership |

usually no longer than one page. Targets must be as simple and clear as possible, and their achievement should be measurable. This excludes targets that are general by nature, or the achievement of which cannot be completely monitored, or that can only be regarded as being fundamental principles of an orderly firm (eg, fulfilment of the firm's policies or partner decisions etc).

Targets falling under the 'Financials' heading will be drawn up by the firm's management. They will vary to a certain extent depending on the size of a given partner's team, his practice area and the jurisdiction in which that person works, as revenues and profits can vary substantially from country to country.

Targets based on the perspective of 'Clients' depend on which strategic goals a given office or practice group or industry group pursues, and on the client team to which a partner belongs. They may relate to further developing and expanding existing client relationships, the pursuit of new targets, or to the building up and development of new practice areas or industry specialisations.

Under the heading of 'People', targets in the 'Team Development' sub-category will depend on the specific human resources development plans that have been drawn up with respect to a given partner team. All partners are expected to participate in training activities both within their own team/practice group, and many also on a firm-wide basis within the firm's own training institution, the 'School of Excellence'.

In the 'Firm and Process' category, targets might encompass the assumption of managerial and administrative functions within the firm. They could, however, also consist in the development of new tools, products, and fields of work. Examples of such new products developed by the firm in recent years are the foundation of 'Re-Structure', an advisory company that specialises in real estate restructurings and workouts in the CEE/SEE area as a subsidiary of Wolf Theiss, the development and programming of a new arbitration software tool, and the foundation of the Wolf Theiss School of Excellence.

A certain maximum number of weighted target 'credits' to be achieved will be allocated to each criterion and sub-criterion. For example, in the standard form target agreement, a total of 200 possible credits is allocated to the criterion 'People', out of which 90 are allocated to the sub-criterion 'Team Development', 30 to the criterion 'Training', and 80 to the sub-criterion 'Interpersonal Skills', and so forth. Figure 2 provides a screenshot of an excel worksheet showing this standard form of target agreement.

What can be seen from the worksheet in Figure 2 is that, depending on the specific targets of a partner in a given year, a certain adaptation of the target credits can be agreed upon. For example, when a partner assumes a role on the firm's management board, a certain number of additional target credit points will be allocated to him under the heading 'Firm and Processes' (because he will undertake increased responsibilities in this category). Thus, his target credits in this subject field might, for example, increase to 400. In contrast his financial contribution may not be the same as if he were not involved in the firm's management; therefore the number of target credits under the heading 'Financials' might, for example, be lowered to 200. In other words, he cannot be expected to achieve the same amount of turnover as he would without the additional responsibilities. In this case, the partner's target credit figure of 300 in the 'Clients' field might have to be reduced, for example to 200, because he will not have the same number of hours to spend with clients as in previous years.

To summarise, the fundamental concept is to have a total of 1,000 target credits for each partner and to allocate them to the different 'fields' of the balanced scorecard (ie, to the Wolf Theiss partner criteria matrix) in a manner that reflects the individual weighting of the individual targets. Important targets are obviously allocated a higher number of target credits. Conversely, less important targets will be allocated a lower number of target credits.

At the end of the year, partners are invited to hand in an 'achievement report' in a condensed bullet point form, providing an overview of the specific achievements made by the individual partner in general, and also vis-à-vis their target agreement. In addition, they are invited to perform a 'numerical' self-assessment, filling out the 'credits worksheet' and awarding themselves credits for their achievements.

The firm then proceeds with the evaluation of the individual partners. The EC

Figure 2: Screenshot of a standard form partner evaluation worksheet

| Criterion | % | Standard | Adaptation on Basis of Target Agreement | Individual Targets |
|---|---|---|---|---|
| 100% | | | | |
| 1000 Credits 4 Key Criteria: | 100% | 1000 Credits | +0 Credits | 1000 Credits |
| 1. Criterion: Financials | 30% | 300 Credits | +0 Credits | 300 Credits |
| 2. Criterion: Clients | 30% | 300 Credits | +0 Credits | 300 Credits |
| 3. Criterion: People | 20% | 200 Credits | +0 Credits | 200 Credits |
| 4. Criterion: Firm and Process | 20% | 200 Credits | +0 Credits | 1000 Credits |
| Control | 100% | 1000 Credits | +0 Credits | +0 Credits |
| 100.00% yet to be distributed | 0.00% | +0 Credits | +0 Credits | +0 Credits |
| 100% | 100% | 1000 Credits | +0 Credits | 1000 Credits |
| 30% 1. Financials | 30% | 300 Credits | +0 Credits | 300 Credits |
| 1.1. Use of Human Resources | 10% | 100 Credits | +0 Credits | 100 Credits |
| -1.1.1. Individual Turnover | 1% | 10 Credits | | Credits |
| -1.1.2. Team Turnover (exclusive Partner Individual Turnover) | 5% | 50 | | Credits Credits |
| -1.1.3. Team turnover/personal cost ratio (exclusive Partner salary) | 4% | 40 | | Credits Credits |
| 1.2. Management of Clients | 11% | 110 Credits | +0 Credits | 110 Credits |
| -1.2.1. Managed Work and Turnover (TO generated by clients and/or matters managed) | 8% | 80 Credits | | Credits |
| -1.2.2. AiC Turnover | 3% | 30 Credits | | Credits |
| 1.3. Cash Management | 9% | 90 Credits | +0 Credits | 90 Credits |
| -1.3.1. Unbilled WIP | 2% | 20 Credits | | Credits |
| -1.3.2. Write-Offs | 3% | 30 Credits | | Credits |
| -1.3.3. Fees outstanding | 4% | 40 Credits | | Credits |
| 30% 2. Clients | 30% | 300 Credits | +0 Credits | 300 Credits |
| 2.1. Acquisitions | 14% | 140 Credits | +0 Credits | 140 Credits |
| -2.1.1. Turnover acquired for oneself | 7% | 70 Credits | | Credits |
| -2.1.2. Turnover acquired for others | 7% | 70 Credits | | Credits |
| 2.2 Business Development | 4% | 40 Credits | +0 Credits | 40 Credits |
| -2.2.1. Client identification and pitches | 2% | 20 Credits | | Credits |
| -2.2.2. Development of industry expertise | 2% | 20 Credits | | Credits |
| 2.3. Client satisfaction | 8% | 80 Credits | +0 Credits | 80 Credits |
| -2.3.1. Client feedback | 4% | 40 Credits | | Credits |
| -2.3.2. Client retention rate | 4% | 40 Credits | | Credits |
| 2.4. Market Standing | 4% | 40 Credits | +0 Credits | 40 Credits |
| -2.4.1. Publications/Lectures | 2% | 20 Credits | | Credits |
| -2.4.2. Listings/Rankings/Media reports | 2% | 20 Credits | | Credits |
| 20% 3. People | 20% | 200 Credits | +0 Credits | 200 Credits |
| 3.1. Team Development | 9% | 90 Credits | +0 Credits | 90 Credits |
| -3.1.1. Recruiting | 3% | 30 Credits | | Credits |
| -3.1.2. Retention | 3% | 30 Credits | | Credits |
| -3.1.3. Promotions | 3% | 30 Credits | | Credits |
| 3.2. Training | 3% | 30 Credits | +0 Credits | 30 Credits |
| -3.2.1 Training | 3% | 30 Credits | | Credits |
| 3.3. Interpersonal Skills | 8% | 80 Credits | +0 Credits | 80 Credits |
| -3.3.1. Feedback within team | 4% | 40 Credits | | Credits |
| -3.3.2. Feedback outside Team | 4% | 40 Credits | | Credits |
| 20% 4. Firm and Process | 20% | 200 Credits | +0 Credits | 200 Credits |
| 4.1. Management and functions held within WT | 10% | 100 Credits | | Credits |
| 4.2. Innovation and Improvement | 6% | 60 Credits | | Credits |
| 4.3. Support of Partnership | 4% | 40 Credits | | Credits |
| CONTROL | 100% | 1000 Credits | +0 Credits | 1000 Credits |
| 100.00% 1000 Credits yet to be distributed | 0.00% | +0 Credits | +0 Credits | +0 Credits |

0 credits: Negative outcome of evaluation
0-20% of possible credits: very poor, consistently below expectations
20-40% of possible credits: poor, below expectations
40%-60% of possible credits: meets the basic standards
60%-80% of possible credits: good - sometimes exceeds standards and expectations
80%-100%: regularly outperforms; consistently above expectations

performs this assessment on the basis of the materials handed in by each individual partner, and on the basis of a number of different sources. These sources include detailed financial figures regarding each individual partner as prepared by the firm's accounting department; information based on an annual '360-degree feedback process' performed throughout the firm each year, a process in which each staff member and each lawyer throughout the entire firm is invited to provide anonymous feedback (on the basis of an electronic questionnaire and feedback tool) with respect to each individual partner; structured comments that each of the firm's administrative departments (eg, human resources, billing and collection, marketing and business development) provides with respect to each partner on the basis of an electronic survey; and finally a number of interviews held by the EC with each partner, and, if deemed necessary by the EC, also with other lawyers and staff members of the firm.

Based on all of this information, the EC then awards the partners credits in the different categories of the performance matrix. As regards the members of the EC themselves, the exercise is carried out by the management board of the firm.

This process sounds burdensome and time-consuming, and it is indeed a strenuous, time- and work-intensive exercise, despite the fact that there are continuous efforts to streamline the procedure. To set meaningful targets, to align them with the strategic goals of the firm and its practice groups, and to make partners buy into them is a challenging exercise and requires time and effort. It is also difficult fairly to evaluate the performance of partners in relation to the achievement of their specific targets on the one hand, and as regards the general standards of the firm on the other.

It is a major advantage, however, that the partnership is still small enough to carry out this exercise. The process ensures that the strategic targets of the firm are a first step in the top-down process of target setting for individual partners and made specifically achievable for each partner. It also ensures that the achievements of the partners are thoroughly reflected and reviewed, and that both the process and the results of performance evaluation are logical and transparent. Such stringent target-setting processes and performance evaluation may also explain why, since the firm's introduction of this formal partner evaluation process, there has not been a single occasion where a change of status of an equity partner – be it the (very rare) exit from the partnership, or a change of position within the firm's lockstep – has ultimately not occurred on a consensual and agreed basis, thus saving the firm all the detriment involved in having to litigate with present or former partners.

The annual process of target setting and performance evaluation also helps the firm to obtain detailed insights into the work of partners, their achievements and what they could do further to improve their work and work results. This in turn provides the firm with a regular and very detailed personal and organisational 'health check' and analysis.

## 6.    Lessons learned; improvements and evolution of system and process

In the first year in which the new performance matrix became operational, the process ended with the publication of the number of credits that each partner had been awarded, and thus with a detailed ranking of all partners. As the self-assessment of partners – perhaps unsurprisingly – showed that the majority of partners considered themselves as 'regularly outperforming' in all relevant categories, the EC adopted a rather strict approach to counterbalance what was perceived to be a lack of self-criticism by partners. This caused frustration with the results of the process among many of the partners – even those listed in the top tier of the ranking, but who had the impression that the number of credits they achieved in various categories should be still higher.

This was partly related to the fact that critical feedback within a group of generally ambitious and performance-oriented attorneys will always be received reluctantly. But it also had to do with the fact that, despite all attempts to apply a balanced and logical system, it was almost impossible to find a perfectly balanced relative weighting of evaluation criteria. It proved very difficult to allocate a certain number of target credits to each criterion in such a way as to allow an evaluation pursuant to a mathematical formula that not only factors in hard numerical facts (such as financial figures), but also relates equally to 'soft' factors (eg, a partner's qualities as a team player, or his innovative skills).

Another potential weakness of the above system – when applied mechanically by merely carrying out partner evaluation by adding numerical credits – would be if it were possible for a partner to offset a complete 'failure' in one of the four categories of criteria by performing well in the other three criteria of the balanced scorecard. This, of course, would be counterproductive.

In Wolf Theiss, the EC anticipated this problem and communicated with the partners early in the process to explain that the results of the evaluation would be deemed to be negative if a partner – irrespective of the number of credits achieved for other core criteria – either completely failed to achieve credits in any of the four core criteria, or only had very low credits in at least two core criteria.

In this first year of the new system, the overall results of its application were subject to intensive discussion concerning the higher 'bands' of the numerical outcome. It showed that whoever was not ranked at the top was dissatisfied with the evaluation and questioned the whole system. However, the results were by and large perceived to be fair and correct regarding the partners who received the lowest credits.

As stated at the outset, Wolf Theiss adheres to a lockstep system where there is no 'merit' element to profit distribution, and where there is no faster progression in the lockstep in the event of highly positive evaluation results. Nonetheless, it is of primary importance for the partnership to have an accurate view of any non-performing partner, just as it is to have a precise view of who is perceived to have performed best – by applying whatever yardstick.

Therefore, an important adjustment for the future when applying the system is that the EC will no longer circulate a ranking of all partners as a result of the evaluation. The general communication to the partnership will consist in flagging which partners the evaluation has shown to have major problems, and also by what measures the EC would propose to remedy these problems. It is not always – and not even usually – the case that a negative outcome of an evaluation in a given year leads to negative consequences within the lockstep. It is more likely to be the case that a partner will have to undergo a coaching programme to overcome certain problems, or that his next target agreement will focus on precisely the issues where major problems have been identified.

One of the problems of a purely numerical allocation of credits in an excel sheet is that evaluation results must not only be seen to be objective, but they must also be deemed to be fair when applying a reasonable 'common sense' judgment. In light of this, the EC of Wolf Theiss decided that, in future, the credit allocation worksheet should only be used for internal working purposes, to assess the individual criteria of the partner performance matrix on the basis of a kind of 'traffic light' system. Under this system, green would indicate when a partner is outperforming on a given criterion; white when a partner meets the standards expected; yellow when he performs below the required standards, but not to such an extent as to raise grave concerns; and red, when performance is very clearly below expectations, and outside the 'bandwidth' that can be expected of each comparable partner.

## 7.   Conclusions

Over the last decade, Wolf Theiss has invested a great deal of time, effort and commitment in developing and implementing suitable target setting and performance measurement processes. It may be thought that this does not have to be a high priority for a lockstep-based firm, but we are convinced that the reverse is the case. A lockstep-based system of profit distribution can be a solid basis for a strong partnership that provides all the incentives necessary for the development of talent, for specialisation, for putting the firm's interest above the individual partner's interest, for cross-selling and for incentivising partners to do things that may not be in their short-term financial interests but have a long-term impact etc. A lockstep system can do all of these things when it is well managed and maintained, and when there are high standards within the lockstep. But a lockstep system must not mean an end to measuring and improving the performance of the players within the system.

It is quite easy to identify underperforming partners within small groupings. However, the larger and more geographically diverse a partnership grows – as has been the case with Wolf Theiss over the past decade – the more important it becomes to standardise and to objectivise the processes enabling this.

In Wolf Theiss, balanced scorecard has revealed itself as a system that currently enables the firm to combine the need to set strategic targets for its partners, and then to monitor and assess the performance of partners against those targets. The firm was not able to pick an 'off-the-shelf' product to enable this, but had to develop its own system, geared towards fulfilling its specific needs acting in a specific environment. After two years of using balanced scorecard in Wolf Theiss, experience shows that the system can never be completely finished. What works within a group of around 50 partners will not work the same way for a group of 100. What works for a firm spanning 15 countries is unlikely to work for a global firm, and might not make sense for a firm that only works in one or two countries. What works one year might not work in another, when the economic environment has changed.

On the basis of the experience in Wolf Theiss, I would therefore encourage any firm that is actively searching for the best solution for target setting and performance measurement to keep an open mind and to look at what others are doing, but ultimately to choose its own way. Within a world as diverse as that of professional services providers, best practice must emerge on a case-by-case basis, and is more a permanent process than a matter to be developed once and never to be touched again.

# Career paths in law firms – the need for flexibility

Jaime Fernández Madero
Fernández Madero Consulting

## 1. Introduction

Ever since law firms stopped being just friends-and-family businesses, designing an effective career model has been a key aspect of their economic and professional success. That is not only because a career is essential to the life of individual professionals but also because law firm business models are closely related to the way careers have been structured, given the centrality of professionals and their knowledge in the life of the professional service firm.[1]

Since most law firms are based on the hourly billing system, where associates work billable hours for rates that exceed their cost to the firm and the profits go to the partners, the answer to the question of how and when associates are promoted to partner becomes of central importance. Moreover, the increasing use of non-equity partner devices to accommodate a variety of cases out of the traditional partner/associate two-tier model has brought the analysis of career structures to the partnership level.

Many of the relevant studies on this subject carried out in recent decades have focused on large law firms that are based on the United States (mostly New York firms) or the United Kingdom, due probably to the predominant influence of such firms in the largest legal markets (both local and international). Strong competitive and institutional forces have meant that most of these firms use relatively similar structures regarding career paths, namely the 'up-or-out' model (see below), albeit that market conditions that have made it more flexible in recent years.

This chapter attempts to address a variety of issues that impact on the concept of career paths in law firms, and particularly how some forces emerging in the last two decades are challenging the traditional models that have prevailed in legal markets for most of the previous century. Although I will follow some of the most relevant and recent studies on the subject which have been made on prime markets, I also intend to provide some perspective from the standpoint of professionals and law firms in other jurisdictions (ie, Latin America), that are in a less developed stage of their evolution.

I will first seek to analyse the traditional promotion-to-partnership 'tournament model', its assumptions and driving forces, and also the weaknesses that have

---

1    "Changing Career Models and Capacity for Innovation in Professional Services", Michael Smets, Timothy Morris and Namrata Malhotra, *Handbook of Research on Entrepreneurship in Professional Services*, August 8 2012.

required that firms introduce flexibility in its application, although it still remains the main metaphor that describes how large law firms recruit and retain high-quality associates.[2] Secondly, I will formulate certain propositions for a flexible career path model. Lastly, I will explain how this model could help in overcoming these challenges.

As markets become more unstable, and firms have to cope with periods of growth that are followed by harsh recessions, law firms must periodically revisit their models and assumptions to maintain stability and success. While clients experience radical changes and lawyers modify their professional and personal wishes and expectations, law firms need to adapt and think in new ways, perhaps subscribing to novel solutions that were unthinkable in the past.

## 2.      Introduction to the tournament model: general strengths and weaknesses

The tournament structure is used in one way or another by firms that offer their associates a career path to partnership. Under this scheme, tournament candidates compete against each other for a limited number of positions at the next grade. In firms that have more structured systems, this process occurs within identified cohorts and pre-established periods of time, but this is not essential for the application of the concept. What is important is that promotion is based on a relative ranking within the cohort (or group of eligible candidates), rather than on any individual's absolute merits,[3] since only some and not all the eligible candidates will be promoted.

As long as the business model of law firms is based on leverage (ie, a greater number of associates than partners that generate billable hours over and above their cost to the firm), a system will be needed where only some of the associates can reach partnership and the others have to leave (or, as an exception, stay as salaried professionals), creating the classical pyramid structure used by most law firms.

This system (known in the market as 'up-or-out') comes from the 'Cravath model' and its application by leading New York firms in the early years of the twentieth century. It worked a key element for institutionalising their employment models, ownership form and governance.[4] The beauty of the 'up-or-out' system is that it simplifies the monitor and incentive mechanisms that apply to work that is complex and intangible. It is not easy to control and evaluate what a lawyer is doing, or to relate the effort applied and the results obtained. During this period, associates work hard to develop competence and acquire the partners' trust in order to win the tournament prize. Effort works in many ways as a proxy to quality since the criteria for promotion is complex and relatively subjective.[5] Firms use this period to train associates into the culture and practices of the firm in a bonding process, while they

---

2       "The Elastic Tournament: A Second Transformation of the Big Law Firm", Marc Galanter and William Henderson, 60 *Stanford Law Review* 1867, 2007 to 2008.
3       "New Career Models in UK Professional Service Firms: From Up-or-out to Up-and-going-Nowhere?", Namrata Malhotra, Timothy Morris and Michael Smets, *The International Journal of Human Resource Management*, Volume 21, No 9, July 2010, 1396 to 1413.
4       *Tournament of Lawyers: The Transformation of the Big Law Firm*, Marc Galanter and T Palay, Chicago, IL: University of Chicago Press, 1991.
5       Molhotra, *et al*, 2010.

evaluate their current and prospective capabilities and associates acquire professional training and human capital.

The tournament model and the resulting pyramid structure have started to be challenged in the last decade as a result of:

- a highly competitive market – for both clients and talent;
- clients becoming increasingly sophisticated and exerting pressure to receive more value for less cost;
- disruptive technologies that commoditise types of work that used to be performed by lawyers less efficiently; and
- a significant change in professional and personal aspirations by new generations of lawyers, namely 'Millennials'.

In the past, relationships used to be more stable and institutional and clients rarely questioned the quality and price of legal services. Competition was moderate since prestigious firms tended to stay with the same clients and did not seek to steal clients away from competitor firms. Service was personal and based on trust. Loyalty was something valued by both clients and firms.

Nowadays, clients have become more sophisticated and generally unwilling to have strong personal or institutional ties with particular firms. Decisions to hire a firm are mainly based on cost and expertise (the order of importance varying depending on clients and cases). General counsels and in-house departments have grown and have a much greater involvement in the client s legal affairs. Moreover, clients are increasingly unwilling to accept junior associate hours, claiming that it is unfair to pay for their training; and the use of other models driven by technology and efficient processes, such as LPO (legal process outsourcing), or firms such as Axiom, are making greater – although still moderate – inroads.

Millennials, for their part, seem to have quite a different perspective from the baby boomers who formed the ranks of law firms for many decades. The most important, in my opinion, has to do with the time paradigm. Young lawyers who went to law firms in the previous century were mostly interested in a career that would get them to partnership. The long-term objectives were stronger than any other and the related sacrifices were more acceptable. Those were the days when long careers in firms and companies conveyed a good image and were something beneficial for professionals. This no longer seems to be the case. In my professional experience as a managing partner and also in my recent academic research,[6] I have found that the time paradigm has changed and what used to be desirable is no longer so.

Young lawyers seek new and exciting experiences in the working environment. And they want them immediately or within a time frame that they can manage, which never goes beyond two years. So, challenges, sacrifices and rewards have to come together within the same period of time. The promises that law firms propose (economic, professional and reputational) in the traditional model are simply too far into the future to care about. Moreover, the equation of sacrifice and rewards that

---

6   "Identification Processes in Professional Service Firms", Thesis for Masters in Organisational Studies, Universidad de San Andrés, Buenos Aires, Argentina, 2011 (written in Spanish).

underpinned the life of partners is not so appealing for many Millennials (including the more talented ones).

In summary, there is a growing pressure at the bottom of the pyramid for reduction of costs and better service, which triggers the need for more seniority and expertise while still keeping an eye on costs. This situation challenges the traditional pyramid model, where firms could train their associates over a long period of time, but within a system where those associates would bill hours in values and quantities sufficient to sustain the business model in the short term.

## 2.1    What happens in other jurisdictions?

Law firms in other regions tend to be smaller. In Latin America for instance, 300 lawyers would be a very large number for a law firm and only Brazil has a handful of firms with over 200 lawyers. Also, in many jurisdictions a large number of firms are young and inexperienced, with only first and second-generation partners. In this scenario, firms' organisations tend to be more informal and less structured. Given that partnerships are smaller and geographical dispersion is not significant, the personal relationship among partners is essential and many decisions, especially the most important, are resolved at a political and informal level. Career, as a structured proposition, has gained some ground over the last two decades, but remains substantially informal in many firms.

However, these differences do not mean that the tournament system does not apply. The essence of the model is still used in many or even the majority of medium or large firms across regions, meaning that:

- they have more associates than partners;
- they live predominantly on the hourly billing system and therefore depend on the leverage effect of the associates' billable hours; and
- only some of the associates reach partnership by whatever system or decision-making process the firm decides to apply.

Do the challenges and limitations for prime markets described above apply also to smaller firms in other jurisdictions (or even in the same jurisdictions)? I believe the answer is in the affirmative in what relates to a war for talents and clients, sophisticated clients that require a more competitive service, and the young generation's challenges. The pervasive effects of globalisation have reached almost all markets and societies in the world. Complaints and concerns from partners are heard everywhere regarding these issues, and although the level of impact and specific characteristics change from place to place, they all share common ground.

On the other hand, the effect of disruptive technologies is still less significant than in prime markets, but nevertheless a powerful force that will increasingly affect and change professional practice in law firms in the future.[7]

Large firms have responded to pressures from the market by introducing one or more exceptions to the two-tier partner–associate structure. These include concepts such as counsels, salaried partners, legal directors, permanent or staff associates[8] and other similar denominations.

---

7    *Tomorrow's Lawyers: An Introduction to Your Future*, Richard Suskind, Oxford University Press, 2013.

The reasons behind this solution could relate to both firms' and individual lawyers' needs. On the firm's side, it works as a response to the question as to why a firm should relinquish a valuable professional even if he is not capable of performing at a full-track associate or partner level, especially from a business development perspective. This flexibility would allow firms to use experienced professionals for lower costs. From the individual's perspective, lawyers who are not attracted by the full partnership track could still remain in the firm and provide valuable services, adjusting compensation to the level of effort and exposure his work would have.

However, on many occasions solutions have been applied only partially and with little determination. The results have been poor and sometimes even damaging for the firm, when alternatives have been applied in an attempt to solve short-term problems, mostly financial. If the model is to be revised, a deeper and more structural view is required.

## 3. Revisiting the traditional system: a more flexible model

Despite the benefits that the tournament model has brought to law firms for many years, its application has also rested on the fact that lawyers assume that this is the only possible structure for law firms and there has been very little questioning of its basic assumptions. The system is not only one of the pillars of the business model on which modern law firms have developed, but also a deeply ingrained structure in the cultural and professional mindset of partners. The fact that everybody is structured more or less in the same way has a powerful influence on law firms and lawyers. Changing practices and structures that have been shown to work in the past may risk the reputation and economic viability of a law firm.

For over a decade, professional service firms have been under pressure to become more corporate and businesslike in their structures and systems, including the career model. Many HR managers believe that the tournament model contradicts the new economic and social environment and that innovation in career systems is necessary to accommodate the emerging needs of young lawyers.[9]

Law firms are structured more on professional than business values. Consequently, changing the model is not only a discussion about potential tools or strategies, but also a philosophical posture regarding the profession. Law firms need to find the right balance between professional and business objectives, whilst bearing in mind that:
- a business perspective does not mean only – and not even primarily – short-term financial objectives; and
- lawyers are naturally less inclined to consider business aspects of the firm and tend to feel more comfortable from a professional perspective.

Although much of this discussion is addressed so far to the largest firms, since presumably they have the biggest exposure to the changes the market is going through, smaller firms are not exempted from this process and the claim that

8    Malhotra *et al*, 2010.
9    Smets *et al*, 2012.

professional and business objectives should be better balanced in the new reality applies to everybody, one way or another. For the largest and most geographically dispersed firms, the changes discussed here might severely affect the very essence of the traditional law firm, in terms of partnership culture.[10] But smaller law firms, concentrated in one or a few offices, should keep and even reinforce the cultural aspects of law firms, albeit adapted to the new environment. Professional values, partnership culture, collegiality and other similar concepts are not essentially opposed to the rationale of business criteria, although many lawyers do not feel that way. Searching for a compatible balance is one of the biggest challenges for today's firms.

Using some of Galanter and Henderson's insights (2008) about the changing model as an 'elastic tournament' and some changes that can be observed in the market in recent years, a flexible law firm model could have a structure as shown in Figure 1.

**Figure 1: Flexible law firm model**

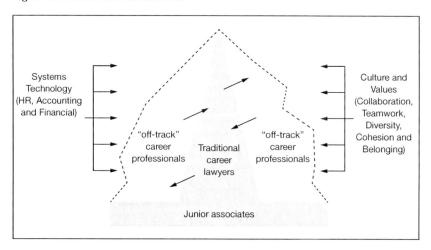

This model would be based on some of the following ideas and propositions:

- Firms will become more flexible from a career model standpoint. The traditional tournament would still apply, but off-track alternatives would gain considerably more space in the structure. Instead of looking like a plain pyramid, firms will take a form similar to an irregular diamond, with a thinner pyramid within the diamond.
- There will be a base of junior associates at the bottom of the structure for the first years. During this initial period, they will not be part of the traditional or off-track alternatives until a later decision is taken. The idea is that junior associates will work more freely from a career standpoint during their first years, thus not forcing them to define what they want in the long term. As

---

10    Galanter *et al*, 2008.

they make progress in the firm, they will find out which options are better for them.

- The thinner pyramid would represent those professionals that take the traditional career path. This would represent the core group of partners that handle clients' relations and associates that run for the full partnership track. Tournament concepts would apply to this group substantially in the same way as firms use them today.
- Outside the thinner pyramid, firms will have lawyers (and other professionals) who are not pursuing the full partnership track or have left it for a variety of reasons, including lack of interest in a long-term career and its related efforts, or lack of skills for a full partnership position. Compensation will be determined depending on seniority, added value to the practice and level of effort to be required. This will make firms appear as an irregular diamond because these professionals could be at different levels of seniority and hierarchy within the firm, depending on the firm's needs and professionals' expectations in different moments. Professionals could stay a long period in the firm under these conditions, but conceptually they are not developing a long-term career. Their situation is more dependant on working conditions at any given time, and flexibility for both firm and professional is essential to the model.
- The system should encourage the participation of non-lawyer professionals, to help in various tasks in which lawyers do not have specific proficiency. This could include management areas, not only at a staff-operational level but also with more strategic responsibilities, especially professionals with a finance background, and also in some areas of practice where other professional expertise could bring value to serving clients. As service and client relationships become more sophisticated, some of these professionals could have direct involvement in client matters. Normally, these professionals would be part of the off-track group, but as the system evolves some could be part of the traditional career track.
- The key with the off-track group is that the core partners who manage the firm and the clients can combine the service and business needs of the firm with the expectations of professionals (both economic and professional). Team and project management would be crucial for an efficient use of all the firm's capabilities.
- Subject to the firm's financial and professional restrictions and objectives, there will be a flexible relationship between both groups, and professionals will have the opportunity to change from one scheme to the other. Off-track professionals could choose to move to the 'full career' track, to the extent that the firm would benefit from that change. That means that tournament conditions would have to be more flexible than the traditional model, although maintaining the strong meritocracy ethos that sustains the model.
- Governance would be handled mostly by core partners, but with an increasing democratic style to allow more diversity of views and ideas.
- In order to have common standards and a shared sense of belonging, firms

will need to put more emphasis on cultural aspects such collaboration, team play, the training needs of junior associates, and other social and professional elements that enhance an experience of shared work and destiny. Individualistic behaviour should not be acceptable. Cultural concepts will compensate for a looser and more fragmented structure.

- The structure could use part-time professionals, including some that have previously worked as full-time lawyers, to work on a case-by-case, as-needed, basis. This would partially resemble the Axiom concept, but adapted to the specific needs of the firm. Compensation would primarily be variable in this group. Lawyers may or may not be exclusive to the firm, depending on the workflow and other aspects in each case.
- Technology and processes (knowledge management and project management) will be very important as management of the system will require fluent information and communication. HR, accounting and financial management should change to make sure that the system stays profitable and that bureaucratic processes do not make it too costly to manage.

The most challenging areas in this model would be how to combine in an efficient way more process and management without losing the professional essence that drives law firms. Also, a growing population of off-track professionals will require a much deeper integration and motivation effort than most firms have used hitherto.

Lawyers working in law firms are used to career paths to partnership, no matter how unclear or dubious the given path may be. And that is because being in that track is what makes you a peer and a member of the pack. If you are suddenly off-track that could mean that you are no longer part of the group, and you could immediately lose the related privileges, which are informal but very important. Consequently, off-track professionals could suffer from isolation and lack of prestige unless it is decided in the context of a professional's retirement.

To make efficient use of this tool, law firms should work hard at partnership level to ensure that these professionals receive full recognition for their role, as well as cultural acceptance and respect from the rest of the firm. Otherwise it will be difficult for lawyers – especially good ones – to accept positions of this kind, even if it suits them from other perspectives (eg, personal and economic). Peer recognition is at the core of every system based on lawyer self-esteem, so law firms need to ensure that none of their professionals are treated like second-class citizens and that their work is valuable both for the firms and their partners.

Some firms have been successful at creating side-track careers for associates, their main features being: finding good attorneys – some from within the given firm – who wish to work less for less remuneration; giving them intellectually rewarding work; releasing them from the obligation to manage clients' matters; placing them in less expensive locations than the principal offices; and making sure that partners respect the arrangements and the professional esteem of the relevant attorneys. The last of these is probably the hardest to achieve, but these firms make sure that partners are onboard because these attorneys help them with their business. Since off-track attorneys can bill less costly hours than regular attorneys, partners can offer a good service for a cheaper price. However, this can only work to the extent that firms develop an efficient way of allocating work and resources, avoiding the creation of a bureaucratic system that brings problems instead of solutions for partners.

## 4. How is this model addressing legal industry challenges?

In general, this model would aim at creating a more flexible structure, with more options for professionals which would allow the firm to use valuable (and less costly) resources that would otherwise not be available in a strict two-tier, partner–associate model. This could be particularly valuable in times of recession when fixed costs become a significant burden for the firm.

To the extent that clients increase their preference for alternative fee arrangements other than the traditional billing system (AFAs), a more flexible structure which is less dependent on a leverage model may allow firms to experiment with more market-driven formulas for income and profits (as opposed to the firm-driven system that results from the purely leveraged model).[11]

For the reasons explained above, it is difficult to visualise at this point how established law firms might adopt this system in its entirety. Moreover, it is likely that these changes may be beneficial only at an initial stage for some firms. Galanter and Henderson (2008) suggest that flexible (or elastic) models could be more applicable to semi-elite (ie, second and third tier) firms seeking protection from salary wars or other competitive dilemmas. Cost and management will be higher in the beginning and firms may resist this. However, as the influences of forces driving change become more pervasive, it is likely that larger portions of the legal market will need to evaluate structural changes of this sort.

As indicated above, since many of the market changes are impacting in all jurisdictions, this analysis is substantially valid across regions. However, those markets and firms that are less developed and institutionalised might find it harder to adopt a more systematic and orderly approach. They probably have relatively flexible systems already, but the type of flexibility that this model implies requires a significant level of organisational commitment since lack of order would probably make flexibility more chaotic and less productive. But less evolved markets such as Latin America already have institutionalisation as a pending agenda, so present market conditions only make it more necessary.

Firms can start by implementing some changes in the model and see how they work. In the beginning, law firms will remain with the same pyramid structure since many associates also tend to be reluctant to change the tournament rules (despite their criticism of it).[12] But lawyers might increasingly accept the alternative status – instead of just leaving the firm – and the rest of the organisation could adapt to this scheme, both from a professional and cultural perspective.

---

11    "A Market Approach to Law Firm Economics: A New Model for Pricing, Billing, Compensation and Ownership in Corporate Legal Services". William Kummel, *Columbia Business Law Review*, Volume 1996.
12    Smets, *et al*, 2012.

In this way, careers will be more holistic and imply a more encompassing proposition, which is important considering the evidence that larger proportions of associates do not seek long-term careers but rather an interesting working experience and training.[13] This system will also simplify the life of many female lawyers who struggle to reconcile family and career objectives. Retention of valuable professionals is likely to increase in the medium term.

From the career standpoint, the emphasis would be on achieving objectives related to learning and performance within shorter periods. So partnership would not be a main target for associates in the first years, even for those who would end up as partners. This involves a different set of ground rules and a much larger set of players. Lawyers who opt for the traditional partnership track will be subject to the traditional standards, although adapted to the new model. Lawyers who do not meet the required objectives could stay in the firm, but they will still need to comply with quality and efficiency standards.

In addition, this model could be more flexible and allow greater focus on typical associate concerns. Such concerns might include more interesting work, higher quality work, shorter working weeks, a more family-friendly workplace, a higher ratio of non-equity to equity partners and better communication on career prospects.[14]

Another topic to consider is how this model would affect work quality. Recent studies suggest that a more flexible model with off-track partners might enhance innovation in law firms, as these partners are able to dedicate time and expertise to developing original knowledge and solutions to clients' needs which other more productive partners that handle clients cannot do. They will also be able to dedicate more time to training younger associates.[15]

The aim of balancing the professional natural inclinations of lawyers with the business approach that is required in the current market is attained in this approach by combining novel structural and operating ideas driven by business objectives and strengthening traditional professional values such as quality service to clients, collegiality, firm collaboration and development of knowledge and young talent.

It is important to stress that this is not a closed model that should be applied in its entirety to be able to work, but more a combination of related ideas that address the type of challenges that firms are encountering in dealing with their career and organisational structures. Since many of the proposed changes involve dealing with important and ingrained cultural values, putting them into practice is not likely to be straightforward. Changing cultures is difficult, so the chances of success are higher if changes are introduced progressively.[16]

The proposed model is therefore based on three fundamental pillars:

- A more flexible career model that would incorporate two distinctive tracks. The traditional track would apply the typical standards of the current tournament model – with or without strict up-or-out – although

---

13    Molhotra, *et al*, 2010.
14    Galanter, *et al*, 2008.
15    Smets, *et al*, 2012.
16    *Organizational Culture and Leadership*, Edgar H Schein, Third Edition, Jossey-Bass, A Wiley Imprint, 2004.

professionals within that track could move to the off-track lane for a variety of reasons. Off-track professionals could be a significant portion of the professional force, depending on areas of expertise, client work and other considerations. This alternative career would be strongly defined by flexibility, productivity and short and medium-term objectives, seeking to accommodate the needs of both clients and professionals.

- This double career track would be supported by a combination of systems and technology in HR, accounting and management (adapted to the size of the firm and its type of work and clients) that would aim at enhancing efficiency, productivity and quality of service to clients.
- A strong set of cultural values would apply, bringing cohesion to the system while supporting the flexible and business-driven approach that the model proposes.

This career model maintains some of the traditional tournament features and criteria, but gives a more flexible and businesslike approach. The emphasis on processes, management and technology is meant to improve the way work is handled and organised. The strong professional ideology of law firms would evolve, combining it with a more practical and businesslike approach. But culture would still be very important to avoid an atomising effect in the system. All successful law firms (and professional service firms in general), attach great importance to the collegial relationship that partnerships develop and the culture that results from it.[17] This would have to be maintained and even reinforced. The difference will be that the institutional aspect, represented by the firm, will be less significant, and work and practices will take the leading role. The naturally informal nature of partnership will coexist with higher levels of coordination. Management, from this perspective, will not primarily be concerned with controlling lawyers' work in a vertical fashion, but rather with helping areas of practice with processes and technology that will make them more efficient.

It could be argued that lawyers always gather around work and clients, but tournament gives a strong institutional perspective, since career incentives focus on the long-term relationship with the firm. Therefore, relations with clients are heavily influenced by that ideology. In a new scenario, the main focus would shift to the current needs of clients and efficient ways of managing work in a more flexible business and professional structure. Culture would focus on values that enhance those objectives, while keeping a sense of belonging and shared destiny. The modern professional scenario does not need a strong institutional reference to develop motivation and commitment from professionals, but rather a stimulating working environment in which professionals can achieve their personal objectives while enjoying a shared work experience.

---

17   *The Art of Managing Professional Services. Insights from Leaders of World's Top Firms*, Maureen Broderick, Prentice Hall, 2011.

## 5.   Conclusions and further investigation

There is much evidence to show that the professional landscape in law firms is changing radically.[18] In a heavily institutionalised market such as that in which law firms operate, changes never occur rapidly and they are normally resisted in their early stages, particularly if they imply questioning deeply ingrained ideologies.

The tournament model is the basis on which medium and large law firms (ie, those which are not family-and-friends businesses) have been structured for many decades. Professional and business objectives and criteria melted into a system that worked well until economic, technological and generational changes started to challenge its validity. These challenges have created a sense of crisis and stress for law firms in trying to deal with a new environment.

Many partners in law firms downplay the impact of the changing scenario and try to describe it as a temporary crisis – mostly related to the impact of a market recession – that only requires temporary adjustments and certainly not a major reshaping of the model. Like any big change that lies ahead, it is always hard to predict how and when it will manifest to its fullest extent. But if you take a look at the big picture and see how whole industries have radically changed in recent decades, and how change itself has become the norm rather than the exception, it is difficult to imagine how the legal industry will remain immune from this wave of new standards.

None of the elements that are being analysed in academic and management forums as affecting professional organisations (changes in clients, technology and younger generations' cultural and social traits, among others) look like temporary phenomena. They indicate trends that are here to stay, and likely to increase their influence in coming years. This does not call for immediate and urgent measures, but at least it seems healthy that law firms and academics in this field dedicate even more time and resources to the analysis and investigation of how the legal industry can confront these significant challenges. This would contribute to reduce the fears that substantial changes might jeopardise the very essence and life of law firms.

Further investigations should focus on the adaptation of new generations to the law firm model, short and long-term objectives in professional careers, the role of technology and management, how knowledge and innovation are created and used in law firms, and how cultural traits help or hinder in facilitating this process.

One thing is certain: the legal profession is experiencing significant change in the world and law firms need to deal with this change in an effective way if they want to continue being the prime organisational model for private legal practice.

---

18    Galanter, *et al*, 2008. Malhotra, *et al*, 2010.

# Strategic challenges of new firm leadership

Patrick J McKenna
McKenna & Associates Inc

---

1. **What are the most common mistakes new managing partners make when they take over?**

We need first to acknowledge some possibly fundamental differences between the overall situations that pertain to a successful firm, versus what might be seen as a strategically complacent firm or a firm that confronts severe and immediate competitive challenges. Each situation may require putting the new leadership accent on a different syllable and with an entirely different sense of urgency.

One of the more common mistakes is arriving on the scene believing that you already know what the issues are and that you already have the answers. If you take that approach, we can pretty much guarantee that you will not only discourage your partners and staff from sharing important information, but that your people will interpret the information you do get in ways that support your pre-existing views.

Secondly, you have to be careful how your relationships are perceived. If you are coming to the top leadership position after stints as a practice or industry group head, or if you reside in some foreign office, you will likely be perceived as maintaining obvious loyalties to established friends. Once you are identified as being on one side of an issue, it becomes even more difficult to solicit disinterested perspectives.

Finally, one of the tough challenges is to acknowledge what you do not know. Identify those around you who are the experts in various important areas and do not be afraid to lean on them. No one really expects an incoming leader to know everything.

2. **What are the biggest challenges all new managing partners face? What are the best ways to overcome them?**

There are so many challenges. Most professionals really do dramatically underestimate the scope and responsibility of managing an entire firm. One thing we should insist on is that the managing partner has a detailed job description. That description must get widely circulated throughout the firm so that everybody gets a true sense of what the job entails. Most thorough descriptions would encompass around 60 bullet points relating to responsibilities.

Few managing partners understand that they will probably go through a transition defined by identifiable and typical emotional stages. The first stage is 'anticipation', or what one leader we have worked with called the "peak of inflated expectations". You have just learned about your new appointment or selection as the firm leader. You are excited, justifiably proud that you have been chosen, and you are busy making physical and mental to-do lists.

The traps that some managing partners can fall into at this stage derive from not fully understanding the full scope of the responsibilities that they have just agreed to be responsible for. They fail properly to prepare, they underestimate their own need to change, and they may not begin the transition soon enough.

The most important stage, however, is the second one which we call 'adjustment', and which the firm leader just quoted, referred to as the "trough of disillusionment". You have begun to serve as firm leader but the realities of the daily tasks do not align with your preconceptions of how managing partners are supposed to operate.

It begins to occur to you that this role is going to require developing some new capabilities. As a new leader, you may be surprised to feel confused and indecisive just at the time you want to appear clear and strong-minded. You may feel overwhelmed and anxious just when you would much rather be seen as composed and dynamic. There are, as a result, a number of what we could call 'leadership tensions' – the more-or-less ongoing dynamics of the job that incumbents wrestle with, to handle the job of being a leader.

As you pass through this second stage, remember that your people are not interested in your title. They want to know if you care about them as individuals, if you care about helping them solve their problems and enhancing their career success. Consider building and maintaining relationships as a critical part of your leadership role. Remember that leading is always done with others, not to them.

Everyone wants a cheerleader – someone to believe in them, to help them have a can-do attitude. What can you do to let every partner know that you believe they can become even more of a success?

As a leader, you are under a microscope. Your decisions, how you make them, the people you consult with, are all viewed very carefully; likewise, everything you say, and the signals you send. You will be inundated with phone calls and e-mails; with questions, requests and advice.

You may need time to transform some relationships. Good leaders customise relationships with each individual on their radar screens.

### 3.    What makes transitions go wrong and how can mishaps be avoided?

A recent example of a new managing partner's false start comes to mind when, on day one, he charged off determined to implement his personal vision of where the firm should be going.

Typically, any new firm leader is someone with a great reputation within the firm. It is anticipated that he will create momentum quickly and deliver the desired results. Expectations are high and the new leader does not want to disappoint, and will therefore mistakenly enter the fray with a given strategy in mind.

New leaders believe that their successful track records, combined with their mandate, guarantee the support of the partnership. They focus attention on the technical aspects of implementing their strategy, wrongly assuming that a critical mass of support is in place. The higher the expectations, the more they believe that everyone is behind them, and the more likely they are to assume that they are on the right track.

As a result, they act first and ask questions later. In the situation mentioned above, the rush to deliver results caused the new leader to neglect taking sufficient time to learn important information, and to gauge more carefully what we call his partners' 'appetite for change'.

As a new leader, it is understandable that you will feel that you already have the information you need about how people think and feel. After all, you have been a partner in the firm for many years and may have even served on the executive committee or board prior to accepting this mandate. But how much do you really know?

It is all too easy to step on people's toes and, as a result, abort even the most promising firm leader's agenda. New leaders must use the time before their actual transition to gain significant information that will refine and perhaps redefine their strategic agenda going forward. In most situations, the new leader's initial concern should not be to hit the ground running, but to hit the ground listening.

The lesson? As early as possible as a leader, you must get input from your people on what they see as the preferable direction. Conduct one-to-one interview sessions with your partners (and other professionals in the firm), asking each one the same questions to get their insights, solicit their advice, and see what themes emerge.

Clarify what they want to see you 'shake up' and what they want to see you 'preserve'. It is wise to have people see that you are genuinely engaged and willing to listen before you say the first word about where you think the firm needs to go.

4. **What is the outgoing firm leader's responsibility during a transition? How can they ensure a smooth transition?**

Outgoing managing partners have at least five critical responsibilities.

First, one common delusion every departing leader may hold is that they are indispensable or at least that the firm will stumble without them. Every one of us who has ever held a leadership position may maintain some secret fantasy of one day announcing our plans to resign, and then leaving office amidst sorrowful tears, a standing ovation from partners and staff, and general consternation about the future, now that we are leaving.

Chances are, the firm will survive and even thrive without you. You should therefore compose a 30-second 'elevator speech' to tell people, in a positive way, why you are stepping down and to convey your excitement about your future and that of the firm.

Secondly, the leadership transition period is a good time finally to deal with annoying operational problems or troublesome personalities, so that the new leader can come in and immediately begin to address the more important, strategic issues. Conferring with your successor and, with their agreement, confronting these often sensitive and sometimes messy situations now, is one of the best gifts you can give your replacement – a clean slate from which to work.

Thirdly, think about what information you would want if you yourself were now about to embark on this new leadership position. As the incumbent, you typically know more about the firm and its operating nuances than anyone else. Much of that information, or at least how to find it, is stored in your head. Think about how you might codify and share everything you wish you had known when you first took office.

Fourthly, to ensure the success of the new leader, you should under no circumstances speak with anyone at the firm about his performance. Being perceived as negative or unsupportive only reflects poorly on you. You must also not allow anyone to say, 'Well that's not how we handled things when you were the boss'. That is disloyalty, and you must take issue with it. It may be gracious of partners to acknowledge your good work, but your focus should be on supporting and cultivating the strengths of the new leader.

Finally, the best advice we can frankly give any leader leaving office is to simply let go. Never mind all those lovely things they said about you at the resignation dinner. You are now a beloved part of history. The firm must learn to live without you, so the sooner you get out of the way, the sooner they get down to business.

## 5. What is the biggest surprise that new managing partners face that they had not thought about beforehand?

The biggest issue we hear about from new leaders is always the amount of time it takes to do the job right. Many of them are not full-time managing partners, so they struggle with trying to maintain some balance between the time needed to manage the firm and the time required to maintain some modest personal practice.

Here is a tip: create a stop doing list. Take a look at your desk. If you are like most hard-charging leaders, you have got a well-articulated to-do list. We have all been told that leaders make things happen – and that is true. But it is also true that great leaders distinguish themselves by their unyielding discipline to stop doing anything and everything that does not fit.

Beyond this overriding time issue, there are subtler, more subjective perceptions and issues that catch new managing partners by surprise. The best way to describe them is with a few direct quotes from men and women who have experienced the transition first-hand …

*"I realised that fundamentally my relations with my partners would never be the same. Everyone has an agenda when they talk to you. As managing partner, you can never again just be one of the guys."*

*"The sheer number of requests for meetings and for discussing issues, both petty and major … is absolutely staggering."*

*"You realise that, if people ever begin to say, 'This firm is no good', it's not the firm, it's you. It suddenly becomes unbelievably personal."*

*"You don't know all of the answers when you assume this position and some of the answers you thought you knew, you soon discover aren't really that workable in the real world. What worked for you or your predecessor in the past may not work tomorrow."*

*"A surprise for me was that what you say is not always what the partners hear and that constant reinforcement of the message by word and deed is critical."*

*"Notwithstanding all of the qualities I believe I have, I'm often feeling like a fish out of water. And yet how do I tell anyone what I'm going through? I need them to go on believing in me and trusting that I know what I'm doing."*

6. **What are the best management practices for new firm leaders? What are the best action points for new managing partners from the moment they are named to the moment they take over? For the first 30 days on the job? For the first 90 days on the job?**

Again, from the day you are first appointed through the first 100 days, the best practice is to listen and learn.

Travel throughout your firm. Look for patterns in everything you see and hear. Spend as much time as possible asking questions, talking to people, and getting feedback and thoughts on what is right and wrong with the firm's operations. Do not be afraid to listen to people who disagree with you. Listen, actively, to those who challenge your assumptions.

Based on what you have been hearing, settle on a few major priorities. You cannot fix everything at once or do everything you want to do, so you need to make some strategic choices. Here is where you begin to align your firm around a shared direction for the future.

Make time during the initial 30 days to meet with clients. Balance the big picture vision with frontline views. There is no reconnaissance more important than client relationships.

Do not be afraid to look for ideas in unusual places. Cast a wide net for insights. Sometimes, for example, the breakthrough idea lies in the successful experiences of other professions.

Within the first 100 days, you need to target a few early wins. Momentum counts and nothing succeeds like success. Pick a problem your firm has not been able to address and figure out a way to fix it quickly. That is how you enhance your reputation and ensure perceptions of a successful transition.

Contrary to what some recent business literature suggests, real leaders do not worry about legacies. They care instead about the long-term competitive vitality of their firms. If you are focused on fashioning a legacy, you will be remembered as ... the man/woman who was focused on fashioning a legacy!

7. **What are the specific challenges and concerns facing a new managing partner who is taking over for a founding partner?**

The challenges and concerns are the same whether it is a founder or whether it is a longstanding incumbent who is revered throughout the firm. In any event, at issue here is whether the new managing partner was hand-picked by his predecessor; that is whether he is an heir apparent in a virtually ordained succession process. By contrast, the dynamics are very different if the new leader emerges as a result of internal campaigning and/or an election. In that case, patriarchy has given way to democracy.

When you are handed the keys to the kingdom by a successful incumbent who has groomed you for the job, there is a temptation to play your predecessor's 'mini-me'. In some ways, you will feel indebted to this managing partner who gave you the opportunity, and you will feel obliged to try to carry on in the same style. But that defeats the purpose of the succession. When people see a new leader who looks exactly like the old one, they may be lulled into thinking the old managing partner has simply been cloned, which, in turn, encourages a mindset that is less than receptive to innovation and independent initiatives.

Hand-picked leaders can also be reluctant to take the organisation in a new direction because, after all, the existing approach worked. That too can be a mistake as it reinforces the old model which, even if effective in the past, sends the message that there is really only one way to get things done.

A leader hand-picked by a founder needs to be particularly aware of pent-up concerns that no one has previously been brave enough to express. A high-profile predecessor may have been so dominant that people in the organisation have been chafing for more participation and involvement in the decision-making process.

Whether hand-picked or elected, you must honour the success and ideals of the person you are replacing. But it is important to communicate that you are still setting your own course, and to make it clear that you are up to the challenge. If the founder was revered, and if he personifies all the growth and success that the firm has enjoyed, the natural concern is that that energy should not dissipate. So rely on simple reassurances to the effect of, 'While I have big shoes to fill, I am determined to fill them.'

Always remember that the team will have played a big role in the success of the departing leader. One of the biggest problems in any firm led by a high-profile managing partner is that too much credit for success is accorded the charismatic individual, and the broader resources of the firm that facilitated the success are overlooked.

8.    **What lessons can be learned by comparing the new managing partner's experience to the first months of other executives, either in business or government?**
We often tease new managing partners by asking them what they could possibly have been thinking when they took on such responsibility. For all the burdens they are willing to shoulder, their willingness to do so is often disparaged. Many partners see management as pure overhead, as drudgery that does not really reflect the legal professionalism that defines a lawyer, and does not generate revenue in the way that actually practising law does.

Meanwhile, partners at law firms often bristle at any suggestion that they can or ought to be led. Firm leaders feel they are making sacrifices for the betterment of the firm and should be appropriately appreciated. The partners think of you as serving at their pleasure; they are allowing you to hold the leadership title, so you should be beholden to them!

Such dynamics convince us that the playbook for new leaders of professional services firms is fundamentally different from the guidance that new corporate CEOs must have. There is a huge difference between operating in an environment where you say jump and people actually jump, and what happens in our world.

In our world, if you dare say jump, your partner will jump all right – right into the arms of a waiting competitor.

# Crafting and executing better strategy: emerging systems and structures in law firms

Rob Millard
Venturis Consulting Group LLP

**Preliminary note**

Diverse and occasionally confusing terminology exists across law firms, even in the same market, when referring to leadership and management roles. In this chapter, 'shareholders' refers to those who own the firm (usually equity partners). 'Executive committee' refers to the body to which shareholders have delegated the governance and management of their firm, especially setting strategy and ensuring that it is executed. 'Managing partner' refers to the individual, almost always a shareholder, who holds overall accountability for the management of the firm. 'Chief strategy officer' refers to a senior person, usually at director or shareholder level, whose primary role is to support the firm's leadership in driving the processes of strategy development and/or execution across the firm's functions and practices.

## 1. The essence of law firm strategy

At its most fundamental level, law firm strategy can be reduced to two questions:

- What mix of clients, services and markets will deliver the best sustainable competitive advantage for our firm?
- What business model/organisational design do we need to have in place, in order to deliver our best economic performance?

The simplicity of these questions belies the complexity involved in answering them properly. Traditionally, law firm strategy has involved a periodic assessment of the firm's market positioning and performance with respect to the three dimensions in the first bullet, with the setting of objectives and development of business plans to improve that. Over the past decade or so, we have seen innovations such as the adoption of industry-sector specialist groups and key client teams, the emergence of business process outsourcing (BPO) and legal process outsourcing (LPO). Since the onset of the global financial crisis, we have also seen aggressive headcount reductions as business services strive to become more efficient and practices discard underperforming areas and fee earners.

It seems clear though that most changes in business model and organisational design (the second bullet) are, so far, nowhere near transformational enough to deliver the efficiencies that are needed to compete sustainably in what some are calling 'the new normal'. It could also be argued that many of the measures that law firms are adopting are tactical rather than strategic in that they are squarely focused on short-term performance, sometimes at the cost of long-term strategic objectives. A good example is pricing strategy where, despite rhetoric, the majority of firms still have exactly the same systems in place as before the global financial crisis and in reality rely simply on discounting to meet client demands for reduced legal spend.[1] At an extreme, even some quite reputable firms are discounting at levels that may be strategically suicidal, in order to preserve revenue flows.

Deep change is almost always uncomfortable and fraught with risk. Unanticipated consequences are commonplace. Firms must be careful to pace their rate of change, balancing short-term economic performance with steady progress towards clearly defined long-term strategic objectives, to enable them effectively to manage the tensions that emerge. In today's rapidly changing and ever more complex world, this is more difficult than ever. Many different kinds of businesses (not just law firms) are finding the processes that they have in place to develop and drive strategy to be inadequate. Such strategy processes typically have two thrusts:

- to ensure that the leaders of the business have the accurate, relevant, objective and timely information that they need to make the best possible decisions; and
- to ensure that those decisions, articulated in the strategy of the business, are translated into action and results (ie, enhanced competitiveness in the market and the required level of sustained economic performance).

Traditionally, strategy development has consisted of episodic discussions, perhaps annually at the firm's 'strategy day', or when something has gone wrong. Mission-critical decisions have been made largely on collective gut feel, based on management accounting and other largely historical data. Even in some quite large, sophisticated law firms, the empirical evidence and hard analysis underpinning important decisions has been considerably less than other kinds of business would likely have applied under similar circumstances. Of course, one should never underestimate the value of gut feel of experienced leaders in tune with their situation. The personal knowledge of the shareholders or function leaders who are promoting a particular course of action is also obviously essential input to the decision-making process. Because of the personal interest, though, such input is seldom objective. All too frequently, different decisions might have been made and greater value created for the firm, had better information been available.

Over the past few years, the concept of strategy itself has also been undergoing quite radical transformation. Traditional approaches to strategy have relied upon the assumption that one can predict the future with sufficient accuracy to fix a clear strategic direction and end-state. We now know this assumption to be dangerously wrong. A 'cone of uncertainty' extends from the present out into the future, with the ability accurately to forecast diminishing exponentially as time increases. This is illustrated in Figure 1.

---

1    Altman and Weil's 2013 *Law Firms in Transition* survey report states that only 29% of law firm leaders polled reported that their firm had significantly changed its strategic approach to pricing since the global financial crisis and that the primary response to pricing pressure appears to be discounts. Non-hourly billing, although used by almost all firms, represented only 10% of fees collected.

**Figure 1: The cone of uncertainty**[2]

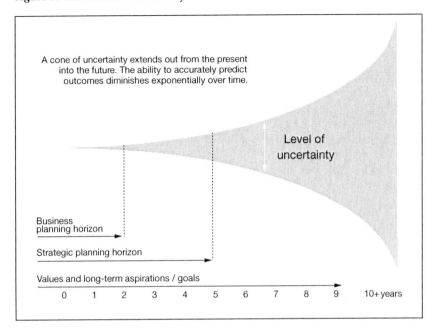

A cone of uncertainty extends out from the present into the future. The ability to accurately predict outcomes diminishes exponentially over time.

Level of uncertainty

Business planning horizon

Strategic planning horizon

Values and long-term aspirations / goals

0  1  2  3  4  5  6  7  8  9  10+ years

We now know that strategy needs to be a continuous process, iterating between making sense of what is going on, defining or fine-tuning the direction that the firm needs to take, developing strategies and plans and executing them. Nor is that the end of the cycle. In order for the strategy processes to be truly effective, firms also need to have systems in place so as to be able routinely to review and learn from their experiences and feed that learning back into the next iteration of the strategy cycle (see Figure 2 overleaf).

## 2.   Law firm leaders need help

Managing partners and executive committees need help if they are to make the best strategic decisions as rapidly and as accurately as is necessary; and then to translate those decisions into actions and results. When one looks at the spectrum of challenges that law firm leaders face when thinking about the best strategies for their law firms, there are several that snap into particularly stark relief:

- maintaining focus on core strategic objectives while fostering entrepreneurialism, collegiality and innovative thinking amongst the firm's shareholders;
- conserving cash to bolster short-term profitability while funding strategic investments to ensure the firm's long-term economic sustainability;

---

2   The cone of uncertainty is a generic concept that was applied in the late 1980s to scenario planning by Clem Sunter, then Chairman of Anglo America's Gold and Uranium Division. He has since articulated this further in several books, perhaps most notably in *The Mind of a Fox* (2001, Tafelberg Publishers).

**Figure 2: The strategy cycle used as a thought framework at Venturis Consulting Group**

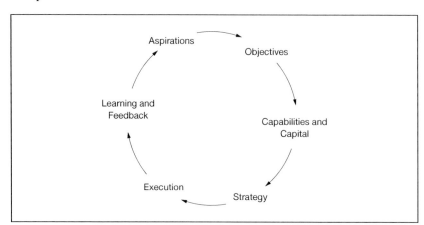

- sorting through the 'noise' to discern the 'signals' that indicate what is really going on in the firm's markets and with its clients, to improve their assumptions about the future;[3]
- watching for new opportunities and threats as they emerge, often unexpectedly; then quickly developing a deep enough understanding of them to be able to formulate the best possible response – and to execute that more rapidly and more decisively than the firm's competitors;
- deciding when to cut the firm's losses and stop investing in an underperforming area of the firm, be it an office, business system, client or practice;
- deciding how the processes in the firm, both in the practice and the business functions (and including the strategy function) should best be sourced, so as to achieve the required level of performance at the lowest cost to the firm;
- assessing the range of strategic options that almost always exist and correctly prioritising them so that the firm's investments are focused on those that will deliver the best return;
- understanding how new markets that the firm enters differ from home markets, and what needs to be done differently as a result;
- developing a deep understanding of what really drives client behaviour when purchasing legal services and how to align the firm with emerging client needs more quickly and more closely than competitors do;
- fostering the creative tension necessary to ensure that complex issues are healthily and deeply debated and challenged, without allowing collegiality

---

3    For an excellent treatment of this topic, see Nate Silver's book *The Signal and the Noise – The Art and Science of Prediction* (2012, Allen Lane). The author is a statistician and political forecaster whose primary claim to fame is that he correctly predicted 49 out of 50 states during the 2008 US presidential elections, trouncing many professional pollsters. He missed Indiana, which Barack Obama won with a 1% margin. In the 2012 US presidential election, he correctly predicted all 50 states.

and inter-partner relationships to suffer. Long-established research shows[4] that one of the key ingredients to achieve this is to focus the debate on objective, up-to-date data that is focused on the issue in question, rather than on personal opinions;

- balancing careful, deep (and therefore time-consuming) thinking about strategic issues and other strategy-related activities with the pressures of their own client work and other shorter-term priorities.

These challenges are not new. What is new are the pressures and the more severe consequences of failure induced by economically depressed, hypercompetitive markets. The emergence across business sectors generally of a new senior management role of chief strategy officer (CSO) is a response to that. Strategy processes and functions are becoming tighter, better defined and more organised. Experience in several prominent law firms is also beginning to show that investment in an effective CSO (typically at director level in business services) supported by a small, well-focused team can deliver disproportionately large returns. It seems highly likely that this trend will accelerate.

## 3. Defining the role of the CSO in law firms

### 3.1 CSO roles can vary significantly from firm to firm

A 2008 McKinsey Quarterly article[5] noted that "CSOs are cropping up in organizations of every size as companies struggle to balance their short and long-term goals in an increasingly complex and volatile business environment." A 2007 Harvard Business Review article[6] described the CSO loosely as a "senior executive whose main responsibility is to ensure that execution flows from strategic planning". A 2012 article in the MIT Sloan Management Review[7] notes that "by understanding how the duties of the chief strategy officer can vary significantly from organization to organization, boards and CEOs can make better decisions about which type of CSO is necessary for their leadership teams".

Being such a new concept, best practices for the roles of CSO and/or strategy teams are still emerging, especially insofar as they apply to law firms. Approaches are evolving rapidly and different law firms (as indeed other kinds of business) are defining the role of their CSO in very different ways. This chapter draws upon interviews undertaken with CSOs and senior leaders to whom they report in law firms ranging from among the largest in the world down to some with a few hundred lawyers. It explores how different law firms are dealing with their adoption of a more systematic approach to strategy and what emerging 'best practices' might be distilled from that.

4   Eisenhardt, Kathleen M, Kahwajy, Jean L, Bourgeois, LJ, "How Management Teams Can Have a Good Fight". Harvard Business Review, July–August 1997.
5   Renee Dye, 2008, "How chief strategy officers think about their role: A roundtable". McKinsey Quarterly.
6   R Timothy, S Breene, Paul F Nunes and Walter E Shill, 2007, "The Chief Strategy Officer". Harvard Business Review, October 2007.
7   Taman H Powell and Duncan N Angwin, 2012, "The Role of the Chief Strategy Officer". MIT Sloan Management Review, September 18 2012. Massachusetts Institute of Technology, Sloan School of Business.

The MIT research suggests that the CSO role is determined by two key dimensions:

- Whether the role was focused mostly on developing strategy, or executing it. Most of the law firm CSOs that we interviewed were focused primarily on executing strategy, although some had multiple responsibilities.
- How the CSO engages with the strategy process. Some are facilitators, advising business units during the process of formulating strategy or assisting in its execution. Others are enactors and far more likely to take a proactive role in driving the process.

Different law firms require different kinds of CSO and even the same law firm may require different kinds of CSO at different stages in its development. In times of transformational change, an action-orientated project manager may be best. During times when the firm is consolidating its position, the focus may be more on analysis and seizing opportunities that emerge – in which case a more thoughtful, research-driven and analytical CSO may be better. The roles that law firm CSOs adopt may be categorised as follows:

## (a)    *Internal consultant*

Where a significant amount of work is outsourced to external consultants, an adequately resourced 'internal consultant' CSO is sometimes a more cost-effective option. An internal CSO also knows the firm better and the firm may be more comfortable trusting that CSO with more sensitive information than it would be with trusting outsiders. On the other hand, the lack of independence may compromise such a CSO's objectivity. The role works particularly well where responsibility for strategy in all but the most macro issues is devolved to business units. An internal consultant CSO may focus on research and analysis, or on project management of initiatives or change management. Rare individuals may have the skill sets that allow them to manage both equally well.

## (b)    *Specialist*

The 'specialist' CSO is appointed because of unique skills or experience that the person has. The MIT article mentions, for example, an M&A specialist brought on board to drive a merger. A CSO who is a specialist in 'Lean Six Sigma' or project management may be brought on board to drive execution and with it efficiency initiatives. Such CSOs may have more portable skills and may be brought on board only to see the firm through a period when this kind of specialisation is required. In contrast to internal consultants, they are more likely to be recruited from outside and to move on to similar roles in other firms once their skills are transferred.

## (c)    *Change agent*

Focused very heavily on strategy execution and effecting organisational change, this type of CSO works closely with and across the various practices and the business services functions to drive transformational projects that deliver execution of the strategy. Such CSOs come into their own particularly where projects are cross-functional, complex and difficult. Effective people skills are essential and success is reliant on the strengths of the CSO's networks across the firm and their deep institutional knowledge. Such CSOs, most especially, need to be clothed with sufficient authority to be taken seriously, either directly through the seniority of their position or through overt and clear support from the firm's leadership.

*(d)*    ***Facilitator***
A 'facilitator' CSO (the MIT article uses the term 'coach') operates between the firm's senior leadership and its functional units and practices, acting as a conduit both upwards and downwards. This role variant works well when strategy is formulated centrally, but execution is devolved and where the actions required to execute the strategy have firm-wide implications. It is also an appropriate kind of CSO when the changes are difficult or traumatic and likely to encounter significant resistance. Because such CSOs typically develop both a wide and an in-depth understanding of the strategies and issues across the firm, they would be well placed to advise on systemic synergies, redundancies and conflicts.

*(e)*    ***Analyst/administrator***
In many cases the CSO may, despite the title, be little more than an analyst combined with a business manager. Such a person is capable of doing rudimentary research; for instance, producing briefing packs on specific issues. He typically focuses heavily on the strategy development side in a support role to the decision makers. Frequently, the role also involves significant administrative/secretarial duties, which can create a situation where the person does not have the seniority in the organisation to be able to influence the execution process. There can surely be few, if any law firms where such a CSO would be appropriate in today's world.

3.2    **Key attributes of a law firm CSO**
During our interviews, we discovered that most CSOs are highly qualified, but not necessarily legally trained. While a general understanding of the legal services that the firm sells and the clients to whom they are sold is obviously necessary, it is far more important that the CSO has the proper credentials in strategy (frequently a good MBA degree plus appropriate experience). CSOs also cannot be truly effective in their role until they have a good understanding of the law firm – its power dynamics and its culture. It is particularly important for the CSO to develop the trust of the law firm's senior leadership. For a lateral hired CSO, especially if from outside the legal sector, all that can take a year or more. In the case of a CSO focused on strategy development, some of the important skill sets and personality traits include:
- getting quickly to the root causes of complex challenges;
- strategic problem solving, complex and innovative analysis;
- effective management of analysts and other team members;
- ability to develop a strong network across the firm and beyond and to leverage that in order to drive initiatives that execute the firm's strategy – this is particularly important because the CSO is likely to have a far smaller team than one typically finds in other law firm business functions;
- communicating effectively with the firm's most senior leadership.

For a CSO focused on strategy execution, the required skill sets would include:

- translating strategic objectives into properly defined projects with action plans, resources, responsibilities and time frames documented and coordinated;
- the ability to understand, analyse and re-engineer/optimise processes both in the functions and the practice;
- anticipating and solving problems that can derail initiatives;
- overcoming resistance and managing stress;
- lateral thinking, creativity and the ability to deliver innovative ideas;
- the confidence, strength of character and professional empathy required to influence and to leverage others in the firm to achieve the required objectives.

Confidence and empathy are in fact essential ingredients for all kinds of CSO. Much of the strategy process is about balancing competing priorities. This is as true in relation to developing strategy as it is when deciding how it will be executed – and then actually driving that execution.

We have already noted the creative tension that is frequently necessary to ensure that complex issues are healthily and deeply debated and challenged before a decision is made. It is only through such deep debate that the full ramifications of an issue can be comprehensively understood. When the opposing views are deeply held though, these debates can become intense – sometimes even acrimonious. While decisions remain the responsibility of the executive committee, the CSO needs to have the professional confidence and gravitas to encourage, guide, even gently provoke such debate, combined with the fortitude to withstand the buffeting that this sometimes involves.

Unsurprisingly, CSOs come from a diverse range of backgrounds and the most effective have significant previous work experience. Some have been recruited from other consulting firms, including premium global firms. Others come from an investment banking background. Still others have been recruited from within their firms or even laterally hired from other law firms.

So far as we have been able to ascertain, the first significant law firm to appoint a CSO was Atlanta-based McKenna Long & Aldridge, in 2004. In this case, the CSO was somebody who started in a marketing role and who demonstrated the ability to operate effectively in a broader, more strategic role. Jeff Haidet, the firm's chairman, commented as follows on the need for the CSO to be able to interface well with the firm's leadership:

"For me, the person in the CSO role must be a good fit with the CEO. They must effectively communicate with one another, be of a similar mind regarding vision and the CEO must have total trust in that person. This is not something that I think I can determine in a couple of one hour interviews but rather requires some time to work together."

## 4. The key roles of a strategy function

Especially in larger law firms and where the role is well defined, CSOs typically have small teams supporting them, to form a discrete 'strategy function'. The composition of the function is fundamentally based on what that particular law firm seeks in its CSO. At its most developed (eg, at Linklaters), the function provides a quite comprehensive strategic support system that covers both strategy development and strategy execution, with the aim that the firm be as effective as possible in:

- basing its strategic decisions on the best possible information;
- translating strategic objectives into executed action that delivers results required;
- capturing innovations and creating change to differentiate itself from competitors.

These three areas and their interrelationships are illustrated in Figure 3 overleaf.

In several firms, the competencies required are present and well linked to the CSO, but not actually located in the actual strategy team, nor reporting to the CSO. This arrangement can work equally well. In smaller firms, such 'multi-tasking' may be the only cost-effective way to develop an effective strategy function.

## 4.1    Business intelligence (BI)

Although the term 'business intelligence' is most frequently used in an IT context today, at its most basic level its simply means the translation of raw data into accurate, relevant and timely information that is meaningful and valuable as a basis for strategic decision making.

The issue for most firms today is not so much where to find relevant information, as where to find the 'signal amidst the noise' or put differently, those truly valuable pieces of information in the sea of data that continually floods into the firm. A well-designed BI function has two primary purposes:

### (a)    *Ongoing monitoring of a number of pre-identified key strategic issues*

To maintain a continual focus on, and to keep the firm's leadership properly briefed about, pre-defined issues of central strategic concern, about which the firm's leadership requires constant updates.

The process involved in delivering this includes identifying the kind of information that needs to be collected; the sources to be used; how those sources are to be to utilised. To be clear, this does not imply anything illegal or unethical. Almost all the information required is openly available in public sources or the firm's own records, if one knows where to look. Other sources may include clients, recruitment agencies, internal focus groups, external consultants and academics.

This information is then collated, analysed and combined with other sources to generate knowledge or intelligence that is directly relevant to the issue in question, to create a work product that can be used to support strategic decision making.

Finally, that work product is disseminated to the firm's leaders, in a form that is most useful to them. Issues requiring the treatment described above might include:

- Monitoring of key client industry sectors: changes in industry sectors frequently spawn changes in legal needs amongst key clients. Competitive advantage can be derived from anticipating such changes or tracking them as

Figure 3: The three components of a well-balanced strategy function

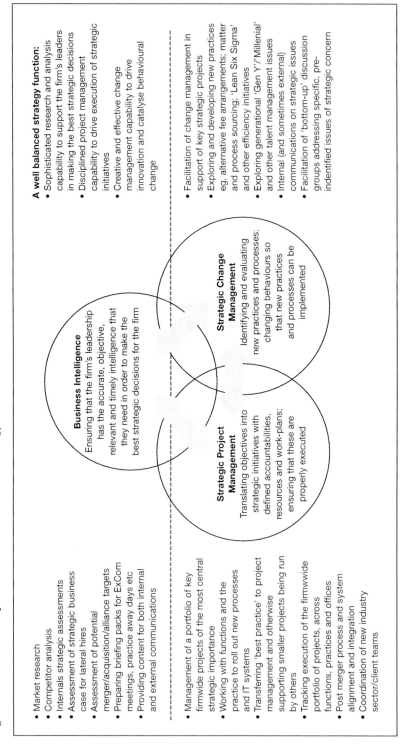

they occur and feeding that information to shareholders servicing clients who are active in those sectors. This is particularly valuable if it engages clients about risks or opportunities about which they are unaware.

- Monitoring key clients: at a superficial level, this may involve maintaining media clipping services on key clients and feeding relationship-building intelligence to the lawyers serving them as it becomes available. At a deeper level, this could involve monitoring client behaviour and even using predictive analysis to gain a better understanding of likely client behaviour.

- Monitoring key markets: some of the more volatile emerging markets especially can experience rapid changes in risk profiles both for clients and the firm itself. Such changes can also translate into new legal needs for clients in those markets. Such monitoring may also be required where it is useful to have a good view of market trends over time, for instance where the firm has earmarked the possibility of a future office or where something specifically relevant to the firm's clients or its own business is expected.

- Monitoring key competitors: few firms track competitors rigorously enough for the intelligence to be truly useful. At the most superficial level, monitoring would involve benchmarking the firm against key competitors in terms of published economic data, Chambers or IFLR rankings or lateral hires or departures. At a deeper, more useful level, it could mean proactively tracking competitor activity in servicing the firm's clients and markets, or trends with their major clients (especially where those clients are also of interest to one's own firm) and other developments that could change the competitive balance between one's own firm and those competitors. Experiments that competitors are undertaking in efficiency enhancement and strategic pricing.

- Tracking specific emerging trends in legal services: in markets such as the United Kingdom, changes in the regulatory environment are inducing changes also to the competitive balance between law firms. Alternative business structures (ABSs) are still in their infancy, but their impact will probably become more profound as they mature and evolve. Any responsible firm obviously already tracks regulatory changes from a compliance perspective, but perhaps not from the point of view of how such changes might be exploited to create areas of advantage over competitors. Other examples of trends that a global firm at any rate may want to monitor might include the step-wise liberalisation of the market in the Republic of Korea, the awarding of Qualifying Foreign Law Practice (QFLP) licences in Singapore, or the convergence of legal services in the ASEAN region or East Africa, amongst others. There are many more.

*(b)* *Providing an in-house management consulting function*

Specific strategic questions will inevitably arise from time to time and another core role of a strategy team would be to act as an in-house management consultancy. Some of the periodic questions that a BI team with the correct mix of skills could address as internal consulting assignments include:

- Alternative fee arrangements (AFAs): as the collective experience deepens in fee arrangements not involving billing by the hour for complex and formerly bespoke legal services, so the opportunities to use the more common forms of AFA as a source of competitive advantage will diminish. Strategic pricing frequently falls under the finance or business development functions, but it could make more sense for this competency to be housed within a strategy team. This would be particularly appropriate where the firm is actively seeking ways of being strategically proactive and innovative with AFAs. In section 1 above, we note the results of Altman Weil's 2013 'Law Firms in Transition' survey (see footnote 1), which states that still only about 10% of fees collected are in the form on non-hourly billing and that most law firms are still responding to price pressures from clients simply by (ever deeper) discounting.
- Assessment of the strategic business case for lateral hires: lateral hires are usually expensive and they have a relatively poor rate of success. This is driving many law firms to apply a lot more rigour to the process of recruiting and integrating lateral hires. Several firms interviewed reported that they were taking a far more strategic view of this than before. Lateral hires with a very significant and portable book of profitable business are more sought-after than ever, but if the business case for a lateral hire is in any way marginal, then firms appear to be applying far more rigour in testing to see whether a truly compelling strategic business rationale exists for the hire. The strategy function can play an objective, impartial role in assessing lateral business cases.
- Assessment of merger, acquisition and alliance opportunities: a competent BI team can be very useful at all stages of a merger process, from conducting an initial strategic appraisal of the opportunity to playing a significant role in the due diligence to supporting the process of integrating the firms afterwards.
- Market research: assessing the potential for legal services in particular markets in which the firm may be interested, which are not already being tracked as an ongoing assignment. This is an obvious precursor for a deeper strategic assessment of the firm's strategic objectives and performance in those markets.
- Options for matter and process sourcing: more and more BPO/LPO service providers are emerging and besides them, other options also exist to source matters and business processes more efficiently.
- Internal strategic appraisal of practices/offices/industry groups/function: working with other functions, an effective BI team can mine into the firm's practice-management systems for data that provides different perspectives to the standard financial and other reports, bringing new insights into what drives profitability in those areas and their potential to enhance the business performance of the firm.

## 4.2    Strategic project management

Most of the CSOs whom we interviewed were tasked with roles focused upon the execution of the firm's strategy. In the case of White & Case, for instance, the strategic initiatives team (headed up by a 'Director of Strategic Initiatives') was developed in order to drive strategic projects that moved the firm from being organised as 35 highly autonomous offices, into 14 regional groups and 16 global practices.[8] In other firms, project management teams have tackled strategic initiatives as diverse as rolling out new technology platforms, integrating processes, systems and structures across legacy firms following major mergers, developing captive BPO and LPO centres and more.

Not all firms have specific project management teams for this purpose. Even some of the largest premium global firms, including Latham & Watkins and Allen & Overy, utilise existing internal resources to drive strategic initiatives, supplementing these where necessary with external consultants and other service providers. At Allen & Overy, significant business projects are used as a testing ground for upper mid-level business services managers to prove their mettle and earn promotion to director.

Other firms have teams that are focused on one particular aspect of strategy execution. Clifford Chance is an example, where execution lies primarily with the relevant partners and business personnel. It also has, however, a team of four managers across the firm who are primarily focused on driving firm-wide efficiency projects, including the practice. In fact, the firm's programme was initially piloted in document review in litigation, investment grade syndicated loans, M&A due diligence and IPO due diligence. Over the past three years, this team has undertaken roughly 60 projects and 'Lean Six Sigma' training is being rolled out into all parts of the firm where a business case exists for it.

Seyfarth Shaw have taken an even more significant approach to Lean Six Sigma, using it as a central component of the firm's business model.

Those firms with dedicated project management functions reported generally that they were valuable assets, as long as they had a good supply of strategic initiatives to keep them engaged. Problems sometimes ensued where boundaries of teams became blurred and members became engaged with lower value activities. A tension existed in several firms as to whether strategic initiatives should be driven by a single, firm-wide team or by regions, individual offices, functions or practices.

'Best practice' would seem to be that there are specific circumstances under which a strategic initiative should be centrally driven, but in most cases it should be driven by those who are going to have to live with the results afterwards. As a general rule, those who will be responsible for managing the system should have a direct role in implementing it. At the very least, this builds buy-in and reduces resistance to the changes involved. Cases where central control may make more sense include:

- the initiative is likely to encounter significant resistance, but its successful execution is essential for achievement of the firm's strategic objectives;
- the initiative requires specialist knowledge that is only available centrally or needs to be imported;

---

8    Ben Hallman, 2008, "White & Case to Undergo Major Reorganization". *The American Lawyer*, December 3 2008.

- the initiative is truly firm-wide or significantly multi-functional;
- the initiative is such that, for any other reason, it makes more sense to drive it from the central team – for instance if it is a project being driven out of the managing partner's office or otherwise involving the central structures of the firm.

This does not preclude the central project management function from supporting projects elsewhere in the firm, or providing an oversight or trouble-shooter role, or monitoring progress so that the executive committee can be kept easily apprised of progress of all projects firm-wide.

### 4.3    Strategic change management

Strategic change management is perhaps the least understood of the three components of the strategy process presented in this chapter, yet it is as important as the other two. Change management as a discipline is well understood and much has been written about it. In law firms, those seeking to drive change encounter particular challenges because of the unique culture and structure of the business (including the fact that many lawyers would object even to the firm being referred to as a 'business').

The simple fact, though, is that many law firms are failing dismally in their attempts to effect the changes that are required to transform their business models and organisational designs, to align with modern market demands. Without detracting from the truly brilliant examples of innovative thinking that some law firms submit to the FT Innovative Lawyers Awards or the InnovAction Awards presented by the College of Law Practice Management each year, most of the offerings are, at best, slight improvements and variations on existing themes.

A well-conceived 'innovation and change management' capability in an in-house strategy function can go at least part of the way towards remedying this. One might ask whether the BI team or the project managers could not fulfil this role and in truth, they probably could at least partially – and in some cases do. The skill-sets and personality profiles required to be good at managing change and driving innovation may be quite different to those that make excellent analysts or project managers, though. Because of the very need for new ideas, this component of the function probably needs to include more external input into its processes than the other two.

Some of the specific tasks that a well-conceived strategic change management component can undertake include the following:

- supporting project managers tasked with driving strategic initiatives by introducing measures to reduce resistance and build engagement;
- deeply exploring new concepts such as alternative fee arrangements, matter and business process sourcing, efficiency enhancements aimed at lowering the cost of doing business and finding innovative ways of making it more attractive for clients to remain with the firm than to move to competitors (building so-called 'exit-barriers');
- facilitating workshops aimed at building partner and employee engagement,

enhancing cross-generational relationships, finding collective solutions to organisational issues (including strategic issues) and business-driven action learning.

**5.    To whom should the CSO and strategy function report?**
The answer to this question depends largely on the governance structures and the culture in place in the individual firm. A compelling argument can be made, though, that the CSO should report to the executive director/CEO/COO, at least functionally. From time to time, the CSO/strategy team may be called upon to produce business intelligence or other analysis upon which difficult, contentious strategic decisions are based. In such cases, the difficulties surrounding such decisions can be exacerbated if the veracity of the supporting data is questioned, because it is perceived that undue influence was exerted over the process. Making the strategy team functionally independent of the central strategic decision-making structures can reduce the risk of this occurring.

A deep level of trust between the CSO and the most senior leadership echelons of the firm is clearly essential, though. Irrespective of what the firm's organogram indicates, this suggests that the reporting needs to be directly to the managing partner or firm chair and/or the executive committee, as is most appropriate from law firm to law firm.

**6.    Challenges**
Given the pressures in most law firms today, establishing a new director-level position overseeing an entirely new function is something that would typically require very significant justification. Cost is perhaps the most immediate issue, but not necessarily the most significant. Some of the other challenges include:

**6.1    Turf wars with the finance function**
Heavy emphasis on cost-cutting and efficiency in recent years has made law firm chief finance officers (CFOs) far more influential. Many have taken on far more substantial roles in both the development and execution of strategy. This is quite understandable and even appropriate, given the current drivers of law firm competitiveness. The boundary between budgeting horizons (typically one to two years) and strategic planning horizons (typically three years plus) can be indistinct, though. This, together with balancing the need for short-term profitability with longer term investments generally may cause conflict between the two functions. These tensions obviously need to be managed, but the tensions themselves can generate creativity and yield innovative solutions when high trust exists between the finance and strategy functions.

**6.2    Sourcing the function**
The processes in the strategy function need to be designed and sourced with as much care as any other business service processes, if they are to deliver results cost-effectively. Much depends on the scale of the law firm, its particular strategic challenges and objectives, the kind of information being processed and the strategic

initiatives being implemented. Some global firms that have developed captive business process outsourcing (BPO) capabilities in less expensive markets outsource at least part of the analysis needs to those centres. For smaller law firms, this can be an option too, if work can be commissioned in such a way as not to compromise security. External consultants can also be utilised for aspects of the processes, especially if they have the right balance of analytical skills and the broad industry experience to bring truly new insights to bear. Ultimately, the solution that delivers the best results at the optimum level of investment is likely to be a combination of in-house staff and a range of carefully selected specialist service providers.

6.3    **Securing the trust of the shareholders and function heads**
One of any law firm's greatest assets can be the entrepreneurial spirit of its partners/shareholders. The strategy function must not be allowed to become a platform for stifling that. This can happen if the firm's strategy processes or the function itself become too bureaucratic and shareholders perceive it as hindering rather than advancing their practices. Having a CSO with the gravitas and demonstrated competence to earn and keep the trust of the shareholders and function heads, and the ability to understand their perspectives, is also essential.

6.4    **Avoiding perceptions of hidden agendas**
It has already been noted that strategy teams sometimes have to develop strategic cases and plans that may be unpopular. These may include closure of under-performing offices or practices, changes to the firm's partner compensation system or reductions to the equity partner ranks. In such cases, the close relationship between the CSO and the managing partner may expose the CSO to criticism that the strategy function is acting simply as an extension of the managing partner's wishes, rather than in the firm-wide interests. This point has already been discussed in section 5 above, but it is worth emphasising. To be truly effective, the CSO needs to avoid the perception developing that the strategy function is partisan in its approach.

7.    **Conclusion**
As noted at the outset, CSOs and 'strategy teams' are a new concept. Much of what has been written in this chapter represents work in progress on the part of law firms that are in the early stages of experimenting with them. As the pressure to deliver truly transformational change increases, and so too the realisation that law firms cannot achieve this without utilising subject experts, so it is likely that the components focused on strategy execution will become more prominent. Likewise, if those firms that are paying serious attention to the quality of the information underpinning their strategic decisions begin to derive significant advantage over competitors who do not, so business intelligence functions are likely to become more widespread.

*Input from the following law firms in particular is gratefully acknowledged: Allen & Overy, Baker & McKenzie, Bird & Bird, Blank Rome, Clifford Chance, Faegre Baker Daniels, Latham & Watkins, Linklaters, McKenna, Long & Aldridge, Parker Poe, Webber Wentzel, White & Case.*

# Improving efficiency in law firms in times of flat turnover and increasing costs

**Ashley Balls**
LegalBestPractice

## 1. Introduction

In 2006 Coudert Frères, widely regarded as the first multi-national law firm, was dissolved due to demands on the partners' retirement fund exceeding the capacity to pay. This was a visceral shock for many in the law as the spectre of an insolvent law firm was an alien concept – one that was experienced by clients, not lawyers. Whilst it is not possible to establish a causal link between this event and fluctuations in supply and demand for legal services it was becoming clear to a few legal commentators that change was underway. For decades law firms were in the comfortable position governed by supply and demand in terms of having more instructions than the legal market could service. The market, such as it was, varied from city to city and jurisdiction to jurisdiction and the gains were unevenly spread. However, the signs were there in the years prior to the global financial crisis of 2007 to 2008, primary mechanisms were starting to change and the ability to increase prices year on year by an amount equal to or more than inflation was coming under strain.

In December 2004, the Clementi Report was published in England, resulting in the Legal Services Act 2007. That act saw the separation of powers for the Law Society and set out the basis on which alternative business structures would enable non-lawyers to have equity stakes in law firms. England was not the first significant jurisdiction to embark on a reform process; Australia saw the first law firm anywhere raise capital through an Initial Public Offering (IPO). Slater & Gordon Limited was the first law firm to be listed on a Stock Exchange.

## 2. The traditional business models of law firms

For the majority of practitioners, whether a rural sole principal or a partner in a major international firm, the prospect of change or the need to raise funds for further acquisitions was simply not on the agenda. The small to medium size (SME) law firm typically had an established relationship with its bankers, and credit was readily available when required. When comparatively plentiful and cheap credit dried up following the global financial crisis, the reaction of many was to cut costs. With staff salaries consuming around a third of fees in a great many firms it was a simple matter, in the face of falling instructions, to halt recruitment and then lay-off or retrench staff. Many firms of all sizes took to cost-cutting with gusto, considering this to be sufficient to wait out the crisis, and thousands were laid off. Most practitioners got on with their jobs and kept a close eye on the routine outputs of the practice management system (PMS) whilst watching the fallout from the global financial crisis and assuming they were now safe.

The business model that had served the professions (including accountants) for decades was based on a presumption whereby every 100 'units' of fees would be consumed as follows:

- one-third on salaries and wages;
- one-third on fixed and variable costs (eg, premises, PI cover, telecommunications, utilities, third-party services and IT);
- one-third distributed to the partners as profit.

The sustainability of this nostrum was rarely questioned.

General management theory has rarely delivered a productivity 'silver bullet' and law is no exception. Productivity improvements come from the application of innovation and minor but cumulative process changes. Legal practice has seen significant productivity improvements from innovation and the application of IT has, over the working life of older lawyers (60 plus) seen the ratio of lawyers to support staff change from 1:3 to better than 1:1. The introduction of online library and precedent research and the completion of discovery and document management can now be electronic, but the core processes by which the basic interaction between client and lawyer take place have barely altered in decades. Most lawyers in private practice are still desk bound and clients make appointments and conduct meetings in meeting rooms or occasionally via teleconference. The situation is so similar across the profession that were a lawyer to awaken today from a 20 or 30-year coma s/he would, once accustomed to new legislation/case law, be quite comfortable about going back to work. Meanwhile other professions have changed. The notion of 'hot-desking', whereby staff do not have their own room/workspace but share resources is alien to the legal profession, but not to accountants. Were all employed personnel at a leading accountants to turn up at 'the office', there would be serious breaches of workplace occupancy legislation.

For decades prior to the global financial crisis, lawyers' fees had been rising faster than the prevailing rate of inflation and were rarely questioned by the client. Demand for legal services seemed to be increasing unabated. Law schools continued to produce new, eager young lawyers and the professions (at least those in the Common Law world) grew in raw numbers by approximately 4% per annum. In this environment, there were beacons of business proficiency and well-applied management theory but for many the disciplined approach to management was spread somewhat thinly. This is not a critical comment, but a normal reaction to business trying to satisfy growing demand for its services. In times of plenty when there is a plenitude of work and profits, attention to process improvements has a low priority. The operating metrics whereby some 30% to 40% of revenue (fees) was converted to profit was an enviable position to be in when contrasted to companies listed on bourses who were pleased to see profit margins of 7% to 12%. At a more granular level other metrics were similarly perverse. Following the lifting of restrictions many countries had imposed on the size of partnerships (typically 20), growth in partner numbers was prodigious; firm size and partner numbers have continued to rise exponentially. Few partners and legal commentators have asked why any business would need hundreds of 'directors' to function effectively. Human resource (HR) leverage models have changed, with many larger firms having as many as 10 to 15 lawyers per partner; but few meaningful changes have taken place in the career structure. Lawyers are either employees, with some having a title to denote seniority, or have some form of partnership. With the changes in HR leverage, the route to partnership has become progressively (mathematically) less likely. Whether this has been a significant impetus to the increasing mobility of lawyers is unknown, but whenever a lawyer is replaced major costs are incurred, covering:

- advertising;
- recruitment fees;
- training; and
- loss of productivity (the final and most costly component).

Whenever lawyers move employment, there is a loss of productivity for a variety of reasons that few calculate even to this day. The disruptive effect means other staff have to assist the new employee to come to terms with a new operating environment, to learn how to operate the PMS, to learn new client care protocols, to become familiar with precedent databases, to learn client hierarchies, intra-office relationships, to get on top of office politics, learn billing protocols and become accustomed to the expectations of managing work in progress (WIP) and debtors. Once the lag between moving to a new post and despatch of the first bill has been factored in, all these disruptions frustrate productivity. The economic impact of the disruptive effect, when coupled with paying a third-party recruiter, plays havoc with profit margins and whilst there is only anecdotal evidence, claims that senior new recruits generate no profit at all in the first year are probably correct.

Few have questioned the business model, presumably believing an operating structure that had withstood recessions, world wars and more had no need to restructure. However, the global financial crisis was different – the result was a credit squeeze as banks stopped lending. Local bankers recognised that the business of law is a 'lagging indicator' in that the work being carried out today may not materialise as fees for four to nine months. When the credit with which many firms were content to finance partner drawings dried up, costs were cut and the largest costs – like any service business – were salaries and wages. Once staff reductions were underway, other costs were examined and further cuts made. Making cuts in premises is not easy, as leases cannot be surrendered speedily without penalty, making it easier to cut elsewhere. The list of spending targets was enormous and included:

- deferring or freezing pay rises;
- deferring capital replacement (IT, printing, telephony, software, cars etc);
- reducing library and knowledge management (KM) spend;
- reducing continuous professional development (CPD) budgets;
- cutting benefits (pension contributions, health benefits, expense accounts, travel);

- outsourcing 'back office' function services (eg, business processes and document review/management).

When the flurry of staff reductions and cost cutting was over, little had changed except on the cost side of the ledger. Very little attempt was made to address the income or fees side of the ledger and lawyers accepted that they had become 'price takers' as opposed to 'price makers'. New ways of working were not adopted with anything like the zeal of cost-cutting. As a simplistic observation, many law firms were leaner, but little else had changed.

Falling profits in real terms is always a stimulus for self-examination and to establish whether one firm is suffering more or less than others. The self-examination in the large firms had two outcomes:

- a significant growth in legal process outsourcing (LPO) and business process outsourcing (BPO);
- a change in the HR leverage ratio – more lawyers per partner.

Unlike other businesses, which were experiencing the same economic pressures, little change took place in terms of productivity – the proportion of lawyers' working day that was spent carrying out chargeable activity remained constant. For many, the fees billed by a staff lawyer equate to approximately five hours per day at the nominal or 'rack' charging rate. In some jurisdictions (eg, New Zealand and Australia), this figure is lower and has been for more than two decades. (It is acknowledged that US lawyers lead in this area and they consistently bill closer to six hours a day at full charging rate. Coincidentally, government statistics departments show that the time lawyers spend working is remarkably similar across the Common Law world and averages some 10 hours a day or 50 per week. It is the proportion that is billed that varies.) These are average figures and it is acknowledged that some lawyers and law firms produce more, but not by a significant margin. This contrasts with other business sectors which have routinely produced more revenue per worker year on year and have productivity measures built into their annual budgetary processes. For example, volume car manufacturers made five cars per employee per annum in 1980 and today make over 30. The differences in the budgetary process for a law firm and a manufacturing business are very similar in that both start from the basis of projected fixed and variable costs and available resources to achieve anticipated sales.

For a production or manufacturing director, there is an expectation that salaries and wages will rise by 3% to 5% and that the board of directors expect an increase in profit of 10%; but prices must rise at a rate lower than inflation. The production director is tasked every year to find ways of making more from less – productivity increases are demanded. This explains why almost every material item purchased has fallen in price in real terms for decades whether it is groceries, cars, clothing or almost any day-to-day expenditure. Real prices for most goods, net of inflation have fallen. Service industries too have achieved similar gains – air travel and telephony make for good examples. Both have achieved significant reductions in real prices, despite significant increases in their fixed and variable costs.

## 3.    Pricing issues

Law is something of an exception and I well recall attending a budget meeting in the City of London when the managing partner opened the session by asking, 'How much are we going to put our rates up this year?' Those days may be long gone, but the legacy has been the near obsessive concentration on finding a pricing mechanism that works for both sides of the legal services delivery supply chain. Many law firms have wrestled with this for some years and still consider there is something of a panacea in pricing – if only they could get it right. Whilst pricing is important, price is nothing more than an output metric; it is not a business process. For a number of years, lawyers have been assailed with pricing nostrums, and three alternatives have emerged:

- time and cost-based or cost-plus;
- value;
- fixed price.

Taking each in turn, all have inherent weaknesses and none offers any significant alternative; nor is pricing delivering a new business model.

### 3.1    Time and cost/cost plus

This is well understood and despite well-researched data is still considered to be the principal method for the determination of pricing. It also underpins the income side of the ledger when it comes to budgeting. As a pricing tool it is akin to using a sledgehammer to crack a nut. It is inherently inflexible and when applied to an individual or work type presumes that the outcome has a constant or fixed value, where the complexity/value of the matter is irrelevant. Lawyers are frequently given a pricing rate based on seniority and are forced to apply it to all (or most) of the work they carry out. The idea that a day in the life of a lawyer has a constant or fixed value assumes that all their work is the same and carried out equally efficiently. Cost-plus has a place, principally as a comparative metric, as it provides an intuitively simple basis for measuring the outputs of lawyers; but for clients it is a blunt instrument and the cause of some disquiet. This is all the more noticeable now that legal regulators around the world have increasingly adopted 'client care' regimes where some pricing transparency is mandatory. At an operational level cost-plus is open to abuse and is dependent on individual lawyers being highly disciplined in its application and ensuring all billable activity is billed 'live'. The realities of the way the modern lawyer operates work against this and many account for their time retrospectively, with the result that many 'units' are lost when telephonic and other interruptions occur. The list of circumstances where suboptimal time management occurs is almost endless.

### 3.2    Value billing

This is misunderstood by many and complex in its application. At its simplest it can involve a dialogue with a client at the opening of a new matter, whereby an outline of the objectives are discussed and the lawyer enquires as to the client's perceived understanding of the value for the completion of the task. It is never an easy task as too few lawyers have any meaningful preparation for discussing value with a client and pricing in many law firms is a process carried out by partners or project managers. It is particularly difficult where large complex matters are involved and project management skills are required. A pseudo-science of value billing has evolved and delivers a process whereby as many as 20 variables have to be considered before coming to a pricing decision. Others use value as a reward by allowing the client to make an additional payment over and above a pre-set minimum if they consider the lawyer/law firm has delivered an especially elegant or beneficial outcome – a process that is open to abuse in a market where the capacity of the legal services industry is believed to exceed the demand. Value billing clearly has a place in the pricing lexicon, but it does not offer a solution to a business environment where the inexorable increases in fixed and variable costs at law firms are being tempered by incessant client demands for lower prices. It is not surprising that in major matters, especially in the public sector or where panels exist, requests for proposals (RFPs) have flourished and a whole new range of third-party advisers has emerged who claim to be able to increase the likelihood of responding successfully to RFPs. In many cases they merely add cost and their very existence virtually confirms the extent of pricing confusion and client apprehension.

### 3.3    Fixed price

The concept of a lawyer being asked to state a fixed price for the delivery of a service is one that is alien to a great many lawyers – particularly litigators, many of whom opine that to do so is a high-risk strategy that has the capacity to bankrupt a law firm. Others, particularly those delivering transactional services, consider it possible, but again many are of the opinion that to work for fixed prices somehow 'cheapens' their role as professionals. Setting fixed prices – particularly for transactional services (ie, property purchase/sale, company formations, debt management, estate administrations, trust formations and more) readily lend themselves to fixed-price billing, especially if delivered using commoditised or systematised processes, frequently referred to as work-flows. Setting prices for such services need not be overly taxing and requires some data 'mining' of past transactions and a reasonable understanding of the fixed and variable costs involved. At its simplest it could mean nothing more than calculating the average price charged for the 50 previous similar transactions and setting that as a base price plus disbursements and taxes, though the application of such a simplistic approach is not recommended. Effective pricing for a transactional service should take account of:

- market trends;
- the maturity of the service in the product life cycle;[1]
- the number of anticipated transactions;
- the seniority of the person carrying out the work;
- whether a work-flow is in place or can be developed;
- the quantity of time required to complete a typical matter;

---

1    All products and services have a product life cycle that conforms to a 'normal' distribution. Products and services have finite life cycles from introduction to redundancy and it is axiomatic that the application of a fixed price combined with a work-flow to a service nearing its natural redundancy has few if any advantages.

- where the work is to be carried out (at the client's premises, at the law firm or some other remote location);
- the degree of risk involved;
- the value of the consideration;
- urgency;
- the likelihood of cross or upselling opportunities;
- the value of the client;
- the cost of sales.

The weighting of the above items is still a judgement call, but when carried out on an informed basis following discussion with the client should result in the delivery of predetermined absolute profit and margins.

The demand from clients for pricing certainty is gathering momentum and likely to increase. This should be a spur to offering more fixed-price billing, but the profession is showing some resistance.

As with most elements of management there is no definitive right or wrong solution to pricing, but resistance to client demands is neither wise nor recommended. Client demand for certainty of pricing is becoming ubiquitous. Attempts to resist this application to legal services may not end well. Whilst it may appear counter-intuitive, the application of fixed-price services, especially when coupled with work-flow applications, has the capability of delivering significant increases in margin and absolute profit. It is possible to deliver greater volumes of services, using less qualified personnel in less elapsed time. This should be sufficient incentive, but for many the act of commoditisation is an anathema and infers 'pile it high, sell it cheap' even when fully satisfying client demand.

The whole concept of pricing and its relationship to profit still causes some managing partners difficulty, as the concept of variable margins is not well understood or widely accepted – especially in the SME sector. Firms, routinely asked what the overall profit margin is, will reply with an accurate figure; but when asked how it varies across service streams (property, litigation, commercial, estates etc), they are frequently unaware of any variation. This can be seen in the fee budgeting process that is applied to their individual staff lawyers. It is not unusual for practice managers and managing partners to apply fee targets based upon a multiplier principle whereby the lawyer is required to bill a sum that equates to three, four or five times their salary. Some use a one-size-fits-all approach and require the same multiplier with no regard to the variation in margin generated by each work stream. Intuitively most partners understand that different work is priced differently with a consequent impact on profits, but are unaware of the mechanisms required to monitor and manage these variations or set prices and margins accordingly. It is worth mentioning that many PMS systems have the capacity to manage large numbers of work streams and record the data accordingly, but experience shows that most firms manage effectively with fewer than 20. Contrast this with a supermarket where there are anything from 25,000 to 40,000 product lines on the shelves at any one time with hundreds of new types arriving and disappearing every year and where a store manager, when presented with any single item, will be able provide the

following data with a few mouse clicks:
- purchase price;
- selling price;
- margin;
- absolute profit;
- cost of sales;
- length of time on the market;
- maturity in product life cycle;
- sales volume;
- ordering history;
- customer profile.[2]

The resulting information tells the store manager where to display the product, whether some marketing initiative is justified and for how much longer the product will be stocked. Few law firms have this level of financial sophistication, but many have the tools to achieve it already in place.

4.    **Cost management, financial controlling and new work processes**

It does not follow that this is an invitation for law firms to micro manage on the scale of a supermarket, but it illustrates how the annual fees budget round could be improved and it starts by gaining more and better information about where the profit in an individual firm comes from. All lawyers and law firms should actively shun low or no margin work unless there is a deliberate policy to loss lead, but only when the overall margin meets defined objectives. It is worth mentioning that if a firm is unable to make a profit from a particular type of work, there will be others that can. Identifying low or no-profit work requires a lot more than merely observing fees billed per lawyer; it requires the following on each member of staff:
- salary;
- share of fixed and variable costs;
- fees;
- basis for charging and if relevant the charging rate;
- types of work carried out and the profit margin on each.

The above list presupposes that a firm is able to reverse engineer its accounts and measure profit margin by work type. When this data is managed, realistic and meaningful fees budgets can be set and monitored. Importantly, no new investment is required to do this even with an older PMS. If the system cannot provide the relevant data at a granular level it is a relatively straightforward exercise to allocate costs and apply variable profit margins with a spreadsheet containing some active formulae. When variable profits are better understood and applied, the monthly routine whereby the practice manager or chief operating officer conducts a tedious progress through the firm seeking explanations as to why certain individuals are under or overachieving can be avoided. The issue then becomes one of finding a

2    This is only possible if the customer uses a 'loyalty' card.

mechanism to explain to staff members why Bloggs has a lower fee target than Smith yet may have the same salary. This single action highlights what many overlook when considering all the various dynamics of law firm management – communication. The suggestion that salary information is confidential from the law firm management's view is correct, but staff readily and routinely discuss and exchange pay levels.

Whether it is staff supervision, matter management, communicating matter progress with clients, needs analysis, capital management or routine management reporting, better communication is the one area that enables any firm to deliver a productivity gain.

Below are some techniques that can assist in building productivity through improved communication.

## 4.1    Staff supervision

In an operating environment where HR leverage ratios are growing, staff management skills are increasingly important. When a busy partner can have anything from one or two to 15 other lawyers and paralegals to supervise it is tempting merely to look in on a staff member once a week and utter that pointless interrogative, "Is everything all right?" Whilst it may seem obvious to mention this, it still happens and the response can only ever be "yes", as anything remotely negative implies that the question was misunderstood, or worse, that a problem is being hidden. Effective staff supervision is a learned skill and when carried out diligently can ensure employed staff have a full understanding of expected outcomes. For example, staff must understand how long a matter should take, what resources are required, what precedents are available and what to do if something unexpected or unforeseeable occurs. This results in matters being completed to higher standards, faster. It is also about managing client expectations. Moreover, less time is wasted by staff blindly going off in the wrong direction which, whilst it may be a learning exercise, results in high write-off levels. An additional few minutes explaining what and how a matter is to be handled always pays dividends; problems only arise when the partner loses patience, believes it is not worth explaining and retains the matter personally. Supervision is an ongoing exercise and does not stop once the matter has been allocated and the expectations explained. The use of leading and presumptive questions is to be avoided as the 'servant' may feel constrained from making constructive comment. Supervision is not a natural skill and those who do it poorly should be dissuaded as it is counterproductive and alienates the staff. Where high supervision workloads are involved allowance should be made for the supervising partner's loss of personal productivity.

## 4.2    Matter management

Once the matter is allocated and the expected outcomes understood (and communicated to the client), the next most important stage is the ongoing review process. There is no right or wrong way to do this as the management input will vary according to the complexity and duration of each matter. The key elements of matter management are to provide a standardised reporting function designed to minimise the likelihood of variation to anticipated time and cost expectations, to speedily identify whether additional resources may be required and if unforeseen circumstances have arisen. It is vital to check progress periodically and carry out a review of these issues on a weekly or fortnightly basis. To save time, the review should adopt the default position that if matters are progressing normally there is nothing to report. Only the variations to the norm are required. Careful preparation of the checklist is vital to ensure all 'live' matters are present but only variations are reported.

### 4.3 Communication

The most important item is communication between staff and partner and between the lawyer and client. The client needs to be kept informed about satisfactory progress and any changes, particularly if it impacts on cost. All of this can be systematised and is easily managed by support personnel. It is not good enough to say nothing to a client when matters are progressing satisfactorily – they should never be left to guess. To borrow a phrase from the medical and nursing professions, 'Always keep the patient informed.'

### 4.4 Management reporting

Routine management reporting varies from firm to firm, even when they have the same PMS. The range and granularity of data reported on varies according to many factors, including:

- firm size;
- structure, including ownership;
- the number of offices;
- specialisation;
- standard operating procedures/protocols used;
- the financial strength (or otherwise) of the firm;
- whether management reports are available to non-owners;
- the complexity and capacity of the PMS system used;
- the purpose for which reports are routinely prepared.

The final two points above are perhaps the most significant. Times have now moved on and PMS systems have become the central platform upon which all law firm activity is measured, recorded and managed. Today it is usual to deliver the following via a desktop network/portable devices, over the internet:

- time and cost recording (fees per lawyer/team, write-off rates);
- client database management;
- client relationship management (CRM);
- online knowledge library access and knowledge management;
- case and matter management;
- marketing;
- client billing and accounting;
- intranet and extranet;
- word processing;

- eDiscovery:
- management reporting;
- precedent management and work-flow creation/delivery.

The size/profitability of a firm was once a consideration in whether the functionality of the above was available through a PMS, as fully featured systems were expensive and not designed for firms with only a handful of desktops. This is no longer the case and fully integrated and high-functioning systems are now available to firms of all sizes. Firms are no longer required to have the entire hardware infrastructure, as hosting and cloud solutions have removed the need for in-house data storage.

The issues today are in selecting the system, deciding on the data storage/back-up facility and adopting a process whereby the firms' needs are reconciled with those of the client and the way in which the lawyers and support personnel work. In a world where personnel have 'flexible' working options and where clients want some services delivered from their offices, secure remote access to the PMS is essential. Budgetary determination is not straightforward given the number of variables, but the allocation of some 2% to 3% of fees per annum works for many. The solution will involve finding the best compromise between functionality and affordability.

These factors illustrate the need for process throughout the legal service delivery supply chain. For many older lawyers this is an anathema as there is a well-entrenched attitude that all legal work is unique and requires a bespoke solution. Many in that generation have controlling or senior management interests in their firms and in some cases frustrate twenty-first century systems and solutions.

## 4.5 Capital management

Managing work in progress (WIP) and debtors continues to haunt firms of all sizes and there are still partners who persist with the notion that WIP is an asset able to be converted to cash as and when needed. Reducing WIP and debtors to best practice standards is neither complex nor onerous. The first decision to take is the establishment of an acceptable quantum for total lock-up (WIP + debtors). A figure of 70 (70/365th) days is achievable and the strategy to realise it is based on a default process whereby billing and collections occur according to a strict set of protocols and where only exceptions are reported on, monthly or more frequently if required. The following protocols – which are already in use – are offered as a guide:

- Remove billing from all fee earners – regardless of seniority – and appoint a billing 'Tsar', giving them the necessary authority to act. All fee earners to receive a monthly report setting out their interim and final billing.
- Educate and inform the clients of your policy – include the policy on your website/Facebook page.
- Ensure your client engagement protocols reflect exactly the WIP and debtor management settings you adopt, including that bills are payable on receipt. Undertake credit checks on new clients as part of the routine anti-money laundering requirements. Adopt a standardised billing protocol whereby the narration on the bill is taken from the engagement letter.

- Bill disbursements in advance and inform clients that work on a matter will cease if any due disbursements remain unpaid.
- Bill all WIP on a monthly cycle – if a matter commences on the second Tuesday of the month all WIP should be billed on the second Tuesday of the month following. (An exception policy will be required for routine transactions where fees are taken from the net proceeds of a sale/purchase of property, for legal aid/public defence cases and where funds are held on account of costs for a sum in excess of any 'time-on-the-clock'.)
- Ensure any final bill is sent within 72 hours of matter completion and as part of the matter completion process ensure that all contributing fee earners log all outstanding time and costs to the PMS.
- Adopt a credit collection policy (eg, send a statement in 14 days and a letter at 21 and if necessary another at 28 days; and if still unpaid at 35, pass the delinquent account to a third party. Cease all work on any matter where 28 days' credit has been taken.)
- Develop a management report showing where any matter and fee earner has not followed policy.
- Name and shame all fee earners who ignore or flout the policy – regardless of seniority.
- Calculate and report the cost of non-compliance (eg, where a firm may ordinarily have lock-up at 140 days (a quite usual occurrence) and has a T/O of say €10 million, the 'value' of lock-up at any one time will average $10,000,000 \div 365 \times 140 = €3.835$ million). If this is reduced to 70 days the value of lock-up declines to €1.918 million. This may seem small, but at current overdraft rates of say 12%, a saving of €230,136 in bank interest is achieved every year.

Some firms have gone further and impose penalties on partners who exceed specific targets, even to the extent of restricting drawings.

There can be no 'special cases' when it comes to WIP and debtor management and firms are advised not to act for clients who will not pay.

4.6    Needs analysis

In an industry facing over-capacity (as evidenced by a new round of lay-offs in England as at May 2013), and where interaction with clients is largely reactive it is surprising to see that so few firms carry out an informal client needs analysis on a regular basis. Whether this is as a result of the ingrained habit of waiting for client instructions or the pressure to record as many chargeable units is unknown, but it continues.

If the well-bruited assumption that 80% of a law firm's marketing effort should be directed at its existing clients, then it follows that needs analysis can be part of this process. The process is straightforward and can be applied at any law firm, regardless of size or complexity. It involves nothing more than checking past financial metrics to identify the clients who consistently generate the highest billings. It is helpful further to examine this group – typically the top 10 or 20 – and confirm that they are also the clients who generate the most profit; some firms lack routine procedures to accomplish this. However, once the list is compiled the relevant client relationship partner should then be tasked with scheduling a lengthy informal meeting with the client 'off-site' at say a sports match, or theatre, over lunch/dinner or a round of golf and talk about the client's future activities. After the first 20 to 30 minutes of small talk, conversation will eventually revert to the one subject they both have in common, the law/business. During this period careful and considered conversation should reveal whether their economic activity is to carry on 'as before', or if some expansion/downsizing is planned and over what period. A commercially minded partner will then talk about the consequences of the future and what it might mean in terms of lease renewals, the most appropriate business structures, what impact it will have on labour, what standard contracts may need to be revised, what litigation avoidance techniques to consider and basically to get comfortable with what the client is doing and planning. It need not and should not be an interrogation – more a detailed familiarisation process and entirely devoid of advice.

When next in the office the lawyer is advised to construct a simple report and time line, setting out the potential pitfalls and legal 'events' that will be encountered as the future plan is rolled out. Next, send it or present it, without a bill, to the client and ask if it accords with their ideas and whether anything is missing. The time involved in this whole process will amount to several hours and should be recorded as marketing or business development. The object of the exercise is to become more informed about the client, create a social obligation and develop a closer commercial connection between the two parties. The *quid pro quo* from unsolicited interest will, in most cases, ensure the lawyer will be top of the list when next a lawyer's services are required.

Recently published research among the SME business sector carried out by the Legal Services Board suggests the scale of unmet legal need in England (defined as the value of business costs incurred where no legal advice was sought) may be as much £100 billion per annum.[3] This suggests that a significant business opportunity is being missed through a lack of enquiry and communication by lawyers.

## 5.    The future

Any attempt to second guess the future shape and operating style of the profession is always going to be an inexact science, but one thing is certain – the post-GFC operating environment is new and any hope of a return to the past is futile. The future is almost certainly going to see the introduction of IT/process-driven applications for transactional work, clients demanding and expecting certainty of pricing, a wider acceptance of the English ABS operating structure/ownership, much high HR leverage, lower profit margins, frozen or declining prices, a slowing of the numbers entering the profession, growth in the role and functions of paralegals/legal executives and a significant reduction in the number of providers through

---

3    See research.legalservicesboard.org.uk/wp-content/media/In-Need-of-Advice-report.pdf

amalgamation and consolidation of law firms. The good news is the emergence of new roles and functions for lawyers in areas such as project management and legal process engineering.

Will young people still want to take up legal careers in this environment? Again a difficult question to answer, but the challenge of new and perhaps more interesting careers than what many perceive as 'traditional' is likely to see interest maintained. As for career structures and opportunities for partnership, some younger lawyers are already reluctant to take positions 'leading to partnership' as these posts are perceived as not family friendly and too high risk when considering the rewards and liabilities that attach to ownership. Salaried functions that come with ready access to high-quality work and clients, coupled with a secure and high income, is for many 'Gen X' and 'Gen Y' lawyers sufficiently attractive. Perhaps these two cohorts have already worked out that further consolidation of law firms and higher HR leverage will not only further diminish partnership opportunities; they may also recognise that in reality, partnership may confirm status among your peers but that for most it carries no real managerial responsibility.

The consolidation of law firms has been underway for a while already. In England and Wales law firm numbers peaked in 1997 and have declined ever since.[4] Recent reports suggest the comparatively benign rate of decline is set to increase dramatically. John Llewellyn-Lloyd, head of professional services at investment bank Espirito Santo is reported to have suggested at a conference in April 2013 that as many as 8,000 firms could disappear in the European Union over the next 10 years.[5] Further comment suggests the Solicitors Regulation Authority may play a part in reducing the number of law firms in England as a result of economic failure and the increasing risk of theft of client funds.[6] With the exception of the moral crisis of possible future theft, other commentators have suggested failure to raise capital will force law firm consolidations as the sums required will be beyond the capacity of partners.

The scale and extent of change is unprecedented and it is better for the profession to embrace and manage the process than have exogenous forces determine future direction. Hitherto, change has been at an evolutionary pace and the delivery of legal services has fundamentally continued unquestioned for generations. The future, however, will not be a continuation of the past; change is inevitable due to pricing pressure, lawyer demographics (a younger profession), client pressure, new methods of delivery (including online) and the new and unknown business structures yet to emerge as the regulatory restrictions are lifted. It will be an exciting time to be a lawyer for those who approach the future with an open mind and a willingness to accept change.

---

4    See: https://research.legalservicesboard.org.uk/wp-content/media/In-Need-of-Advice-report.pdf. Also see Mayson and Balls, Chapter 2, "Legal Services Reform", in *The Business of Law 2009*, R Pol and A Balls (2009) Thomson Reuters.

5    See business.financialpost.com/2013/05/03/investment-banker-predicts-8000-law-firms-will-disappear-in-next-decade/ and www.lawgazette.co.uk/news/private-equity-spurns-law-firm-advances.

6    See www.legalfutures.co.uk/latest-news/sra-expect-large-law-firms-go.

# Law firm strategy: serving the results-driven in-house law department

Richard Given
HSBC
Paul Lippe
OnRamp Systems

## 1. Introduction

If you have got this far in the book, we assume that you recognise that the traditional law firm approach is no longer 'fit for purpose' and that something different is required. We also assume that this is not your first foray into what is required for the future.[1]

That said, in our experience most firm leaders are way ahead of their partnerships in recognising the need for change, and are experiencing a lot of stress in trying to bring their partners along. So it is an interesting challenge to write about law firm strategy for managing partners.

We have organised this chapter in three parts:

- a brief discussion of strategy;
- a longer discussion of what is happening with clients that should drive your strategy; and
- a roadmap on how you can develop your strategy organically, given the constraints you face.

For the impatient and busy reader, here is a (140 character) summary:

*"Law firm strategy: listen to clients and internal innovators; do new things to boost value for clients; risk (micro) failure and do more of those things that work."*

## 2. A brief discussion of strategy

The best way to start thinking about strategy is to borrow from Peter Drucker, perhaps the pre-eminent management thinker of the twentieth century. Some relevant 'Druckerisms':

- "If you want something new, you have to stop doing something old."
- "Trying to predict the future is like trying to drive down a country road at night with no lights while looking out the back window."
- "The best way to predict your future is to create it."
- "Strategy is a commodity, execution is an art."

---

[1] For more background on change in law, see Richard Susskind's book Tomorrow's Lawyers www.amazon.com/Tomorrows-Lawyers-Introduction-Your-Future/dp/019966806X, or Bruce MacEwen's Growth is Dead: Now What? www.amazon.com/Growth-Dead-firms-brink-ebook/dp/B00AOW6J2M.

That may not feel like a particularly coherent explanation of what strategy is. But that is exactly the point. Strategy is not a panacea or set of Powerpoints. It is the actions and choices that the organisation makes, including very much the things you do not do. Generally, when we say 'strategy' we mean doing something different from what we are already doing, and thinking longer term. This leads us to the issue of why strategy is hard for law firms.

For a law firm that has been around for a while (say 30 years or more), strategy is hard. By contrast, every new law firm has an intrinsic advantage in that it was started by, and is probably still run by, people with an idée fixe (eg, success-based fees or serving a particular niche), that still animates the firm.

## 2.1 Why is strategy hard for law firms?

- *Strategy does not feel very professional to lawyers.* As professionals, we are inculcated with the idea that we have a fundamental level of competence, and our expertise is superior to that of our clients. So doing something different implies somehow we are not already doing things correctly, and listening to clients to hear truths we are not acquainted with feels … unprofessional.

- *Strategy does not fit the law firm governance model.* Unless a firm has been through an (acknowledged) near-death experience, the managing partner will have been selected by a process within the firm dominated by the people who most benefit from the status quo. So how likely are those people to support a leader and a strategy that purports to create dramatic change, that implicitly devalues their strengths and moves to another paradigm that may be for the greater or long-term good of the firm, but may not benefit them in the short term? Law firms are highly federated, with a strong sense of individual partner autonomy, so there is no reason to imagine that the same 'strategy' will fit precisely well for a trust and estates partner in one office as a real estate lawyer in another.

- *Strategy does not fit most firms' financial model.* As a partnership, most law firms must pay current-year taxes on earnings, so there are very few incentives to maximise retained earnings, to keep capital in the partnership and invest in activities that might produce increased profits in future years. In the United States and United Kingdom at least, it has become quite clear that firms are run almost entirely to maximise current-year partner distributions. So long-term changes which require investments today are necessarily much harder to contemplate, let alone pull off.

- *A 2013 strategy does not fit lawyers' mental model.* Most people in leadership roles in law firms are 40 or older. Most lawyers aged 50 or older will have gone through law school and law firms whose mental model did not really comprehend the changes we discuss below. Those aged 40 to 50 will (until recently) have grown up in an uninterrupted legal boom that felt 'normal', so when change came it seemed unfair or unnatural. And by definition any innovative strategy is a minority view at first, so meaningful strategy change is hard to achieve by consensus. The old joke about the law firm management committee that asked a consultant to propose a really innovative strategy and then asked 'who else is doing it?' is only funny because it is true. Since neither clients nor firms have 'consensus' on the right next strategy, it is easy to revert to the status quo. As such it is easier to fail conventionally and in line with everyone else than risk being slightly wrong in a new way.

But strategise you must, because the world is changing. Shortly before writing this chapter, the authors were in New York, walking up Fifth Avenue past St Patrick's Cathedral, and a banner on scaffolding around the building read "Check in On Facebook … Follow us on Twitter …"

Just as few partners would have anticipated today's flat legal market, one suspects few would have anticipated St Patrick's being on Facebook. That does not by itself prove that the future will be very different from the recent past, but it docs suggest that we should approach the future with some curiosity and humility.

Many readers will have taken a picture with a smartphone in the last month. But they will not have used Kodak film. Why not? Kodak was one of the iconic companies of the twentieth century. They dominated film, invented digital photography in 1975, marketed the first digital camera in 1995, had the first wi-fi enabled camera and basically invented photo sharing. Even as Kodak went bankrupt, the number of pictures taken has dramatically increased, the value of photography has dramatically increased. The St Patrick's sign could have easily said "follow us on KodakShare.com". The authors could have taken that picture with a Kodakphone, not an iPhone. Kodak starved to death at the buffet table. Even though they saw digital photography coming, they spent most of their days talking to the experts who said 'the model's working, why change?' Does that sound familiar? Too often, feeling safe by sticking with the old consensus is very risky, especially in the medium and long term. Who knows precisely when that is? No one. Not us. Not you. Not your partners.

3.    **What is happening with clients?**

The essence of law firm strategy is to understand client demand, your own capabilities and your competitors' capabilities and then win more than your fair share of the work you want and deliver it with superior value, profitability and professional satisfaction. If clients' behaviour were fixed, then law firm strategy would not have to change. But of course all clients are not the same, and do not all exhibit the same desire for change. Our focus in this chapter is on large, global, sophisticated clients, who we believe are indicative of ongoing trends. It is quite possible to imagine a strategy that does not contemplate sophisticated clients, but focusing on those clients who are less demanding in order to minimise change just seems to be a delaying tactic, not a real strategy.

• *Law is part of something bigger @ the client.* When we look at where lawyers are wrestling with change, it is almost always when they are required to operate in a 'client-centric' world as opposed to a lawyer-centric world. One of the first things that strikes a lawyer as they move from a traditional private practice firm to an in-house legal department is the fact that being right in a law-centric sense is not the same as being right taking into account the whole range of things (including people and costs) that matter to the client. Quality cannot be measured in purely legal terms, but must be understood in the overall client context. When preparing for the annual Boat Race against Oxford, Cambridge University Boat Club always examine all that they do by asking, 'Will it make the boat go faster?' There are always rowers with high individual performance scores ('ergs'), but they have to contribute to the 'swing' of the boat to enable team success.

- *Increased complexity.* Global clients have to deal with legal regimes in dozens of countries, and with the needs of tens of thousands of employees and perhaps millions of customers. Traditionally, a law firm offers advice as a single issue of complexity to be addressed. This may be managing an acquisition; a disposal; a commercial contract; a dispute settlement; a patent registration etc. Each of these will have many variables and will likely throw up some element of complexity. However, they are all single issue (the 'deal in hand'). In reality, the matter is part of a much larger inter-dependent and co-dependent multi-layered system that is the enterprise. A disposal can have significant implications beyond the transaction. A law firm would consider transitional services to be a part of the transaction but would the implications for stranded costs (as one example) factor into the thinking of the law firm? An in-house lawyer will need to sit across the situation and ensure that all the pieces fit together. Do law firms understand the client's objectives? (And does the client?) Given the likely combination of ambiguity and inconsistency in law, and the involvement of different service providers, is the law firm fully 'engaged' with the client's complexity?

The ability to manage the information demands of the client in a way that enables informed decision-making is critical to the success of the law firm. It is all well and good acting for a client in negotiating, say, a commercial contract for them and seeking the 'best possible' risk profile for the client in relation to this transaction with a vendor. However, the reality is that (with very few exceptions), no single vendor to a client operates in isolation without any interaction with other vendors. As such, is it really possible to negotiate the 'best possible' deal without understanding the circumstances of the engagement with this vendor? It is likely that the true position on risk is changed by the overall landscape with its other vendors.

An additional aspect of multi-jurisdictional opportunities is that companies are often trying to drive consistency and control across the enterprise. This can manifest itself through central engagement by a framework agreement negotiated between the two parents. From this there is the challenge of ensuring that consistency is not sacrificed for local preference (and the local client may be the biggest proponent for the 'it's different here' approach). It can be very challenging managing a client which displays conflicting views depending who you ask. Conversely, it is imperative that the drive for a single approach does not result in local legal complications. A single approach is laudable, but can undermine the overall deal if, in fact, the way in which the deal is structured centrally is unenforceable in the local country (eg, the possible tensions between common law and civil law jurisdictions).

Too often law firms think (hope) that the 'professionalism' of their staff will be all that is required to navigate these challenges 'on a dynamic basis' (which might mean 'we'll make it up as we go along'). This is not to dispute the professionalism of law firms. However, law firms historically are not systematically focused on these types of challenges. Certainly this will not be good enough in the future. How are you going to get ahead of this challenge and make it a 'selling point' for your firm?

- *Increased costs.* The natural corollary to complexity is costs. And, of course, law firms have grown accustomed to hearing clients complain about costs, and clients have grown accustomed to law firms 'stiff-arming' them on costs. But there are many factors that go into costs and the decision about which firm to hire and how to structure fees. These include:
  - total cost of all service providers;
  - whether cost is incurred as part of a 'special event' or where budget is expected to be tightly managed;
  - where cost is budgeted (ie, in the legal department or another part of the business);
  - whether cost is accrued in a particular accounting period or only paid after billed; or
  - who the decision-makers are within the client who determine whether the cost is reasonable.

Lawyers, like any professionals, are deeply imbued with the notion that what they are doing is the most important thing for the client, and therefore any suggestion that 'cost is an object' is potentially offensive. But in any large organisation at any time there are thousands of intensely important activities going on, and they must compete for resources.

- The emerging role of operations. Within a client, it is quite common for there to be an operational department with oversight of the legal function. This may be within the legal function or outside. To that end, it is imperative to understand not just what the business of the client is but how the client operates. Proposing elegant solutions which require hosting information on your systems when they have their own (different) internal protocols for information storage is never a vote winner (and yet it is amazing how frequently this idea is floated by all professional firms). Have you taken the time to understand exactly how the client operates and how you need to integrate with them and their systems? This may be as simple as working out that their regular meeting each week/fortnight/month is on a Tuesday morning and so sending out regular reports very late on a Monday will not help!

## 4.    How to develop and implement your strategy

So all that may start to sound and feel pretty bewildering, but in fact implementing a successful strategy in this context is pretty easy; in the words of Nike, "Just Do It." The good news is that:

- other firms face the same constraints as you;
- clients want you to succeed (although your view of success and theirs may be slightly different); and
- you are already doing lots of things right or you would not be in this conversation in the first place, so you just need to implement a strategy that builds on what you are already doing right. No one needs to (or can) be perfect, but if you simply follow the 'playbook' you will develop and execute your strategy at the rate appropriate to your firm.

### 4.1    Acquaint yourself with the 'conversation'
As described above, lawyers who have spent most of their careers in-house approach the world very differently, and all the trends of the last five years are reinforcing those differences. Try http://adamsmith.jdmatch.com/category/articles/ or www.abajournal.com/legalrebels/new_normal/.

### 4.2    Respond sincerely to clients on value and innovation
Clients deal with all kinds of 'suppliers'. Because of our professional norms, lawyers are a unique style of supplier, but lawyers should not assume that this uniqueness brings only privileges without responsibilities. Imagine for a minute that we are an in-house legal team looking to refresh the company's panel with a 2013 perspective. It might be for general advice or only for a specific area of legal expertise. How are you going to stand out from every other law firm 'pitching' for the panel place or the project? Why would a company hire you rather than another firm?

### 4.3    Try to move some work to success-based pricing models
The most profitable firms in the United States – litigation boutiques such as Quinn Emannuel or Bartlit Beck, and the deal boutiques like Wachtel – do the bulk of their work on something other than a pure hourly fee. That does not mean that non-hourly fees are always and everywhere the right answer, but it does suggest that hourly fees are not always the right answer. The single best way to improve both quality and value in a matter is to commit to rigorous planning up front, and a success-based fee is much more likely to lead to that rigorous planning. Many law firms may argue that there are too many variables in the way a transaction might progress and therefore it is impossible to commit to a budget other than, perhaps, some small token (and so immaterial) sections of the transaction. But improved planning will always sharpen understanding, improving quality and costs.

### 4.4    Find ways to improve value and reduce costs
- *Adjust billing rates.* One frequent complaint from clients is that associate time is over-priced (some clients now refuse to pay for first or second year associates) and perhaps partner time is under-priced. So offer clients an option to pay more for partner time, less for associate time. Use pricing as a way to get information about what works, not as something to be affronted

by. The challenge with billing rates is that too often law firms and in-house lawyers talk about 'value' when really they mean 'cheapness'. For many years, in-house lawyers have felt that they have been over-paying law firms given the (overall) level of complexity of the work being delivered – predominantly because work could not so easily be disaggregated as is possible now. As such there is a feeling (fair or unfair) that law firm partners have, for too long, been overpaid for the complexity of the work product delivered and the risk taken (when compared to other businesses that have to take risk to make a return). It is critical, therefore, that you understand which conversation you are having with your client – good value or just cheaper?

- *Technology.* Various technologies can help streamline processes, share information and avoid redundancy. One of the dreams of any GC is to find a way to create a dashboard of their world such that they have leading indicators from which they can plan their department's utilisation – where to focus resources, where to invest etc. In most cases, however, the vast majority of the department's workload is reactive (ie, someone in the business is coming to them for support).

- *Project management, disaggregation and general contracting.* There are clients now who are mandating that for any project over a certain level of legal spend, the law firm will need to appoint (within their fee) a specialist programme manager or project manager to oversee delivery of the work product – not a lawyer but someone who knows how to run a project. Be clear on what the goals are and who will do what. In a recent M&A transaction, a (large well-respected) external law firm undertook a significant piece of work reviewing the property portfolio of a target company in order to produce a full due diligence report on the offices. This was not asked for; it was just that it was on the template checklist of activities to be followed and so it was done. In fact, the properties were all leasehold with the ability to terminate on very short notice (as had been established as part of the more general commercial engagement) and the buyer was intending to (and did) move the operations of the target into its own premises and terminate the leases. The due diligence report (all 50 to 100 pages) went unread (and unpaid for). Someone had been slave to a checklist designed to aid efficiency. Start to look carefully at the different 'inputs' that go into your work, and find ways to do some of them cheaper, perhaps by turning over to a specialty firm. The disaggregation of what might be perceived to be activities that are the (exclusive) domain of lawyers and law firms is very real and will continue to accelerate; we are on the cusp of technology and efficient mainstream business practices making a profound impact on the practice of law. Just as the pagination exercises that many 20 to 30-year qualified lawyers will recall from their younger days as part of discovery or disclosure exercises would not be something a law firm would expect to have lawyers doing today, there is plenty else that lawyers often do today which, in the (not too distant) future, will seem quaint and old fashioned.

In many cases, the workload that would historically have been undertaken by a junior lawyer (or a team of junior lawyers) would be better undertaken by other professionals or, better yet, by technology. If we were to show you all a picture of a Caribbean island and ask you to describe the colour of the sea, it is very likely that we would get a variety to answers such as blue, green, sea blue, aqua-marine, turquoise etc. And yet, it is only one colour. It is the subjectivity of the individual that has come into play in 'interpreting' the data to provide an answer. When the complexity is a single-issue matter and bespoke advice is appropriate, that is one thing. However, when there are multiple dimensions to the matter then repeatable and consistent delivery becomes as critical as the information itself. Humans are incapable of being truly impartial; we are all products of our upbringing, our beliefs, our ethics, our caffeine intake, and our general well-being. While in many cases, people are able to ensure that the influences of these vectors are immaterial to the work product that they deliver, in cases where, especially, consistent repetition is demanded, then a computer has the edge. In all the studies of these circumstances, the computer aces the test. Humans do not perform as we think we might; computers do not get tired and lose concentration and nor do they find the work dull and tedious!

In pitching to us, therefore, it is imperative that you understand the work that is required to fulfil the brief and the extent to which technology may be a preferred solution. Even where technology is not the answer, there will always be other resources which may be better placed to do the work quicker, better and cheaper. These include legal process outsourcers (LPOs), other advisory firms (whether the big accountancy firms or other boutique firms), or even law schools. In the United States, the Deans of a number of law schools are re-examining how they train the lawyers of the future, as they understand that the 'traditional' three-year course needs revamping. One avenue that is being explored is to model themselves (to some degree) on medical schools and look to include within their training the opportunity for students to work with business in some manner. This opens up a number of interesting opportunities for the schools, for the clients and for law firms. How this plays out is still not clear but it is a salutary reminder that change will happen and it may happen to you if you do not make it happen. It is imperative that the disaggregation question is at the heart of every exercise in developing a support model for a client.

None of this is particularly new or shocking as a general topic. However, this trend can only continue as clients look to drive efficiency into the legal spend. It is getting more common for clients to look to dissect a transaction and parcel up work to different law firms depending on complexity, price-point etc. It may be tempting therefore to consider this decision as the client taking back on itself all delivery risk on the project/transaction. There will always be cases where the client does, indeed, take overall control and responsibility for the matter. However, it will also be the case that law firms will be expected to sort it out amongst themselves. Allowing any form of dissonance between law firms to impact on a matter will not win you or your firm any plaudits. It is imperative that there is effective, open and constant communication between firms just in the same way as there is between departments within a firm.

**4.5     Do not be too quick to dismiss an incomplete success as a failure**
Innovation requires experimentation and persistence. Both in-house and firm lawyers tend to be very quick to lose confidence in new initiatives. To make change, you have to sustain the effort.

**4.6     Integrate client service, business development and client 'account management'**
Trevor Faure from Ernst & Young says that law firms need "professional telepathy, professional prescience, exceptional client service and cost efficiency". Here we want to limit the conversation to communications to your client. The average in-house legal department is appointing you/your firm because they are too busy on other things and it would be an inefficient use of their resources to undertake the project themselves. Even a need for specialist advice is a trade-off; it would take too long and be too inefficient to learn it themselves. To that end, they are looking for effective communication from you/your firm. You therefore need to work out for the client what the client really needs to know and then provide that in a concise way. Long, 12-page memos are a legacy of a bygone era; especially as many of them were deliberately drafted to avoid the law firm taking any position at all!

This issue is as relevant when you have not been instructed as when you have. Relationships between you/your firm and a client are (we all hope) long term in nature and it is a truism to say that reputation takes a lifetime to earn and moment to lose. To that end, how much thought goes into what information is sent to which client? Does everyone at the client want the same information? Do clients even want the information at all? The number of 'client briefing papers' that were circulated during the enactment of the UK Anti-Bribery legislation was staggering. Almost all of them were bland, non-specific documents which were verging on spam and certainly (for the most part) trading on the fears of the client in the hope that the client would come running to ask for help. Much better perhaps is the tailored two-to-three line email which shows that you have thought about the client and their needs.

To that end, we challenge each of you to consider how often you ask to spend time with the client (off the clock) with a view to gaining an in-depth understanding of their business? Nothing shows commitment better than spending time asking questions and having conversations around their business ... provided it is truly approached in this manner and not seen as an extended opportunity to sell!

**4.7     Define a success point five years in future**
Do not try to 'electrify the ocean', but do come up with some idea about how the firm will be different in the future and start to identify the milestones on the path to get there.

**5.     Conclusion**
Until the financial crisis of 2008, lawyers experienced almost a generation of uninterrupted growth in complexity and growth in income. That taken-for-granted

growth has come to an end, and we need to manage a period of professional renewal, focusing on delivering the most value we can and competing for financial success like anyone else. Developing and succeeding in that strategy will be the highlight of your professional life; denying the need for change is unlikely to accelerate success or to develop your talents to the fullest.

*The opinions expressed in this chapter are those of the individual authors and do not reflect their organisations' official view.*

# Professionalising pricing and procurement processes

Silvia Hodges Silverstein
Columbia Law School; Fordham Law School; TyMetrix Legal Analytics

Senior executives in many companies demand that legal departments improve control of spend. From management's point of view, legal departments are cost centres and need to be managed as such. To satisfy their shareholders and owners, companies scrutinise legal spend in ways never experienced before. The view is that the legal department has to be a better corporate citizen, no more 'legal is different' explanations are accepted. In practice, this means that lawyers need to budget and stick to the forecasts, no longer just manage risk and give legal advice. Like the rest of the organisation, the legal department is expected to be efficient, do more with less, reduce risk and save money and achieve desired outcomes such as:

- operational efficiency;
- predictability of spend;
- enhanced client–attorney relationship;
- strategic perspective on the state of their business.

## 1. Aligning interests

Outside counsel and clients share a common goal – to manage matters effectively and achieve a successful outcome by applying their legal expertise. But their goals and priorities can conflict: in-house counsel must find ways to manage legal matters effectively while staying within their budgets; outside counsel need to run their firms and maintain, if not increase, their profitability. In the case of litigation, if outside counsel are paid for their time regardless of the outcome of the case, clients fear they may bring the case even when it is not in the best interest of the client, spend more hours working on the case than the client would want, and reject a settlement when the client would be better off if it were accepted. Alternatively, if outside counsel are compensated according to the conventional contingency fee arrangement, they are paid only a fraction of any trial award or settlement, but bear all of the cost of litigation. In this situation, clients fear that outside counsel may have insufficient incentive to bring the case, spend too little time working on it if it is brought, and encourage a settlement when the client would be better off going to trial.[1] It is, therefore, important to find ways that align the interests of law firms and their clients.

---

[1] Polinsky, A Mitchell and Rubinfeld, Daniel L, Aligning the Interests of Lawyers and Clients, *Stanford Law and Economics* Olin Working Paper No 223 (April 2002) at: http://ssrn.com/abstract=281628.

## 2. Introducing business professionals: pricing directors, legal operations and procurement

These new demands necessitate support on both sides: more and more clients now work with legal operations experts, data analysts, and legal procurement managers, while firms work with pricing professionals:

- legal operations professionals help improve the legal department's processes and efficiencies;
- data analysts collect, organise, and analyse data for the legal department;
- legal procurement professionals oversee the selection, purchasing, budgeting and invoicing of legal services;
- pricing directors help law firms figure out the cost and price for services to ensure profitability for the firm and determine ways to deliver the service for the agreed price.

Business professionals' tools include:

- pricing: alternative fee arrangement (AFA) programme development and establishment of AFA 'playbooks';
- procurement: management of outside counsel, controlling and monitoring of purchasing activities and contracts, as well as sourcing, bidding and requests for proposal and reverse auctions;
- analytics: legal spend analytics to gain insight into how much money a company spends on what types of services, using UTBMS codes;[2]
- benchmarking: comparing the department with industry best practice;
- technology: e-billing,[3] matter management etc;
- outside counsel guidelines;
- reporting, scorecards and dashboards;
- alternative resources: legal process outsourcing (LPO) and contract lawyers.

In this chapter, we will discuss the first two tools: pricing and procurement.

## 3. Pricing

Pricing is the process of determining what a law firm will receive in exchange for its services. Pricing in the legal sector used to be straightforward. For the longest time, law firms billed by the hour. Some argue that the process for determining price is not based on sound business practices: "Firms look at the rates charged by other lawyers with similar years in practice at other firms they'd like to compete with – and then they add on whatever the partners want to make in increased profit per equity partner."[4] While this approach is focused entirely on the firm, it disregards the firm's costs to produce

---

2    UTBMS stands for the Uniform Task Based Management System, a series of codes used to classify the legal services performed by a law firm in an electronic invoice submission. More information can be found at http://www.utbms.com.

3    E-billing or electronic bill payment and presentment, as it is also referred to, is the electronic submission of invoices by outside counsel over the internet, using software. Clients pay these bills electronically. E-billing is common practice in more and more countries today.

4    Susan Hackett, Reconnecting Law Firm Pricing to Cost, Profit, and Value, Corporate Counsel (September 25 2012) at: www.law.com/corporatecounsel/PubArticleFriendlyCC.jsp?id=1202572446358.

the service and ignores what the market will bear and what their clients will pay.

Now more and more clients demand alternative fee arrangements (AFA).[5] AFAs are also called 'value-based fee arrangements', 'alternative billing arrangements' (ABAs), or even 'appropriate fee arrangements'.

AFAs are meant to align the company's interests with those of its law firm, promote efficiency and accurate budgeting, and reward results rather than effort, thereby shifting some risk to the law firm.

Although the concept of AFAs is not new, the push to AFAs has never been more prevalent in the legal sector than it is today. A review of 2.6 million matters from the TyMetrix LegalVIEW® database identified a steady increase in the use of AFAs by AmLaw 100 firms in only two years, from 3% in 2010 to 9% in 2012.[6]

Table 1: Advantages of AFAs

| AFA advantages for legal departments | AFA advantages for law firms |
|---|---|
| AFAs represent an opportunity to<br>• save money<br>• manage legal spend<br>• buy value rather than hours<br>• improve the predictability of legal spend<br>• reduce budgetary pressure<br>• align the interests of the law firm with those of the client<br>• share the risk of lawyer's fees and costs | AFAs represent a chance to<br>• prove their willingness to innovate<br>• partner with clients<br>• improve profitability by rewarding efficiency and quality work |

Fee arrangements come in three main categories: hourly based, fixed fee, and value based. Arrangements can be applied to an entire matter, distinct stages of a matter, or across of a group of matters.

## 3.1    Hourly-based AFAs

Hourly-based AFAs are technically not pure AFAs, but discounts and blended rates are often referred to as AFAs nevertheless:

- *Straight discounts* are rate reductions for a single matter.
- *Volume discounts* are reduced rates based on the amount of work a client gives a firm. They are often utilised in addition to other AFAs. They may ensure work for the firm, but significantly cut into the firm's profits and may even endanger the firm's value proposition.
- *Blended rates* set one hourly rate for all lawyers working on a matter, regardless of their seniority or status. This simplifies billing and eliminates

---

5    AFAs are billing methods based on metrics other than the number of hours worked. AFAs include fixed fees, flat fees, retainers, contingency fees, capped fees, collared arrangements, blended rates, etc.
6    TyMetrix Legal Analytics LegalVIEW® Data Warehouse (June 2013).

the 'penalty' for work done by more senior partners. On the flipside, clients might fear that blended rates incentivise law firms to be 'too efficient' and have more junior lawyers or paralegals do as much work as possible. The feared result is too little senior advice for clients. In fact, blended rates have been called arguably the least effective AFA because the firm's incentive is to push work down to the lowest-rate biller, typically a junior associate, who is in turn incentivised to run up the number of billable hours on a given matter.[7]

- *Capped fees* limit the maximum legal spend by imposing a ceiling under which the firm bills the client hourly. The client is not charged for fees above that amount. Capped fees limit the total cost of an agreed amount of work and provide clients with greater certainty and predictability than hourly billing. This arrangement may signal to the client that the firm does not really need to charge as much for its billable hours as its standard fee suggests. Capped fees typically benefit the client more than the law firm; however, some firms see them as a way to get new work. In effect, capped fees may be used by firms as a (potential) loss leader to retain or win market share. Of all hourly-based AFA models, capped fees offer the most incentive for firms to work efficiently and/or use outsourcing options. Determining the cap is critical to the success of this model. Clients often distrust caps, as they perceive the fees as coming in above the cap and seldom, if ever, below. Firms often dislike capped fees because their lawyers do not necessarily operate more efficiently than they would if the matter were being billed using normal hourly fees and therefore ignore the cap. As a result, firms believe they lose money because their realisation rates go down.

- *Collared fee* or *risk-collared arrangements* are similar to capped fees. Clients guarantee to pay a minimum amount for a particular group of cases, while the firm guarantees it will not bill the client more than a maximum amount. This creates both a fee floor and a ceiling, and reduces the risk for both parties.

- Under *outcome-dependent holdbacks*, firms agree to discount or 'hold back' a portion of their fees with the provision that the client will pay a bonus if the firm meets agreed criteria related to case outcomes. Client and firm establish a metric defining a successful outcome, by reference to quantitative and/or qualitative factors. Work is billed at an hourly rate, but a portion of the fees billed is held in reserve for future payment to the firm according to the metric or at the client's discretion. A holdback is a type of partial contingency arrangement in which the law firm is guaranteed part of its fees, but the other part is contingent upon the outcome. Since success is defined at the outset, holdbacks facilitate risk sharing, which clients strongly prefer. For example, a firm may receive 80% of its normal rates while a matter is underway. At the

---

7    Michael Kozubek, Alternative Fee Arrangements Vary in Effectiveness, Experts Say, Inside Counsel (April 2010) at: www.insidecounsel.com/2010/04/01/alternative-fee-arrangements-vary-in-effectiveness-experts-say.

end, it may receive the remaining 20%, or less, depending on the client's satisfaction with the result. This type of arrangement may also be combined with a success fee that provides a bonus for a positive outcome.[8]

- When using *budget/time-dependent holdbacks*, firm and client establish a metric based upon the perceived cost of the matter or the time frame within which the client wants it resolved. Work is billed hourly, but an agreed amount is held in reserve, payable to the firm for its successful achievement of budgetary or timing objectives. Given the focus on time and money, firms have an incentive to optimise workflow and explore outsourcing options and other efficiencies. A greater amount of risk is shared because the client has a larger role in defining successful results. Since estimating cost and timing is essential, only firms that possess the necessary tools or experience should consider this approach.

- *Contingency fees (or conditional fees)* contemplate payment only if the firm achieves an agreed result for the client. This arrangement aligns the firm's and the client's interests. Traditionally used by plaintiffs' lawyers in litigation, contingency fees can also be used for transactional matters. However, many jurisdictions prohibit the use of such contingency fees generally, or for certain types of legal services. The fee is typically a percentage of the money recovered, saved, or won at trial or on settlement. The client generally pays nothing unless the legal action is financially successful. Such arrangements provide clients who are willing to forego a large portion of a positive result with protection from a bad result. Contingency fees may be appropriate for cases that have a high likelihood of success and a success fee significantly higher than estimated standard hourly billing revenues. It is important to note that success might mean different things to different clients. In the case of litigation, a client may value a quick resolution over a win following a lengthy trial. Contingency fees encourage firms to work efficiently and provide a risk-sharing mechanism. Results can be drastically disproportionate: windfalls occur when the firm's share greatly exceeds the corresponding hourly fees, or when the cost to the client is far less than the value of the representation. The drawback is that clients might be suspicious and assume that if a firm is willing to assume the risk, the lawyers must think they will win, and billing hourly might cost the client significantly less.

- *Success fees (or partial contingency fees)* set a bonus that the firm receives in addition to its hourly, flat or capped-fee arrangement if the result meets agreed criteria. This may be defined as level of success, speed of resolution, or cost savings. This type of AFA is typically used in transactional matters outside of defence litigation work or in high-stakes work. Success fees may be the best example of value billing, where client and firm interests are, on the

8    Jim Hassett, The nine most common types of alternative fees, Legal Business Development blog (September 28 2011) at: http://adverselling.typepad.com/how_law_firms_sell/2011/09/the-nine-most-common-types-of-alternative-fees.html.

face of it, aligned. Problems result if the firm must determine whether to advise a client against a particular course of action (because it is not in its best interests from a legal perspective), but stands to gain financially if the client takes that course of action. In such cases, the success fee may lead to a conflict of interest or lack of independence.

## 3.2 Fixed fees and flat fees

Fixed fees and flat fees set an agreed amount for a distinct scope of work. Firms typically calculate them by applying a mark-up to the firm's estimation of resources for that type of matter ('cost-plus calculation').

- A *fixed fee* can be used when a firm handles a single case (or case portion) for a pre-specified, negotiated amount.[9] Establishing a flat rate for litigation poses challenges due to the uncertainties. This can be reduced, if not circumvented, by breaking a case into specific well-defined phases, and setting a flat fee for each. For example, the firm can set one fee to draft and file a complaint, and an additional fee to cover subsequent stages of litigation.[10] On the transactional side, a flat fee can be agreed for each phase from preliminary agreements to due diligence to drafting the principal documents etc.

- A *flat fee* is an agreed total for multiple similar cases (eg, for all cases within a jurisdiction or geographical area, or of particular exposure or risk). There may be a specific number of cases, or the agreement may cover all cases of a specific type that occur during a set time period. Recurring matters, such as routine loan closings, leases, and collections, lend themselves to flat fee agreements. These matters often involve a well-defined scope of work and limited complexity, and may be handled in volume. This is important to the law firm to ensure an aggregate profit. When using flat fees for litigation matters, firms must handle many of the same type of cases, as the firm will make a profit on some and lose out on others.

Fixed and flat fees give clients incentives for firms to work efficiently by removing the correlation between time expended and profit. Firms need to work with the client in advance to understand and define the scope of the matter as thoroughly as practicable to ensure accurate pricing, cost control and profitability. Both parties must agree to the assumptions and qualifications that govern the matter and the fee. Fixed and flat fees and performance-based bonuses have been said to be most effective at reducing cost and improving client satisfaction.[11]

---

9   In some countries like Taiwan, clients expect fixed-fee billing and are, generally, uncomfortable with hourly billing. Fixed-fee billing is the norm, not an AFA. Paul C Easton, "Legal Project Management is Key to Fixed-fee Billing", Legal Project Management (August 31 2009) at: http://legalproject management.info/2009/08/legal-project-management-is-key-to-fixed-fee-billing.html.

10  Chris Leach, "Alternative Fee Arrangements with Law Firms can be Beneficial", special supplement to the *Denver Business Journal* (October 12 2008) at: www.bizjournals.com/denver/stories/2008/10/13/focus4.html?s=print.

11  Michael Kozubek, Alternative Fee Arrangements Vary in Effectiveness, Experts Say, Inside Counsel (April 2010) at: www.insidecounsel.com/2010/04/01/alternative-fee-arrangements-vary-in-effectiveness-experts-say.

Once the project is underway, the firm must carefully manage it, constantly reviewing assumptions and qualifications. Factors outside the control of the client and the firm (eg, changed economic conditions, acts of government agencies such as competition or antitrust regulators, unforeseeable reactions by the counterparty), and factors within client control (eg, the client changes some element of a deal's tax structure) may affect the integrity of the fee arrangement. Regular communication between the firm and the client is essential. For such a fee arrangement to work, each party must be confident that the other will not take advantage.

- *Flat fees with shared savings* set a flat fee for a matter but include a safety valve by tracking the cost of the work on an hourly basis. At the conclusion of the matter, the client and firm share the difference if the fee based on hourly rates is lower than the flat fee.
- *A fixed fee menu* provides a list of fees for related services or for segments of a particular matter. For example, a fee of $5,000 might be quoted for a particular type of real estate transaction. Then charges would accrue for different situations, such as plus $5,000 for assumption of an existing loan and $7,500 for new financing.[12]
- *Portfolio fixed fees* set a single price for a large number of matters, such as all of a large company's annual labour and employment cases in a particular jurisdiction. Again, success for a law firm depends on having a large volume of matters, so that there will be enough profitable matters to offset any losses the law firm may incur on others. For this arrangement to work, the desire for predictability shifts to the law firm since it will want to have some reassurance as to the number and timing of cases.
- In a *bundling arrangement*, the firm receives a large number of matters simultaneously that it handles for a specific fee.
- *Subscriptions and retainers* allow clients to 'buy access' to certain firm lawyers, or to the entire firm, for a monthly fee. Agreements can include all types of matters or exclude more complex work that will be priced separately. Both client and firm must be clear about which services are included and which are not. Since clients are more likely to call the firm because they will not get charged for every call, firms may develop a more intense relationship and learn more about the client than they would when the firm is used only for discrete projects. This may lead to additional work outside the subscription/retainer. Therefore, some firms see subscriptions and retainers as marketing tools and use them as loss leaders. Firms hope that, eventually, clients will begin to see the difference in quality, and become willing to pay higher fees for higher quality work. This arrangement also sensitises clients to paying their invoices as they are billed on a monthly basis.

12    Jim Hassett, The nine most common types of alternative fees, Legal Business Development blog (September 28 2011) at: http://adverselling.typepad.com/how_law_firms_sell/2011/09/the-nine-most-common-types-of-alternative-fees.html.

### 3.3 Value-based billing arrangements

Value-based billing arrangements seek to reflect a firm's contribution to a case. They assume that the hours spent were not necessarily a relevant indicator of that contribution and may actually create an incentive to distort billings. Value billing must not be confused with flat or fixed-fee pricing. To the client it 'looks' the same in that it results in a set fee, however, the price is arrived at in the opposite manner: by an open discussion of the value to be delivered by the firm. The value determines the price, and the cost (or project management plan) is based on the value proposition.

- *The Fuselage Pricing Model* is a mix of value billing and retainer. It allows clients to choose first-class, business-class, and coach-class pricing. The model works with standard business counselling and corporate matters. Similar to airlines differentiating the level of service flight attendants provide to passengers, the firm offers different levels of service to its clients. For example, the firm's best people in every area of expertise are always at the first-class client's disposal. Coach-class clients, by contrast, do not have on-demand access, and work only with a single, highly trained lawyer. While this lawyer will provide sound legal advice, he may not have the same depth of experience and knowledge in any particular area.[13]

- *Packaging* high-value representation with low-value work helps secure interesting, lucrative work for the firm while enabling it to handle lower value work at a price point that is acceptable to the client. Historically, this work would be sent to a lower cost firm for servicing. In other words, the firm would have lost this business if it had not accommodated the client based on value. Such arrangements consolidate a larger amount of work with the firm, offsetting any economic risk from the low-value matters with the high-value matters, while providing the client with quality representation at a saving. It also allows the firm to determine how to manage low-value matters efficiently and cost effectively and to manage its own costs (and risk) associated with the provision of legal services to the particular client.

- *Secondments* provide in-house legal departments with temporary assistance. Placement of a lawyer on-site with the client is an alternative to handling the work traditionally and billing at hourly rates. The basic premise of a secondment is that if a client has enough of the 'right' type of work (eg, in terms of volume, skill and experience required), but not enough to make permanent recruitment feasible, taking a lawyer on secondment will be cheaper than paying for that lawyer on an hourly rate basis. In return, the law firm gets guaranteed utilisation of the lawyer, a degree of certainty of revenue, and predictable cash flow. In-house counsel are said to love secondments.[14] Clients may rely on the lawyer's specialised skill set that they cannot afford to recruit to help with the 'heavy lifting' on a big deal, or to

---

13    Patrick J Lamb, "Alternative Fee Arrangements: Value Fees and the Changing Legal Market", Ark Group (2010). Exemplar Law Group's CEO Christopher Marston created the Fuselage Pricing Model.

14    Mark Smith, The Joy of Secs (secondments), LexisNexis Communities, Legal Business Community (September 22 2011) at: www.lexisnexis.com/community/legalbusiness/blogs/people/archive/2011/09/22/the-joy-of-secs-secondments.aspx

provide its small in-house team with broader access to their external law firm's resources than otherwise possible. Law firms benefit from the stronger relationship with the client and the secondees' invaluable experience and perspective. The insight secondees get from working in the client's environment cannot be gained from researching the company. Secondments provide an opportunity to understand the clients' inner culture and pressure points, as well as the opportunity to build broader and deeper relationships – not just with the in-house teams, but also with their internal clients. When an ongoing secondment programme is established, it is likely to build a very strong connection over time between firm and in-house team, giving the firm a powerful competitive advantage.

Pricing secondments is a challenge for firms. Due to the intense competition among firms, particularly since the economic downturn, the price clients will pay for secondees has decreased drastically. Firms typically charge 'at cost'. As firms restructured and struggled to find work for their lawyers, farming them out to clients allowed them to retain good people and keep clients happy. However, firms struggle to define 'at cost'. For example, is it salary cost including benefits and bonus, or a proportion of the overhead?

Due to the potential for unpredictability when using AFAs, firms often want to discuss safety valves, look backs, and savings clauses with their clients. These safeguards are meant to allow firms pre-negotiated 'outs' if the unanticipated occurs, but not eliminate all risks. Rather than exercising the safeguard option too quickly and negatively impacting the lawyer–client relationship, discussions about safeguards should encourage regular communication between client and firm.

## 4.     Setting up an AFA
The TyMetrix phased approach of the *Four Pillars of Providing Value* – Scope-Baseline-Benchmark-Value – is useful when setting up an AFA:

### 4.1     Scope
Firms need to discuss the boundaries of a project with the client and analyse the results it is likely to produce. It is important to understand the scope of a matter, which could include:
- client expectations, including best and worst case assumptions;
- metrics used by the client and their respective weight and importance;
- perspectives of the client's stakeholders, as well as business objectives.

### 4.2     Baseline
Firms need to determine the known state of past performance so it can be measured and compared:
- The firm analyses similar litigation matters – including by phase – utilising both internal and external data in terms of cost, duration, timekeeper allocation, rates, number of parties involved, pleadings, etc.
- The firm scopes the matter based on the client's communicated assumptions

to determine the likely number of hours by timekeeper role, phase, and tasks.

- The firm fleshes out the possible division of labour between the client and the firm and suggests milestones. What work will the client do in-house? What will the firm handle?

### 4.3 Benchmarking

Firms need to gain intelligence into how others provide the same services and value. To this end they need to understand their direct competitors for the particular type of work: do only a few firms have the expertise necessary for a certain type of matter, or is it of the 'garden variety' type?

### 4.4 Value

Firms need to ensure that their offer aligns the firm's goals with those of the client:

- What is important to the client and the client's different stakeholders, particularly the final decision maker(s)?
- How are decision makers measured and compensated? What is their autonomy in terms of decision making?
- How will the case outcome influence the decision maker's career?
- What level of risk sharing is the firm willing to accept?

In the end, successful pricing needs to be based on trust and real business partnership. Both law firm and client must be certain that the other party will not take advantage of them. Pricing is also both art and science. It is important to understand your firm's own costs, market prices, and your clients' preferences. Successful pricing requires your firm to understand its own processes and to show a willingness to examine these processes to improve efficiency.

### 5. Legal procurement

As mentioned on the outset, more and more legal departments collaborate with their colleagues in procurement when hiring and managing outside counsel. Legal procurement applies its experience and insight into efficient and effective spending for the legal department.

*"In 2008, when the CEO came in for the annual 'save money' talk, they didn't take 'I can't' for an answer from the General Counsel (GC). Instead, the CEO introduced procurement to the GC and let them know they were there to help."*[15]

This shift is particularly seen at the initial instruction phase, when procurement professionals help evaluate providers and negotiate fee structures. When involved in the purchasing of legal services, procurement typically negotiates on behalf of the legal department, measures value, and provides more objective comparisons.

Procurement professionals are 'buyers' in the classic sense: they are responsible for the engagement letter/retainer or framework agreement and negotiations. Procurement professionals are influencers; they try to affect the outcome decisions

---

15    Toby Brown, "Procurement's Role in Purchasing Legal Services: A Counterpoint … to a Degree", in *Buying Legal: Procurement Insights and Practice* (2012), page 70.

with their opinion. Additionally, procurement professionals also act as gatekeepers for the legal category – they help manage and direct the flow of information between the service provider and client. When effectively using procurement, legal departments do not simply hand over all power to their procurement colleagues. Procurement is rarely the final decision maker. Selecting law firms is still the legal department's prerogative. Rather, procurement is mainly responsible for managing the sourcing process; negotiation and contract development; pre-purchase evaluation of outside counsel (which may or may not be traditional law firms); as well as developing sourcing criteria and purchasing strategies.

More and more procurement professionals are involved not only in purchasing routine services and legal 'commodities', but also in complex and high-value legal services. Exceptions may be emergency situations, where procurement's time frame does not fit.

More and more companies invite outside counsel to bid for their business. Today this is often done electronically, through reverse auctions. Electronic auctions or so-called 'e-auctions' or 'sourcing events' are auctions where the roles of buyer and seller are swapped. The sellers compete to obtain business from the buyer by undercutting each other's price, whereas in a normal auction buyers compete to obtain a good or service by offering increasingly higher prices. Companies often use e-sourcing tools such as reverse auctions alongside requests for proposal (RFP). RFPs are sent to potential sellers of legal services, asking them to bid for the service and specifying service requirements: The company develops a document identifying the need (ie, the type of service they need and why) and specifications. It also lays out the bidding process – how the process will work and how outside counsel will be scored (eg, how different skills are weighed), as well as rules for the bidding process. The company invites potential suppliers to register online and opens the event for a specific time for bidding. At the end, the company awards the contract to one of the bidders. The decision can be based on price or other factors such as skills, experience, geographic reach, fit or 'bench depth'. A recent study found that for procurement, the most critical factors when deciding which legal services providers to select were services excellence, expertise with similar matters, value for money, and fee arrangement flexibility. Interestingly, 'lowest price' was the second least important factor for the participants in the study.[16]

To conclude – both new pricing and the influence of procurement have changed the way lawyers need to manage their firms and provide their services. However, neither using AFAs nor working with procurement means that firms will no longer make money. Yet it is better to understand these changes and be prepared to work in this new way, as the competition will not get less fierce any time soon.

---

16    Silvia Hodges, "Legal Procurement: Sourcing is a Team Sport" Bloomberg Law (2012) at: http://about.bloomberglaw.com/practitioner-contributions/legal-procurement-sourcing-is-a-team-sport/.

# The changing relationship between clients and law firms

**Mark Jones**
Addleshaw Goddard LLP

## 1. Introduction

The professional services environment has changed a great deal in the period since the collapse of Lehman Brothers in 2008. Forces of change were at play before 2008. The great boom in demand for legal services in the years before 2008 not surprisingly led to an increase in service delivery capacity that risked becoming an excess in the event of any significant downturn. The severity of the economic crisis that developed in and after 2008 was such that it had an impact far more profound than anyone – including governments and regulators – had anticipated. The result was almost a perfect storm of changing circumstances, economic challenges and excess capacity. Law firms and their clients around the world have been grappling, and continue to grapple, with the consequences. Clients have come to understand that they are in a far stronger bargaining position than before 2008. The relationship between clients and their law firms has also therefore changed, and is continuing to change, a great deal.

In this chapter, and set against that background, we therefore explore two questions:

- Is it possible to position a law firm, in this changed environment, so as to operate below the group of top international firms, with a value focus and with its services streamlined, so as to improve its competitive advantage notwithstanding the perfect storm?
- If that is possible, given the scale of the demands placed upon law firms for the deconstruction and reconstruction of legal services in order to respond to the forces of change, how might readers set out to build and execute such a value proposition?

To view those challenges in their proper context, we will begin with an external perspective by:

- examining the commercial environment;
- considering the implications for a professional services firm in that environment;
- examining how a firm might begin to respond to that environment;
- taking account of technology, mobility, demographics and growth;
- reflecting upon the influence of new entrants to the market; and
- considering client requirements.

The chapter then goes on to consider how a firm might begin to review its own position in order to set out to build and execute a value proposition in the current business environment.

In doing all of the above within the confines of one short chapter, the reader will appreciate that it is not practical to provide a thorough analysis or detailed recommendations. Indeed, such recommendations would not even be possible without a full and proper understanding of a particular firm and its circumstances. This chapter should therefore be treated as general guidance, setting out issues to explore and take into account and signposts for consideration and development into a robust execution plan by the firm, whether on its own or with appropriate external assistance.

## 2.    The commercial environment

There are three primary drivers bearing upon the business community and society generally, and which, therefore, also bear upon the legal services sector and its clients. It is important to the proper exploration of the two questions identified above that we have a common understanding of those drivers.

The first of the three is globalisation. One definition of globalisation is the "process enabling financial and investment markets to operate internationally, largely as a result of deregulation and improved communications" (*Collins English Dictionary*). The improvement in communications is arguably more important than deregulation. Specifically, the making available of the internet to the global population was an event of great significance in the process of globalisation. It is difficult to believe now, but internet access was offered to the general public for the first time only in 1992. This enabling of financial and investment markets to operate internationally is having – and will continue to have – a profound effect upon businesses operating in the legal services sector and upon their clients.

Furthermore, the ability to offer a global integrated service and respond to changing market demands has been facilitated in recent times through ease of communication. Arguably, professional services providers have been better able to respond to the recent global financial crisis through the use of technology to achieve the re-allocation (rather than relocation) of human and other resources to maximise capacity across their businesses.

There has been a rapid development of legal process outsourcing (LPO) and business process outsourcing (BPO) businesses. These businesses are already big, established, scalable, well run, ambitious and hungry. Law firms have tended to be slow adopters of their services, but ever-increasing pressures on costs have necessitated their use. Even if external providers are not utilised, opportunities to take advantage of the unbundling of services (through internal 'offshoring' and 'onshoring') – essentially internal LPO – now need to be maximised. LPO, BPO and unbundling are in part driven by, or perhaps more accurately the product of, globalisation and the process seems unstoppable. With 59,000 law graduates in India joining LPO offices each year, the question for lawyers, whatever their geographic location, must be: whose bread and butter do law firms think they are going to want to eat? They are also, however, among the challenges that law firms should in any event be looking to address in the light of the other factors identified in this chapter.

The second of the three primary drivers is consolidation, being the merging of a number of entities into one. There can be many reasons for the initiation or continuation of the process of consolidation. These include:

- oversupply,
- production benefits of greater mass or resource; and
- service delivery benefits derived from greater size and geographic reach.

Consolidation can also take many forms, but for the purpose of the challenges examined in this chapter, the two that are particularly relevant are:

- 'vertical consolidation' whereby a single business controls its entire product life cycle from production of 'raw materials' to delivery of the 'finished product'; and
- 'horizontal consolidation' being the amalgamation of a number of businesses into one, thereby facilitating either or both of the benefits of shared resources or geographic spread.

To some extent, the former might be described as a 'client perspective' and the latter as a 'law firm perspective'.

The 'process' of consolidation and merger of legal services businesses has been prevalent for some time and inevitably this will be an area of increased activity going forward, as firms look both to build economies of scale and to respond to the consequences of excess capacity in the market.

Perhaps the most successful example of the consolidator scheme in the legal sector to date has been Slater & Gordon, the Australian firm specialising in personal injury litigation. It was the first law firm to float and thereafter acted as a consolidator in the PI sector, first transforming itself from a small, albeit reputable, firm to a business employing 900 lawyers in 40 offices throughout Australia before, in 2012, moving into the United Kingdom through the acquisition of Russell Jones & Walker.

The dual impact of globalisation and the worldwide recession is to compound the process of consolidation, particularly when there is currently an oversupply both of law firms and of lawyers in a number of developed jurisdictions when compared to other – emerging – jurisdictions and also a drive by clients to consolidate (ie, reduce the size of) their law firm panels.

The third primary driver is commoditisation. For the purpose of this chapter, the word is used to refer to the process whereby something becomes less and less differentiated in the eyes of the purchaser. As a result, purchasers care less about who they buy from. That process of commoditisation reduces the pricing power of the provider law firm, in that if products or services become more alike (undifferentiated) from a purchasing client's point of view they will tend to buy the cheapest. There are only three logical responses to the process of commoditisation:

- find a way to continue to differentiate one's product;
- choose instead to compete on price; or
- get out of the market.

In many cases, law firms are struggling to achieve the first response, are loathe to adopt the third response and are therefore defaulting to the second response. Whether that makes good business sense is, at best, questionable.

All three of those drivers bear upon the legal services sector. This sector does not operate in isolation from the business community generally. In the professional lifetimes of many readers of this chapter, the legal profession will have changed out of all recognition compared to the one they joined.

In addition, from a client perspective, the 'panel game' is increasingly the preferred advisor engagement method of large corporate and commercial entities. This trend has been increasing over a number of years. Taking the United Kingdom as an example, see the annual "Chambers Client Report – Who acts for Corporate Britain?" survey. To quote from the 2012 survey:

*"The average number of firms mentioned by FTSE100 clients this year has fallen ... Of the 30 firms with five or more FTSE100 mentions last year, 23 have fewer mentions this year. None have more."*

Currently a FTSE100 company might typically have a global firm, an upper mid market firm, two mid-market firms and a volume business as the four or five core members of its panel. In a few years' time, a likely alternative scenario is that it will typically have a global firm, an upper mid-market firm, an outsourcer and one or two volume businesses as the four or five core members of its panel. Among the FTSE250, less emphasis on the global and more on the upper mid-market is now and will still sometimes be the norm. For the FTSE350 (being the combination of the FTSE100 and the FTSE250), that model provides a viable long-term future for materially fewer commercial law firms in the United Kingdom than are currently operating in the legal services marketplace. The implications of that phenomenon are by no means confined to the United Kingdom. They are fundamental to the medium to long-term health of the firms occupying what is currently viewed as the upper to upper mid-market. But much of the work those firms do is not genuinely or consistently high-value work if value is to be defined by the client. To quote one FTSE250 company secretary, "For the financial director, of course, the appeal of having fewer firms is that you can demand lower fees. For the company secretary the appeal is that you get better service." An appropriate ability to deliver differently will therefore be vital to the medium to long-term health of many firms.

The globalisation, consolidation and commoditisation drivers have been having an effect for some years and are not therefore new. Progress, of course, will not continue at that same rate. It is almost certain to accelerate and has already been doing so for some time. The opportunities and rewards for firms that prepare and position themselves appropriately in this commercial environment will be very significant. Positioning a firm so that it can become one of the successful continuing legal entities will be crucial to its long-term success and to its ability to deliver what its clients want in the way they want it. And it is, of course, what the clients want that matters. Client requirements are leading to radical change in the legal sector.

## 3.    The implications for a professional services firm in that environment

### 3.1    The value pyramid

Many readers will be familiar with the concept of the value pyramid. It is not new. In a relatively simple form for analysing types of work in a professional services environment, it might appear as shown in Figure 1.

Figure 1: The value pyramid

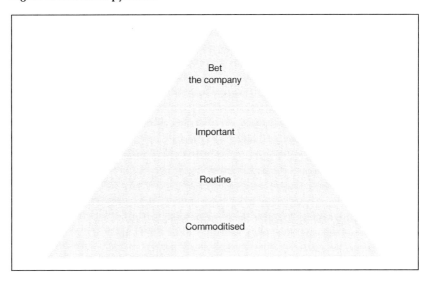

Clients purchase legal services. Over a period of time any given legal service commoditises. What is meant by this statement? A number of years ago now a firm in the United Kingdom invited the general counsel of a client to its annual induction course for its newly qualified lawyers. The client in question was a private equity fund. The general counsel chose as his theme a management buyout transaction and spoke to the audience about what his company required from its lawyers. Over a period of 15 minutes the feedback from the delegates was either 'that's not fair' or 'but you don't understand'. The general counsel took that in remarkably good spirit, given the circumstances. Eventually, after the sixth or seventh interjection, he responded to the effect that the audience did not understand. Some years previously the management buyout had been a new product. It was then high complexity, high value, low volume, high margin work that few firms were able to undertake. The relevant firms could, more or less, name their price. Now, however, the management buyout was mainstream, lower complexity, lower value, higher volume, lower margin work that many firms could undertake. There was a price that the buyer was prepared to pay. The firms had a choice: find a way to do the work and make a profit at that price, or get out of the market. The product had commoditised. The general counsel was met with a number of uncomprehending looks.

That anecdote goes to the heart of the issues addressed in this chapter. Legal services, as a product, are in any event susceptible to the same dynamics as anything else. Laptop computers evolved from being rare, prestigious, expensive status symbols that were difficult to produce in large quantities, to accessories that every student expects to have. Mobile phones started out as rarities worthy of comment and then became ubiquitous. The phenomenon affects not just information technology. Cars, double glazing, insurance policies, audit services and optometry have all followed the same route. So too have legal services. Wills, residential conveyancing and flotations have all commoditised. By way of reminder, by this we mean that they have gone through the process whereby something becomes less and less differentiated in the eyes of the purchaser, with the result that purchasers care less about who they buy from.

Over a period of time any legal service offering 'commoditises' to some extent, with or without an economic crisis. The process has been happening since well before the onset of the 2007/08 global financial crisis. It will carry on impacting upon the delivery of legal services long after the current financial crisis is over. In some ways, the advent of that financial crisis has potentiated the process, in that the buyers of legal services have become more powerful and the drivers of globalisation and consolidation have acted so as, in some respects, to accelerate the issues around commoditisation.

Further, the impact of technology and the internet on mobility and the ability to deliver legal services from a variety of locations has added layers of complexity to the challenges and opportunities facing law firms.

In an environment in which the buyers of legal services demand more for less, the ability to (in the words of that general counsel all those years ago) find a way to do the work and make a profit at the prevailing price, or alternatively to get out of the market, has become even more important – not only as a differentiating factor, but even as a survival factor. In other words, the circumstances have 'raised the stakes' for law firms. Not only is it possible for a law firm to streamline its services so as to improve its competitive advantage; it is also necessary for many firms to do so in order to remain competitive.

## 3.2 The beginnings of a response: mapping one's work on the value pyramid

As part of its risk management and business planning, a firm should in any event regularly be monitoring its services (ie, its products) by mapping them on the value pyramid in Figure 1. When equipped with a proper understanding of where its products sit on that pyramid, a firm can then begin to ask itself whether it wishes to carry on providing commoditised products and, if the answer is that it does, how – and from where – it can deliver them in a way that allows it to make a profit. In the same way, a firm can evaluate how to deliver 'business as usual' products ('important' and 'routine' work), which it will wish to carry on providing, in the most cost effective and profitable way.

In the environment faced by firms since 2008 such monitoring and mapping has become even more important. Indeed, it can make the difference between success and failure.

At any given point in time, services delivered by a firm operating below the top group of firms, when mapped on to the value pyramid, will usually appear as in Figure 2:

**Figure 2: The value pyramid for firms operating below the top group**

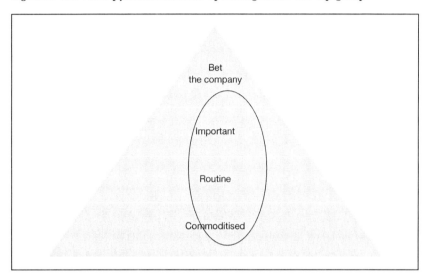

The shape mapped on to the pyramid, and the distribution between the layers of the pyramid, will – or should – determine how a firm goes about delivering its service. Taking the example above, all firms aspire to do as much 'bet the company' work as they can, but few firms can honestly say that such work represents more than a small proportion of what they do. For most firms, 'important' and 'routine' work will comprise the majority of their service delivery. Again, most firms will be doing a proportion of 'commoditised' work; their challenge is as to whether they should in fact be doing it and, if the answer to that is that they should, how they do it in a cost-effective way that allows them to meet client expectations whilst also making a profit.

## 3.3 Technology, mobility, demographics and growth

In 2009, Orange carried out research in the United Kingdom with a view to gaining a better understanding of the impact of information technology on mobility. Two of the questions they asked participants sought to identify where, geographically, participants currently worked and where they would prefer to reside given the freedom to choose unfettered by the need to have to travel to their place of work. If the answers to those questions were acted upon, the result would be some quite significant movements in regional population within the United Kingdom. Many of the respondents declared a desire to reside in another part of the country. The relevance of that to this chapter is that technology has now evolved to a level such that location is no longer the issue it once was in relation either to place of work or to service delivery. A law firm looking to re-engineer its service delivery model is no longer necessarily constrained by the location – whether city, region or even country – of its current office(s). Even within one country, the main operating costs for a professional services business, namely salaries and premises, can be significantly different from one region to another. When one then takes into account the aspirations – in terms of where they wish to reside – of the people who are the talent pools of such firms, location can not only have a powerful influence upon cost but also be a powerful staff recruitment and retention tool.

Several other factors also need to be taken into account.

- Some of the developed countries of the west, and in particular the United States and the United Kingdom, have a greater number of lawyers per thousand of the population than others. There are, of course, a multitude of reasons for that, but in the more mobile environment described earlier one has to ask whether those two countries are now over-supplied with lawyers, particularly when compared to countries such as India. And the lawyer population of the United States and United Kingdom is certainly expensive in terms of comparative salary cost.

- The widespread use of English as an international business language and the availability of university education in countries such as India makes it wholly unsurprising that India became one of the main centres for legal process outsourcing: it has a large number of well-educated and ambitious young people who speak the same language as lawyers in the United States and the United Kingdom. The same is true of other popular locations for LPO providers, such as the Philippines or South Africa.

- Economic growth – and therefore consumption and the resulting demand for legal services – is increasingly to be found in the east rather than the west. McKinsey projects that, by 2025, China will have a middle class of about 520 million people. That is more than the total current population of all 27 member states of the European Union.

Those three factors make the deconstruction and reconstruction of legal services simultaneously both a value proposition opportunity and a competitive threat for law firms. Furthermore, they make it important for a law firm to identify what work it wants to retain in house, what work it wants to outsource to third-party providers and where – geographically – it wants to have both types of work undertaken.

## 3.4    New entrants

Should any reader still harbour any lingering doubts about the assertions above, it is only necessary to consider the emergence, in recent years, of non-law firm legal services providers.

One of the founders of a well-known legal process outsourcing business explained, in interview, that a significant factor in his decision to launch the business had been his experience of the litigation service provided by his then New York lawyers when he was running a previous company. Upon receipt of a six figure bill for work on disclosure he asked himself the question: did I need to have that work done? His answer was yes, but not by associates located in New York with an overhead structure that required them to charge several hundred US dollars an hour for their time. That answer led him to launch a new business.

He was not alone. In the last few years insurance companies, mutuals, private investors and asset management companies have all begun to enter the market for the provision of legal services. As with the more established LPO and BPO providers, a number of these businesses are ambitious, hungry, well resourced, capable and determined. It is unlikely that they will give up, not least because they see profitable business opportunities. If law firms do not respond appropriately they risk losing work and clients. Several trends have been emerging with increasing clarity since 2008:

- Practitioners are coming to realise that market forces are actually capable of 'breaking' law firms in ways that might not have been feasible in earlier times. One way in which some firms are responding is by beginning to outsource – which is to say stop doing – some of the work that they did before 2008; the law firm economics of the years prior to 2008 no longer work in the current environment. And we are unlikely to go back to life before 2008 in the foreseeable future.
- Consolidators and financiers are now creating volume businesses operating on a national and international scale. In the United Kingdom the legal sector is beginning to come to terms with the reality that such businesses will, before too long, threaten to push some of the so-called 'specialist commercial firms' of the period before 2008 out of the top 20 in terms of size and – more importantly – profitability.
- The new entrants such as retail groups, insurers and financial institutions referred to earlier either have now entered or are actively considering entering the market and are offering highly competitive online or telephonic legal services to complement or supplement their existing business lines.
- A number of LPO providers are seeking to dominate the market for commoditised and process-driven work, some having attracted external finance.

Not only are there too many law firms in the marketplace, but the entire upper mid-market only has room for a finite number of law firms – a far smaller number than currently seek to inhabit that space. In recent years, we have seen commercial law firms fail. We will also see commercial law firms disappear into the new entrants. Indeed, if Australia's Slater & Gordon is viewed as a consolidator new entrant, the United Kingdom's Russell Jones & Walker has already disappeared into it.

Against that background, a number of commercial law firms are struggling to thrive in their old forms, and are engaged either in wholesale re-invention of their business models or in partial reconstruction or deconstruction of their services.

All of this points towards a viable, healthy future for fewer law firms than currently exist. New entrants, together with client requirements, are therefore also underlining the importance of deconstruction and reconstruction of legal services in order to respond to the forces of change and to continue to thrive.

## 3.5 Client requirements

Let us now take into account the perspective of the clients. In 2011, the author's firm carried out research among a group of general counsel of large corporate clients. Five messages were of particular relevance in the context of LPO and workflow management. They were as follows, in each case with the message from the clients followed by text referring to points made elsewhere in this chapter:

- *Relationships really matter, regardless of panels and panel positions*
  Good relationships are at the heart of a good understanding of a client's expectations and, therefore, of what is needed in order to meet those expectations. Mediation, facilitation and project management are core skills in relationship management. They also lie at the heart of a sound relationship and are critical to consistency of service delivery (as to which see the fourth bullet below).
- *Sector knowledge really matters – it is crucial to understand the market and know the environment*
  This message is pertinent in relation to service delivery and the client's perception of value in the marketplace as seen by the client. Think back to the anecdote about the general counsel explaining his company's requirements to the newly qualified lawyers. There was a price that the client was prepared to pay. The law firm had a choice: find a way to do the work and make a profit at that price, or get out of the market.
- *True value added really matters – budgets are stretched*
  Value added here is value as perceived by the client, not the law firm. The founder of the legal process outsourcing business referred to earlier recognised that disclosure was a necessary step in litigation but did not recognise it as delivering – let alone adding – value at the price he was then paying. It is a sobering thought that law firms are good at 'reinventing the wheel'. Firms that can find a way to avoid such 'reinvention' will differentiate themselves in the minds of their clients.
- *Consistency of service delivery really matters and can be a commercial advantage*
  Consistency is by no means 'merely' about the accuracy of technical legal advice. It embraces timeliness, teamwork, work flow, chronology, reliability and a host of other elements of service delivery. It is also inextricably linked to the crucial need for the different offices of a multi-site operation to be 'joined up' in the delivery of service. Firms that can both achieve the deconstruction and reconstruction of their legal services and deliver those services in a consistent way will be capable of securing a commercial advantage – and therefore of differentiating themselves.
- *Don't assume that because someone is the incumbent they are doing a good job*
  There are 'retain the status quo' and 'make a change' influences at work in any panel relationship. The 'cost' of switching supplier can militate against a change of supplier and in favour of 'retaining the status quo', even when there might be some dissatisfaction with the service delivered. The opportunity to develop a relationship with an alternative supplier who can demonstrate relevant sector knowledge and an ability to deliver service in a

way that adds value in a consistent manner can be powerful drivers towards 'change', to the advantage of a firm able to deliver in such a way.

The commercial and economic environment; the presence of too many law firms; the impact of technology, mobility, demographics and growth (or the absence of growth); the appearance of new entrants and the demands of client requirements create both risk and opportunity for the law firms that respond appropriately. Choosing whether or not to respond is not an option.

**4. So how might one set out to build and execute a value proposition for a professional services firm in this environment?**
As has been said already, in one short chapter there is going to be no definitive answer to that question! Rather, what follows is a series of 'guidance notes' for consideration and development into an individual firm's execution plan.

In an interview on September 28 2006, David Cameron said, "Lots of people call me Dave, my mum calls me David, my wife calls me Dave, I don't really notice what people call me." Based upon the matters identified in this chapter so far, there are four limbs to a successful response to the messages from clients and the challenges of the commercial environment. 'Dave' is a useful acronym for the four limbs:

- Differentiation of one's firm in the marketplace is vital when there are too many (or, at the very least, an abundance of undifferentiated) providers of legal services.
- Alignment with one's clients' interests and objectives is fundamental to the development of a successful value-based service delivery model and a proper understanding of a client's requirements.
- Value added (to the clients and as they perceive value) by, together with consistency of, one's service delivery can give a firm a competitive advantage.
- Engagement with the client, at trusted advisor/supplier level, reinforces the relationship, as do enthusiasm and energy. In the words of Joey DeMicco, the president of marketing agency AIMG: "It is not the customer's job to get you excited about selling to them, it is your job to get the customer excited about buying from you." And engagement, enthusiasm and energy 'sell'.

A firm with a 'Dave' approach to the delivery of value-focused legal services will improve its competitive advantage. There are five areas to consider in developing those four limbs of a 'Dave' value proposition for a firm.

**4.1 Differentiation**
Differentiation is a frequently used word in relation to the delivery of legal services. True differentiation is both rare and difficult to achieve. Achieving it requires a deep understanding of a client's needs and objectives.

In the United Kingdom, Cranfield School of Management has worked with the author's firm to apply its research into, and understanding of, best practice in key account management to develop a practical approach to planning, analysing and implementing a closer relationship with a law firm's strategically important clients.

A programme such as the one offered by Cranfield School of Management enables a firm to develop a strategic key account plan for specific clients using the best practice Cranfield template, which is based upon its leading position in Europe in the field of key account management research.

Given the changes that the legal market is going through, with an increase in buyer power on the part of clients, the importance of understanding what the client wants and needs, and the importance of gaining real engagement internally, cannot be overstated if a firm is to be able to offer a truly differentiated service to its key clients. A firm needs to equip its lawyers to understand their clients much better and therefore provide more tailored solutions and develop their client relationships.

Tailored solutions then lead on to consideration of an appropriate business model.

## 4.2 Business model

Developing an appropriate business model for a firm is an important part of true differentiation. Research conducted by the author's firm suggests that at least 20% of the work undertaken by firms in the mid-market (the work characterised as 'important' or 'routine' in the value pyramid illustrated earlier in this chapter) does not need to be undertaken by highly qualified lawyers (or even by lawyers at all!). Such work, when done by lawyers (and sometimes significantly over-qualified lawyers), can all too easily result in a firm making very little money on it, or even making a loss.

Examples of the type of work concerned would include due diligence, document review, document management, bundling, bibling, data room management and e-disclosure.

Reworking the business model will involve, among other things, scoping, project management, process mapping, the development of document production tools, flexible resourcing and, where appropriate, LPO. A firm would also need to revisit the 'traditional' career structure, with its presumed progression through levels of role and bands of remuneration which may well be neither appropriate nor sustainable in a reworked business model. In short, there should be a fundamental re-evaluation of a firm's approach to service delivery and to its business model so as better to align itself with its clients.

## 4.3 Alignment

Alignment of the interests of a law firm with those of its clients is a powerful enabler in the development of a stronger relationship between the two. Whilst not – self-evidently – without risk (that is, after all, part of the point!), one way in which alignment can be achieved effectively is through pricing and risk sharing. The threat presented by recent increases in client buying power can, perhaps paradoxically, therefore be an opportunity – to re-work the approach a firm takes to pricing. A firm's pricing menu might offer a range of options, for example:

- The hourly rate which, whilst still used quite extensively for legal advice, is increasingly the clients' least preferred option.
- In certain circumstances a firm might offer a fixed fee. The skills identified earlier in relation to a proper understanding of ones business model and the

steps – processes – involved in the delivery of the service to the client will be crucial to a profitable outcome.

- Engagement can be on an annual retainer basis. This is increasingly attractive to larger corporate clients, and sometimes used in conjunction with a fixed fee approach, for bundles or types of work (eg, all of a client's employment tribunal work or litigation).
- A success fee or deal fee. It will be crucial to agree with the client its objectives, the criteria for success and a fee basis designed to deliver payment to a firm if it helps the client to succeed, but a lower (or, more radically, no) payment if the client does not succeed.

Such a menu-based approach can serve to align a law firm's interests with those of its clients. It requires a proper understanding both of the client's objectives and of the firm's service delivery model. It can therefore also be a differentiating factor, deliver competitive advantage and facilitate the building of 'trusted advisor' relationships.

## 4.4     Project and process management

The streamlining – whether by outsourcing, deconstruction and reconstruction or otherwise – of legal services is not a binary 'do it or don't do it' process. Equally, it is not a bipartite process: a multitude of parties can be involved. Project and process management are therefore key skillsets. Also key is the clear articulation of the roles of the various potential supply chain parties in the delivery of legal services to clients.

There is a clear parallel here with BPO. Whether in relation to 'front of house services' (eg, reception, switchboard or catering) or 'back office services' (eg, finance, IT support or human resources), the experience of law firms appears to vary widely, from very satisfied all the way through to very dissatisfied. The author's conversations with satisfied firms, however, leads him to conclude that they share certain things in common, namely:

- a flexibility of approach to the evaluation of what services should, or should not, be outsourced (and why);
- discipline and rigour in ensuring that any third parties involved truly understand both the cultural approach of the firm and the needs and operating environment of its clients;
- clarity both as to the project and process management skills needed within the firm in order to work as a team with the chosen third-party providers, and as to the service level expectations on both sides;
- the recruitment and/or retention of a small number of key individuals with the skills, passion and enthusiasm to act as the 'bridge' between the firm and its outsourced providers.

Those four characteristics apply equally to the outsourcing, deconstruction and reconstruction of legal services. Referring back to the value pyramid, it is quite common for the 'process' of commoditisation to lead to some types of activity being oursourced whilst other types of activity are retained within the firm and deconstructed or reconstructed. That has always been the case. An example would be the use of specialist counsel in jurisdictions that do not have a fused legal profession. The critical challenge is to have, within the law firm, the capability to deliver in the above four areas.

## 4.5 Partnering

At the same time, precisely because a law firm will almost certainly have a need for some types of activity to be oursourced whilst other types of activity are retained within the firm, partnering for service delivery – with clients, with a firm's own people and with third parties – is also of fundamental importance.

Engagement with the client, understanding of the client's requirements, clarity and communication, project and process management and appropriate quality control all come into play in partnering. And when implemented effectively, they reinforce differentiation, alignment and adding value.

## 5. Conclusion

In a marketplace driven by the forces of consolidation and globalisation, buffeted by an economic crisis the likes of which has not been seen for very many years, there is most certainly the opportunity – and need – for some firms to operate below the group of top international firms, with a value focus and with their services streamlined so as to improve their competitive advantage.

As to how any given firm might set out to build and execute such a value proposition, after first understanding the commercial environment and its implications, taking due account of technology, mobility, demographics and growth and considering client requirements, it will need to:

- rework its business model appropriately;
- clearly align itself with the interests of its clients;
- ensure that it has in place the necessary project and process management skills; and
- adopt a partnering approach to the opportunities identified.

When those steps are implemented effectively, they also reinforce differentiation, alignment and adding value to the firm's clients. When the matters considered in this chapter are taken into account, the value pyramid might appear as in Figure 3:

As noted above, it is not possible in one short chapter to provide a definitive exposition and analysis of the answers to the questions posed in the introduction to the chapter. The series of 'guidance notes' set out in this chapter will, however, hopefully have provided a basis for further consideration and for firms to structure their thinking and convert it into an individual plan of execution.

Because, in the words of the English businessman Allan Leighton:

*"Business is only about two things. Strategy and execution … the only thing that really works in an organisation is execution. If you look at the great businesses in this world, the reason that they are better than anybody else is because they execute better than anybody else."*

## Figure 3: A final view of the value pyramid

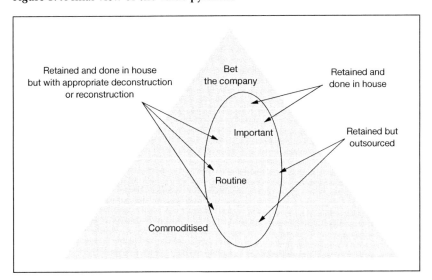

# How to screw up your international expansion: a 15-step guide

**Robert C Bata**
WarwickPlace Legal, LLC

---

So you want to be an international firm? You want to open offices in exotic locales? Good for you. We live in a thoroughly interconnected global economy. Increased access to information, greater ease of communication, expanded global markets and proliferating cross-border transactions and disputes have transformed your clients' expectations. The action is ... everywhere! If you can't look after your most valued clients wherever in the world they may need you, well then it's *adiós, amigos!*

The trouble is that, as it turns out, going international is not easy. The global legal landscape is dotted with flags planted by law firms dashing to establish themselves in the hottest new markets – and littered with the wrecks of efforts gone wrong. There are a myriad of ways to fail at it. In the end, if you foul up, you will have spent an awful lot of time and end up losing money, losing clients, losing colleagues, losing your reputation and quite possibly losing your very existence. So it actually may be viewed as a public service of sorts for us to lay out a set of concrete steps to ensure you will make a shambles of it without investing too much time. And for those inspired souls who prefer to learn from the mistakes of others rather than their own, there may even be a road map here for getting it right.

Not all of the 15 measures described below are necessarily fatal in and of themselves, but they each contain the seeds of fiasco. By the same token, one need not slavishly take each of the actions highlighted by this guide in order to achieve a complete mess. But taken together, these 15 suggestions, or guidelines if you will, are as good as a guarantee that your international expansion will fade, fizzle and flop in pretty short order.

Finally, it may seem to the sceptical reader that some of the scenarios described below are too silly, too outlandish and too implausible to have happened in our learned profession. Please be assured that, while we have named no names, in order to protect the innocent (or just the plain foolish), each example has an antecedent in the real world.

## 1. The vision thing

The accumulated wisdom of the firm's *éminence grise* is one of the treasured assets of many partnerships. These elder statespersons, although still firmly in charge, can look beyond the mundane affairs of firm management and devise strategies for the future. Although well-intentioned, their visionary strategies can sometimes soar beyond the practical and the necessary, and occasionally they are just a means to enshrine the leader's personal legacy. Whatever the motivation, however, the bigger the vision, the bigger the need to achieve 'buy-in' from the partnership. And yet, when it comes to one of the most transformative of strategies – international expansion – senior partners often ignore the fact that it is the firm's most productive partners, the ones in the prime of their careers, with active practices, for whom the strategy must work. If those partners' practices will not be enhanced by an international strategy, if their practices are distinctly domestic, if in fact they see the cost of cross-border expansion as a hit on their profit share and no more, the project is doomed. This is especially so when the leader is held in such high esteem that the partnership goes along with the plan out of deference to their wishes. Once the senior partner exits the stage, it will be curtains for the foreign office too.

A corollary to this phenomenon is that of the passport-happy partner, who insists that a foreign office is essential to their practice, or else all of their clients (who until now had mysteriously been content to work with them without such offices) will disappear into the clutches of more nimble competitors. Is this just someone who wants a lot of air miles, or perhaps live the glamorous expat life? Or is it someone who would like to find a nice hiding place from the rest of the partnership? Or maybe it is someone who has been freshly recruited from an international firm and now claims that their practice will only follow if the new firm opens up foreign offices in the same locations as the old one. (Now *there's* a case of the unasked question coming back to bite the recruiting committee.) Let these characters have their way, and you can be pretty sure the new office will end up as nothing more than a frolic and a detour.

## 2. Geography is overrated

The world is a confusing place. Regimes change, place names change, countries get carved up, people insist on speaking incomprehensible languages. Who can keep up with all that? Even so, a few years ago some partners with a burgeoning practice in Central and Eastern Europe thought they had made a persuasive argument to their colleagues for opening an office in Budapest. The business case was strong, barriers to entry were low, the field was still wide open. It was therefore all the more disheartening for them to be solicitously asked by the firm's management committee whether it wasn't too dangerous to set up shop in such a volatile region of the Middle East … The atlas-challenged firm never did get past its confusion. It ended up losing the lead partner to a competitor, missing out on several waves of groundbreaking privatisations and having to play catch-up when it was too late. This was an efficient failure, streamlined and elegant: if you can't tell your Azores from your Elba, your foreign venture is doomed from the get-go.

## 3. *J'aime Paris!*

Lest we become overly smug in our assessment of those who did not pay attention in geography class, there is plenty of potential for a belly-up when the impetus for international expansion comes from a misguided focus on a particular location. This happens when you think you know something about a market when actually you don't. Take for example the China Syndrome, which goes something like this:

China's population is more than one billion people, so the demand for legal services must also be astronomical. And everyone else seems to be opening offices there. Therefore we should be there too. We'll need to figure out what we can offer, but that's a minor issue: once we build it they will come.

But the truth is that the big numbers in China – huge population, giant country, enormous resources, warp-speed development – don't necessarily translate into big numbers on your bottom line, as many firms have learned. For every firm that has the talent and resources to handle a big-ticket arbitration, or a Red Chip IPO or a behemoth infrastructure financing, there are plenty who have merely bounced along the bottom, handling routine company formations, low-end real estate and rubber-stamp labour and employment matters. If you barge into a market on a wing and a prayer, you're likely to end up crawling and cursing.

Even worse is the wanderlust approach to expansion. Say for example that one of the partners has handled a matter in Laos or Mozambique or Tahiti and has simply fallen in love with the place. She persuades her partners that this could be a fantastic opportunity to get involved in more of the same type work if only they had an office there. Local businesses, ministry officials and a member of one of the leading families have all told her they would send work. Before you know it, a presence is established, and the wait begins … and continues … and continues, because no one in this enchanting locale is willing to pay your home country billing rates. But even if rates are not the issue – and when aren't they? – allowing a partner to commit the firm to an expansion that serves little benefit other than to indulge his enthusiasm for a place, be it Paris, Milan or Rio, all on the hopeful supposition that a practice 'could turn into something', is sheer folly.

## 4.    Seeing is believing

You are well-informed about the difficulty of entering a foreign market. You've heard some horror stories, and you're not too sure you believe the tales of success. What you do know is that your firm needs to be seen to be in a particular location, so your competitors across town don't steal a march on you. It also happens to be a nice recruitment tool to be able to say that you've got an office in an important and possibly fascinating city. But you're not going to risk your partners' money, because that would be imprudent.

So you do the next best thing, which is to rent some space and trumpet an office opening to the world. Your website is updated to show the lawyers 'in' that office, even though when you look closely, those lawyers are actually sitting at their desks in their original locations. You might even give these lawyers a separate identity, like the 'Gulf States Team', or the 'Iceland Desk'. These are superbly evocative designations: 'Team' suggests a well-oiled machine ready to spring into action, while 'Desk' conjures up a busy newsroom, with typewriters furiously clacking, or possibly a kind of foreign ministry warren where diplomats work the night away gathering intelligence and negotiating secret protocols.

Yes. Well, the problem is that the 'teams' and the 'desks' are illusory, and clients catch on to these things. You assure them you can fly hordes of lawyers to your new foreign location at the drop of a hat, but the client won't pay for that, and you can't eat the cost. Local businesses will not take you seriously if you can't make yourself available on short notice. And you can't very well schedule meetings in the back room of the bodega you were able to get on the cheap. Bottom line: if you're renting space without anyone to put in it, you're better off staying home.

This is a good place to mention another smoke-and-mirrors approach favoured by some: the 'International Practice Group'. This can be wholly innocuous in intent – it's a way of advertising that your firm has dealt with matters outside its home jurisdiction and is, perhaps, comfortable with doing so again. Unfortunately it can also turn into an admission that, in fact, you have nothing like an international practice, but that you have cobbled together a hotchpotch of incidental projects you've handled in order to make it appear that you do. An international practice is, after all, not a practice area, like corporate or real estate or tax, unless your firm has a Law of the Sea speciality. A genuine international practice is one where you can routinely find cross-border elements in your substantive practice areas – simply saying you have one won't make it so.

## 5. Reinvent yourself

You've arrived at the decision to enter a foreign market. Your reasoning is pretty sound. You know where you want to go, and you want a real presence, not a Potemkin village. You understand that merely being in some unusual location is not enough to qualify your firm as having an international practice. You've done research, and you know the strengths of particular locations. You've concluded, correctly, that London is a major financial centre, or that Hong Kong is huge in capital markets, or that Ulaanbaatar is the next big thing in natural resources.

In fact, you've gone an extra step. You've looked at your firm's performance in its home market and realised that things are not looking so good there. Your partners are complacent and not working hard enough; your marketing and practice development are non-existent; your brightest associates are being poached by your competitors; and worst of all, your profits have been on a downward curve for some time. So you've found the perfect solution: enter some of the world's most competitive jurisdictions, where no one has heard of your firm, and act as though you belong there. Go ahead, start an energy practice in Houston, even though you wouldn't know a pipeline from a chorus line; start a telecoms practice in Düsseldorf, even if you think a megahertz is a limousine rental company. Hire some locals to provide you with cover, and hope their practice will be good enough to let you survive. And then, your theory holds, you can set to work fixing what's wrong back home and possibly transforming the firm into something completely different.

Wake-up call: never in a hundred years will this work. Firms with a well-thought-through strategy have done plenty of reinventing of themselves, and quite successfully too, whether they were once a standard practice in the Midlands of England now grown into a global megafirm; or a small bankruptcy shop in New York's Midtown that is today one of the world's most successful and sophisticated international capital markets firms. But you cannot magically metamorphose into a different firm – much less solve your domestic problems – by bolting on a novelty practice in a foreign country.

In the first place, you will most likely not find anyone interested in joining your firm in the foreign location. After all, where for the foreign practice group is the synergy, the cross-sell, the prospect of fruitful integration into a firm whose practice has nothing to do with theirs? Even worse if you do find some interested recruits: chances are their business is in the 'rebuilding phase' (ie, they don't have any); or they have no interest in integration, because after they've spent a few years with you they will move on to the next highest bidder.

Secondly, your domestic issues must always take precedence over foreign experiments. An unproductive partner will remain unproductive no matter what a colleague in another country in another practice area may be doing. Your core clients will not suddenly send you new work at home, on the strength of what you may be doing overseas. You want to tell your real estate clients in St Louis that your London office is tops in AIM listings of mining company shares in London? Knock yourself out, but they won't care. What those clients really want to know is how you can serve them better at home. International expansion is not a cure for what ails you at home.

## 6. Goals versus own goals

You have avoided all of the major pitfalls. You know where you want to be; you know why this location is important; you're satisfied that being there is not simply a whim or a masquerade. You are not merely ducking intractable problems at home, and you know you'd better not pretend to be something you are not. All set to go? All set to fail if you don't have a clear strategy for what you want to accomplish once you've arrived.

A particularly big way to fail in this regard is through a merger that is really nothing more than a work in progress. For example, a prestigious City firm learned the hard way that marrying up with a US firm which, although most distinguished in its heyday was suffering declining fortunes, gave it little more than an expensive beachhead in a competitive location. The thought behind this kind of merger is that getting into the market is more important than figuring out how to succeed in that market. Yes, the thinking went, at some stage steps will have to be taken to rationalise the merger, but for starters it was perfectly OK to gobble up an amorphous, undifferentiated mass and put off into the future shaping it into something that made sense. Of course the opposite turned out to be true, a costly and painful lesson for all concerned.

Another but no less effective way to fail in a foreign jurisdiction is to hire everyone who comes through the door and is willing to accept a paycheck from you. You can report staggering advances in your headcount: a bankruptcy team here, a credit card expert there, a litigator or two, some real estate and insurance specialists, online gambling, structured finance, venture capital ... it makes one's head spin just to contemplate the variety. It doesn't matter that the office has no recognisable identity, you say, because you are determined to reach 'critical mass', whatever that may be. Once you get there will be time enough to decide which way to jump, right? Dead wrong. How could you know what size you need to be when you don't know what you want to be? Depending on the practice you are building, a small headcount can be sufficient and still profitable. Yes, size matters – except when it doesn't.

## 7. I've got a secret

However sound your strategy for international expansion may be, you can still drop the ball if you mishandle the way you communicate it to your partners and the outside world.

In the world of law firms, surprises are generally unwelcome and almost always unpleasant. It is therefore remarkable how often a very small group of firm leaders decides it is a good idea to keep from their partners any notion of a potential international expansion, only to spring it on the unsuspecting populace as a *fait accompli*. This is a poor idea for many reasons, particularly because, no matter what the firm leaders say, the rest of the partners will assume they have been cut out of some sweet deal the seniors have arranged for themselves.

Treating sensitive and proprietary information as confidential is of course crucial in any phase of planning an international expansion, especially when it involves a merger. But there is no message more toxic than one that implies that the firm's leaders do not trust the partnership to maintain confidences or to discuss the issues in a constructive way. The result: demoralised and sceptical partners withhold their support, or walk out the door, or take it upon themselves to initiate discussions with third parties, thereby derailing the original plan.

## 8. Alert the media!

Fearing precisely the dire results described in the previous section, the firm's leaders embark on a strategy of letting the sun shine on every fresh idea they come up with. A memorandum is circulated to all staff describing the decision of the management committee to seek to expand internationally. Although the committee has reached no decision on how, where or when the expansion will occur, they are now committed to this goal. The memorandum is circulated to the media, and within a day or two the world is aware that this firm is on the march.

A flurry of press attention, accompanied by a tsunami of approaches from recruiters and law firm management consultants, takes place over the next few months. But nothing happens and the story becomes yesterday's news. Then an announcement is made that discussions are taking place with a particular firm. Rumours fly, partners are preoccupied with how the combination will affect them. Meetings are arranged for practice groups to meet their counterparts. Heads of terms are drawn up and leaked to the press. Speculation abounds regarding name changes, leadership roles, expected lay-offs. Partnership votes are scheduled and postponed. Interest blocs spring up within the partnership – some love the idea of the merger, others see the seeds of their practice's very destruction.

And then the whole thing goes nowhere, the two firms announcing that they part as friends. But a few months later the process starts again with another firm and goes nowhere again. And the same a year later. And again. The continued, repeated and much-discussed failure of the expansion project puts the world on notice that it will never happen. Finally the prophecy becomes self-fulfilling, or, perhaps worse, the firm, now desperate to have its strategy validated, is forced into the embrace of the wrong suitor. It is a long and painful road to failure.

9. **Democracy is wonderful**

Managing a law firm, particularly one with international ambitions, is far too complex to be done successfully by just one person. (There are some notable exceptions, but they are truly exceptional.) Sometimes though the task seems so daunting that major decisions get delegated to a task force or a committee, and the deliberations of these bodies are then supplemented by partnership-wide discussion groups, focus groups, head-scratching groups and of course votes. Lots of votes.

Well and good in the interest of openness, but not so good when it comes to following a straight line toward the goal of international expansion. Take the case of the 'International Committee', which some firms set up to investigate possible approaches to expansion. These committees are usually made up of a handful of partners who meet the following qualifications: they like to travel; they have time on their hands; and they have fixed ideas as to what would benefit their practice the most.

Having spent a good bit of time and money on exploratory travel and meetings, the committee will make a recommendation to the firm's leadership, which is usually too busy to second-guess them. The recommendations therefore either get shelved until some later date, or passed on to another group of partners, or to the full partnership for some kind of discussion or vote. Inevitably someone will have a better relationship with another firm in the target country and will want in on the decision-making process, or will want to form her own committee. In the meantime, one of the members of the original committee retires or gets de-equitised, or worse. Ultimately, another person with a different idea for a strategy emerges and recommends abandoning the entire project.

There is no substitute for well-informed and open discussion among partners; but failure is certain if there is no overarching guidance from the firm's leadership. Without that, any semblance of an international strategy becomes the domain of competing interest groups.

10. **Strangers in a strange land**

Once you've decided on your approach to expansion and are ready to set up your office – whether starting from scratch, recruiting locals, or joining an existing firm – the most important decision you can make is who, if anyone, from your firm should be assigned to the new office. This person or group will be ambassadors for your firm, crucial cultural translators between the new office and the rest of the firm and of course inspirational characters with a strong work ethic and an interest in ensuring smooth integration. Too often, however, these people are not to be found. It turns out that the partners whose practice is most relevant to the new foreign office are too busy to move; or they want to stay close to their domestic clients; or they have young families they don't wish to uproot; or their children are grown, and they want to be close to the grandkids; or the right person never even gets asked.

So you come up with creative (for which read mind-boggling) solutions. An oft-seen one is taking a much-respected partner out of semi-retirement. This will often be a genial figure, delighted to be living abroad, happy to come into the new office, take the lawyers to lunch and regale them with anecdotes about long-ago and faraway exploits. This person will usually know a great deal about the home office and be very helpful with information about the firm, but his contribution is not likely to advance the cause of building the practice.

One otherwise sensible firm decided to send its pro bono partner to its new London office. This partner, who was doing a wonderful job running the firm's pro bono practice back home, but who otherwise had no clients of her own, would have been utterly at sea in this new environment and would have brought nothing to the table for the lawyers in the new office. Even worse, sending her was tantamount to sending the message that the firm did not consider it worthwhile to assign a revenue-generating partner to the office.

In another instance, a firm sent a litigation partner to a busy corporate finance office in Hong Kong. With no litigation business he was qualified to handle in that part of the world, and with no particular cultural fit or language skills, the young man was consigned to sitting in his office, widely assumed by his local colleagues to be serving as the eyes and ears of firm management and therefore to be avoided at all costs.

Each of the situations described above resulted in a potential existential crisis for the foreign office involved. In two cases the problem was resolved and the office salvaged. In the third ... that chapter is still being written, but the office has had a series of departures and is experiencing declining revenues in an otherwise dynamic market.

## 11.    It's my way or the highway

Even when the right person – meaning one with the appropriate skills and practice interests – is transferred to the new office from the home jurisdiction, there is always an excellent opportunity for making a mess of it. Absence of cultural sensitivity can be a tripping-up point, as in the case of the US managing partner of an East European office, who invited the office staff to his home for a barbecue, only to be told that socialising with 'superiors' was considered work and therefore an unconscionable invasion of what otherwise would be deemed free time.

Usually the problem has less benign origins than a friendly barbecue. This normally has to do with the importation of procedures from the home office. If the partner assigned to the new foreign office has no ability or authority to adapt the rules to local realities, confusion will reign. This isn't just about imposing onerous requirements like 2,200 billable hours (which to this author's knowledge is more urban legend than reality). It's about having a centralised billing system that is unable to prepare invoices in local currency. It's about associate reviews conducted on the telephone by people who have never met or worked with the lawyers being assessed. It's about not understanding that for some lawyers feng shui considerations can influence career decisions, and even decisions about which way office furniture should face.

Simply dictating compliance with rules because 'that's how we do it back home', when those rules do not conform with local practices, is a sure way to alienate and create resentment among your foreign lawyers. And if they are seen to be flouting the rules, then the lawyers in the home jurisdiction will sour on the foreign office, and quite possibly on the whole international practice: 'They just don't get how we do business. We'll never make it work.'

So what don't you understand about 2,200 billable hours?

### 12.   This land is my land

Even if the cultural sensitivity quotient is all in order, that does not mean other sensitivities are being attended to. No one appreciates the colonial approach, where the foreign office is treated as a sort of playground or travel agency for visiting dignitaries from the home jurisdiction. Many local managing partners have had weekends spoiled by that breathless call from home, announcing that retired partner Buford B Buford IV was coming to visit their city and would dearly love circus tickets, a stretch limo and Turkish takeaway arranged for his arrival. A favourite of this author is the request to a Shanghai managing partner from the heads of the firm's real estate practice group to arrange for escorts to take them to art gallery openings, specifying that the ladies be ... tall.

Management by remote control also falls into the neo-colonial mindset. Once the foreign office has been established and is more or less humming along, management of growth (revenue and personnel) and of careers, particularly the advancement of younger lawyers, become crucially important. A sure-fire formula for undercutting the authority and self-esteem of the local partners is for the home office to conduct further recruitment without soliciting their advice and participation. Another way is to make unilateral partnership and compensation decisions in that foreign office. Sideline or minimise the roles your foreign colleagues play in the development of their office, and you can be sure they will look for greener pastures.

### 13.   It's good to be the king

Your clients don't really care about all the legal niceties, so long as their deal gets done, their case gets won and their product gets sold, right? So the important thing for your foreign presence is contacts, access, 'who you know not what you know'. So bring on the former ministers, ambassadors, generals, tribal chiefs and shamans, to run your office the way it should be run in their country. How grand it will be to have the inside track!

The trouble is that generals need armies, ministers need factotums and shamans need acolytes. Before you know it, your foreign office will be the principality of a person used to the trappings of power and accustomed to demanding more. Of course she must have a chauffeur. Certainly if the computer system breaks down the IT guy should be flogged. By all means make sure His Excellency has an office larger than a football field. And if they demand to be paid a king's ransom, why just imagine how influential they must be.

This is not to say that employing a distinguished public servant to represent your foreign office is necessarily ill-advised. You are fortunate if you find a talented and prominent figure who has your firm's best interests in mind. But beware the celebrity biding his time while plotting his return to power, and look out for fallen stars seeking to relive their glory days. Your office will be enmeshed in controversy, your reputation will suffer, and you will expose your partners to professional risk.

## 14.   Best of breed

There is really no great mystery to recruiting the right people for your new international office. It's downright easy, and you don't need to find any out-of-work bureaucrats either. The trick is to swoop on the most successful local firm and grab some of their best people. It may cost a lot – these people are not leaving the most prestigious firms in their country for a pittance – but it will all work out when the business starts flowing.

Except that the business does not start flowing, as more than one US firm found out in London when raiding Magic Circle firms. They did bring in remarkably talented and successful lawyers, but they had not realised that, in too many cases, the work that had kept these individuals busy, happy and well paid, came from their firms' institutional clientele. Yes, the lawyers could move … but the clients weren't budging. By the time the two-year/three-year salary guarantees expired, the magic had worn off.

But, one might say, law is a personal service business. Clients want the lawyer, not the firm. That's also true, in part. Ideally, there is a close relationship between the lawyer and her client, which is further enhanced by the services and personnel the lawyer's firm is able to bring to servicing the client's needs. When the relationship is predominantly institutional, there is no one lawyer in the firm who is crucial to the client. When the relationship is predominantly personal, then the client will not feel strongly about the identity of the firm – provided of course that the firm can supply the support the client needs.

It is at this end of the scale that the notion of 'portable' business becomes pertinent. Every firm wants laterals to come with portable business. But if the business is so portable that it has already made its rounds to several firms before landing on your doorstep, you have to wonder. How long before the next portability exercise? Is this work just the same set of balls being juggled by this lawyer year after year, or has there been an effort to expand the scope of representation? Is the work the lateral team is bringing just the last hurrah before it peters out, or is there a realistic prospect of it continuing and expanding into other practice areas of the firm? Sometimes all 'portable' means is 'easy come, easy go.'

## 15.   My silo is bigger

Not sure what your Almaty office does? Then chances are they don't know what your office does either. Or maybe you didn't even know you had an office in Almaty, and why should you? You have a nice energy practice in São Paulo: what could interest you in Kazakhstan, one of the world's leading oil and gas producers? As long as you get along with headquarters, you don't need to understand what these other offices are all about, much less go out of your way to develop relationships.

If the only time you meet the lawyers from other countries is at your firm's annual golf outing; if you maintain that your practice area has no need to hold regular discussions with international colleagues engaged in the same area; if you prize your referral relationship with a foreign firm over your own firm's office in the same city; if you fail to seek out opportunities for cross-selling; if in other words your firm has not made global integration an absolute priority and held you accountable for your share in the effort .... The truth is, if all that happened, the world would not come to an end, because these are common occurrences within international firms. Firms need to deal with integration issues, and some are better at it than others; but it is unrealistic to expect busy professionals to devote too much time to global harmonisation. But firms send the wrong message to their partners when they allow an out-of-sight-out-of-mind mentality to develop. And if that happens, why bother going international in the first place? You might have been better off staying home.

## 16.    Conclusion

This chapter has sought to provide a guide to law firms for making a mess of their international expansion efforts. It is sincerely hoped that these suggestions will be found instructive, timely and cost-efficient. It may also be useful, however, to attempt to distil from the foregoing some rules for getting it right. Here are a few.

- Know your business: how did you get where you are, what makes your firm what it is, how do you keep and grow it?
- Know your partners: what do their clients and practices require now and in the years to come?
- Create and communicate an internal process for evaluating international opportunities, and involve the principal opinion leaders of the firm.
- Ensure the partners are aware you are working up a strategy, without inducing fear or exuberance.
- Make decisions based on tomorrow's needs, not today's fads.
- Find the right people, and conduct extensive due diligence.
- Place practice skills, track record, work ethic and cultural fit above contacts.
- Set compensation fairly, with an upside for success, but no lavish packages or guarantees.
- Understand the pricing tolerance of the local market for legal services.
- Set achievable goals – and then some – and then stick with them.
- Maximise the exposure of the new team to the legacy firm: create global practice groups and industry sectors; ensure the new team's visibility in every office; establish secondment and exchange programmes for younger lawyers among the offices.
- Balance the need to have consistent performance and compensation criteria across all offices against the new team's historical experience.
- Make clear where and how the new team fits into the rest of the firm's current practices and aspirations.
- Open management and leadership opportunities to the new team.
- If things start going wrong, be prepared to make changes promptly and decisively.

# How to merge: lessons from 20 years of law firm mergers

Lisa R Smith
Fairfax Associates

## 1. Introduction

The legal industry has recently been going through an extended period of growth and consolidation. Despite the slowdown due to the global economic downturn, the leading global firms have grown substantially. The 2012 Global 100 (*American Lawyer*, September 28 2012) included 11 firms with more than 2,000 lawyers and 34 firms with over 1,000 lawyers. At least 70% of these firms have completed a merger, and in many cases the firms have been created by a merger or multiple mergers. Of course many firms smaller than these global powerhouses have also completed mergers, further contributing to the consolidation of the legal market.

While domestic mergers continue to drive a significant volume of merger activity we have seen a marked increase in cross-border combinations of law firms over the last few years. Some of these combinations have created new global players, while others have bolstered existing global firms. Firms from China, Australia, Canada, South Africa, Hong Kong and of course the United States and the United Kingdom have been involved in significant combinations.

There are over a dozen firms who have more than 50% of their lawyers outside their home country. There will no doubt be more firms moving into this group over the next few years. And while the leading global firms have traditionally been dominated by US and UK firms, it is likely that we will see significant global firms with an Asian base becoming major global firms as well.

The consolidation of the legal industry is likely to continue for some time. Despite the multitude of mergers over the last two decades, the legal market remains much less consolidated than other professional service sectors. The top 10 investment banks, accounting firms and advertising firms hold a much greater share of their overall markets than the top 10 law firms do of the legal market. While there are some natural barriers to consolidation in the legal industry – conflicts chief among them – it is likely that the market will continue to consolidate for the foreseeable future.

While law firm mergers have become increasingly common, the outcomes of mergers are decidedly more varied. Many have been successful, while some have been spectacularly unsuccessful (to the point of firm dissolution). Some have exceeded expectations, while others have had little impact on the overall competitiveness of the combined firm. Our experience, having consulted on many mergers over the last two decades, indicates that there are two key variables to predict success in mergers. The first is the strength of the business case for the merger. The second is the effectiveness of execution and integration (see Figure 1). A weak business case for merger is unlikely to succeed even with flawless execution. Likewise, we have seen some combinations with very strong business cases take much longer to reach their full potential because execution was weak or an afterthought.

**Figure 1: The key variables for successful mergers**

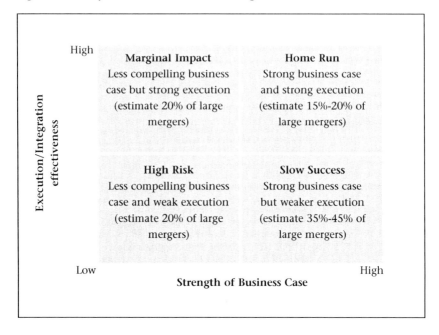

This chapter will address both of these dimensions, as well as the key strategic drivers of mergers and the effective management of the merger process. While the focus is on mergers, many of the principles can be applied to lateral groups as well.

## 2. Why merge?

The answer to the question 'Why merge?' is actually quite simple. A merger between two firms must improve competitiveness in pursuit of specific strategic objectives. A merger is a way to execute a firm's strategy. Of course, there are nuances to the simple answer and a range of reasons why firms pursue mergers.

### 2.1 Build geographic capability

Building geographic capability is one driver of mergers, and is particularly relevant for cross-border mergers. Leading companies are continuing to build their business around the world. The global economic balance of countries is shifting and will continue to shift, with emerging market economies overtaking many western market economies over the next several decades. This dynamic creates a need for global law firms, and perhaps ones that look different to the current set of global firms.

The first question a firm needs to answer is how or if a new jurisdiction will help build competitive strength. That competitive strength could come from a number of sources – does it help you provide services that are or could be demanded by your current clients? Would it build on a particular industry or practice strength that would allow you significantly to raise your profile and attract new clients? Is it a critical jurisdiction in your network?

It is also useful to think about the question from the defensive perspective. What are the competitive disadvantages of not pursuing a global strategy or not being in a particular jurisdiction? Will having only a domestic presence limit the work the firm will be considered for? Is this work that the firm could realistically expect to compete for with a presence in a new jurisdiction?

It is important to remember that not all firms have a client base or practice mix that requires a multi-jurisdictional presence. Some mergers have failed to meet expectations because opportunities for the two legacy firms to work together, whether across state lines or across oceans, simply did not exist. For those firms that do require a broader domestic or a global platform, a merger can be an effective way to build that capability.

## 2.2 Build practice and industry depth

Building practice and industry depth is another key driver of mergers. Most companies with significant legal needs are sophisticated buyers of legal services. They are increasingly buying legal services on the basis of specialist expertise and deep knowledge of the business that can be applied to their specific legal problem. The ability to access information on firm expertise and success has accelerated this trend. Quality of legal services is not a differentiator, but a given. Merger can be a way to build practice depth and to solidify both firms' presence in one or more industry sectors.

Similar to the geographic dimension, the first question that needs to be asked in the context of a merger is how combining practices will build competitive strength. Do the two firms have practices which, when combined, will create or have the potential to create a market leading practice? Or will the combined practices simply be larger, but still lack the critical mass to be competitive in the market? Do the firms bring complementary practices that can realistically be offered to clients? Would the combined firm increase its profile in key industry sectors? Would this industry profile add value to clients in that sector and attract new clients?

## 2.3 Grow with clients

Ultimately, a merger must be driven by the needs of the firm's current and future clients. If a client's business has grown rapidly a firm may find that it no longer has either the depth of experience or the breadth of practice adequately to serve the needs of that client. A merger that brings breadth and depth can help better serve (and retain) the client.

When two firms have clients in common it can help both the client and the firm. Many clients are looking to reduce the number of outside counsel they work with. Combining work in one firm can help them achieve this. It also helps the firm increase its ties to the client and solidifies the relationship.

### 2.4 Address internal issues

Finally, there are some internal factors that can contribute to a firm looking at merger. While internal factors should not be a primary driver of mergers, they can be factors that cause firms to consider merger more seriously. These can include:

### (a) Scale

Increased scale brings with it some advantages, including ability to make investments, be it in technology, process innovation, marketing initiatives or geographic expansion. In addition there can be economies of scale when it comes to costs. While there may be short-term costs associated with a merger, over the longer term the firm can reduce the cost base of the firm.

### (b) Leadership and succession

Some firms find that a merger is a viable way to address leadership and succession issues in the firm. A firm may find that there is no one interested in or capable of taking over the leadership role in the firm. This is not uncommon in closely held founder firms. In considering a merger of this type it is important to ensure there will be an adequate transition and that the clients are likely to survive the retirement of the founding partner or partners.

### (c) Catalyst for change

Some firms find that while they know they need to make certain structural changes in the firm – for example, change the partner structure, eliminate an unfunded retirement plan, close an office – they do not have the fortitude or stability to make those changes as a stand-alone firm. A merger can present the opportunity to move the firm forward and make long-needed changes.

### 3. Building a business case for merger

Once the question 'Why merge?' has been answered, it is critical to build the business case for a specific merger. First and foremost, the discipline of building the business case helps to ensure that a strong case actually exists. Sometimes it is easier to talk about the mechanics of merger than the strategy, so it is not unheard of for discussions to progress to a term sheet without having taken more than a superficial look at the business case.

Secondly, it is critical to be able to articulate the business case for the merger to various audiences during the course of discussions and after the announcement of the merger. Leaders need to build support and enthusiasm from the firm's partners by explaining the business case. Partners need to be able to explain to their clients why the merger makes sense. The chairman needs to be able to explain the rationale for the combined firm to the press and to the marketplace. Associates and staff need to understand what opportunities the combined firm will create for them.

Finally, merger discussions can fall apart when inadequate time is spent on developing the business case, because the negotiating team can lose enthusiasm when the discussions hit the first hurdle if the ultimate objective is not clearly understood and articulated.

The business case for merger starts with a clear strategy for the firm. The strategy should focus primarily on the firm's desired market position, the basis for the firm's competitiveness and differentiation in the marketplace, and the firm's target client base. The strategy should also address internal factors including talent management priorities and cultural underpinnings. A merger is a way to execute the strategy, not a strategy in and of itself. The strategic underpinnings of a business case become more complex in the context of merger because the merger needs to align with the strategy of two different firms.

The business case must address not only the current position of the combined firm, but the likely position in the evolving market. The market is moving too quickly to create a firm that is only competitive today. The firm must be competitive on a going-forward basis as well.

Key components of the business case generally include:

- Strategic aims for the combined firm:
  - basis of competitiveness;
  - market position, including future position;
  - core practices and industry sectors.
- Key practice opportunities:
  - creation of market leading practices;
  - additional depth in core practices;
  - addition of complementary practices.
- Key client opportunities:
  - opportunities to expand the relationship with existing clients through additional services, deeper services, or new geography;
  - opportunities to gain new work (including capturing recent lost opportunities);
  - potential business conflicts which will impact growth of certain practices.
- Key geographic compatibilities:
  - market position in key markets;
  - impact of expanded geography;
  - potential markets for the combined firm.
- Financial profile:
  - key performance indicators and projected performance of the combined firm;
  - merger related synergies and costs.
- Risks and obstacles:
  - key risk factors;
  - potential barriers to success.

The development of the business case will typically be an iterative process. The initial case will be developed in early meetings. Detail will be added as practice groups meet, as pro formas are developed, and as client opportunities are identified. It is important to step back periodically to ensure that the case is still as strong as initially thought, and to communicate that strength to the partners.

## 4. Effective management of the merger process

Managing the merger process is critical. Unlike a corporate merger, where the discussions and negotiations take place at the top levels and are announced to the employees and the market when it is a done deal, mergers of law firms must build support among the partners from the early stages. Not only is it important that the partners be onboard with the merger in order to achieve an effective integration but from a more practical standpoint a majority of partners, and in some firms as many as 90% of partners, must approve the combination.

While this chapter will not address the full scope of the merger process, there are four key aspects to focus on that can help to ensure a smooth process.

### 4.1 Plan the process

Not surprisingly, planning the process and the timetable is the critical first step. This includes identifying the key steps required in the different workstreams, setting the merger teams and sub teams, and establishing a desired target effective date.

The value of the planning process is that it helps to ensure that all involved recognise at the outset the scope and scale of the issues that need to be agreed, and to manage expectations among those directly involved in the discussions and the partnership at large. While discussions rarely go entirely according to plan, the merger plan can establish the framework for moving forward. Planning also helps to ensure that both firms have similar expectations of timing. If one has a greater sense of urgency than the other, both will likely be frustrated.

### 4.2 Be realistic about effort and resources

In our experience there is an almost universal underestimation of the effort and resources required to complete a merger. This can be in part related to the time required to resolve unanticipated issues, but in the main tends to be related to the underlying complexity of merging law firms and the breadth of issues that need to be addressed. The time and commitment required to complete a merger are considerable. Those involved must be able to give sufficient priority to the role or there is a high risk that the talks will drag on too long, enthusiasm and momentum will be lost and eventually the process will stall entirely.

The time commitment will vary with the role a person is playing in the process, and the size and complexity of the merger. The managing partner and/or chairman typically needs to be prepared to devote half or more of his time to the process at key stages.

Because of the time commitment required merger discussions are not something to be entered into lightly. Protracted discussions can distract the management team from other strategic initiatives and can result in the firm treading water for a period of time.

### 4.3 Anticipate and address hurdles

Hurdles and challenges are likely to arise during merger discussions. The stronger the business case and the relationship between the two firms, the more likely it is that solutions will be found. As with all aspects of negotiations the primary consideration in addressing such challenges should be maximising the competitiveness of the new firm rather than adopting the approach of one or the other firm. This is particularly true if the merged firm will be competing in a market position and be of a scale that is very different from that of either legacy firm.

There is sometimes a temptation to defer addressing some issues until after the merger has taken place. While that can be appropriate for some issues, it is important that not too many substantive issues are deferred. The drawback of deferring is that the merged firm starts life with an overly introverted focus – addressing internal issues of organisation and structure or profit sharing or management roles – rather than being focused on the far more important issues of serving existing clients, winning new work for the combined firm and creating opportunities for lawyers to work together.

## 4.4 Keep the partnership informed

Considerations such as the scale of a firm, its culture and the impact of the potential merger will influence the level and detail of communication between the firm's management and the partnership during merger discussions. Experience has shown that in most circumstances it is more effective to keep a partnership informed of progress as discussions proceed and to seek partners' input, endorsement and commitment on a step-by-step basis rather than attempting to 'sell' what may be regarded by partners as a done deal. Keeping the partnership informed and consulting as appropriate requires significant time from firm leadership but results in the case for merger being tested throughout the process and builds partner commitment.

While each firm is different, some firm leaders have found it important to have key influencers involved in the merger discussions from an early stage. This includes those who are potentially sceptical of the combination, as their early involvement in and support for the business case can be crucial for gaining overall partner support. At a minimum the sceptics and key influencers may require additional attention and communication during the merger discussions.

## 5. Merger structure and impact on business case and process

Historically, law firm mergers were expected to be fully integrated and to replicate the model that would have obtained had the firm grown organically. More recently, and particularly in the context of cross-border mergers, an increasing number of firms have adopted firm structures that facilitate cross-jurisdiction combinations. These are typically a 'Swiss verein' structure, although other forms exist as well. A verein firm effectively operates like a holding company with member firms. While the verein is governed by a board under an advise and consent type arrangement, the member firms are separate financial entities and can have their own management structure and compensation arrangements. In fact sharing of profits is prohibited, although sharing of expenses and joint ventures is permitted. Some vereins are highly integrated while others are quite loosely integrated and allow significant autonomy to the member firms. Some have two member firms, while others have many.

A verein can certainly ease some of the challenges that impact cross-border combinations. It facilitates combinations of firms who may have different fiscal years, different tax and accounting methodologies or who operate in jurisdictions with very different financial models. It is also easier to defer the resolution of some issues (eg, a common approach to compensation), as they are not required for the firms to begin operating on a side-by-side basis.

Regardless of the structure a firm might take it is important to approach the development of the business case with rigour. While there may be less immediate financial interdependence in a verein structure, there will certainly be brand interdependence. The strategy of the combined firm and the relative market positions of the member firms must be largely aligned in order to facilitate cross-servicing and cross-selling of clients. The approach to client service and the underlying culture of the firms must be compatible to facilitate strong working relationships. The financial strength is important, even with separate profit centres, because instability in one segment of the firm could be problematic for the whole firm. And comparable financial strength will be critical should the firm move to closer financial alignment at some point.

While there is a set of issues that are *verein* specific, such as the financial structure, the governing approach and structure at the global level, and even branding, we recommend that firms considering merger under a verein structure discuss and address the same issues that firms contemplating a fully integrated structure would be addressing.

## 6. Keys to effective merger execution

The key to effective merger integration is to ensure a balance between client, practice and people integration and administrative and structural integration. Too often the administrative integration becomes the primary focus, and the client, practice and people side is left to its own devices. While the firm may ultimately achieve its expected objectives it is likely to take five years instead of two. The true success of the merger will not be measured by the immediate compatibility of the voicemail system, but instead by the ability to deliver on the potential identified in the business case. This can include, for example, delivering on a competitive strength, delivering integrated services to clients across jurisdictions, and winning new work.

Throughout the integration it is important to keep the majority of the lawyers focused on continuing to serve clients. The merger should enhance client service, not distract from it, and client perceptions can be formed in those early days.

This chapter will not address the full scope of the merger execution and integration but will focus on the three aspects we find to be the most critical to success.

### 6.1 Plan the process

As with the merger process, effective planning of merger integration is critical. It helps to establish the roadmap and expectations, as well as allow the leadership of the firm to delegate where appropriate and focus on the most value added initiatives. Too often leadership gets caught up in the minutiae and then does have adequate time to address the important issues. This is not meant to diminish the importance of getting the small things right. But the big things will be the ones that make the long-term difference.

The starting point for developing the merger integration plan is to establish the gap between where the combined firm will be on day one, and where it would like to be at key future points – six months, one year, two years, and three years. Taking this approach, as opposed to focusing on the immediate steps that need to be achieved in the first 90 days, ensures a longer range outlook and plan. Of course there are aspects of the plan, particularly the administrative integration plan, which will have to be planned out week-by-week in the early stages; but the strategic plan needs a longer term focus.

While the specifics of the execution plan will depend on the size, scale and objectives of the merger, as well as whether it is a Swiss verein or similar structure, we recommend that the following be specifically addressed in the plan:

- Cultural integration:
  - definition of core values;
  - approach to client service.
- Practice group integration:
  - leadership assignments and responsibilities;
  - partner assignments and roles;
  - planning process and goal setting.
- Client integration and development:
  - integration of key client programme and client teams;
  - communication and BD plans for key clients;
  - integrated business development programme.
- Human resources:
  - partner performance expectations and metrics (typically detailed before the effective date but often requiring refinement post-merger);
  - alignment of talent management initiatives and policies;
  - alignment of recruiting initiatives.
- Communications plan:
  - clients;
  - internal;
  - market.
- Financial plan:
  - alignment of financial and billing policies;
  - alignment of metrics and reports.
- Technology and administration.

## 6.2 Be clear about expectations and success metrics

People typically have expectations, often unrealistic ones, about what the merger will deliver and when. It is critical to be clear about what the expectations are around a number of dimensions, and what metrics will be used to define success.

Financial expectations are subject to the most scrutiny, in part because they also often factor in to the public perception of the success of the merger. Setting realistic financial performance metrics and budgets for the first two years of the merger should be done in advance of the combination. The partners need to understand the underlying financial drivers and what performance levels are required to achieve the objectives.

The leadership should also set at least broad expectations and metrics around practices and clients. While it can be dangerous to be too specific (eg, expanding work for Client C by 30%), it can be useful to identify overall expectations for expansion of existing clients, winning of new matters and new clients, growth in key markets, and the like.

### 6.3    Pay attention to communications

Not surprisingly, effective communications are critical in a post-merger environment. There are at least four dimensions to consider in communications – the frequency, the content, the tone and the medium.

#### (a)    *Frequency*

Typically, firms under-communicate rather than over-communicate. Managing partners are often surprised to find that a message that they feel has been delivered has not in fact been heard by the majority of the partners (or others). It is important to keep messages simple and direct, and to communicate them more than once, sometimes in more ways than one. In the early days a weekly leadership update may be appropriate. After the first 90 days or so it may be that monthly or bi-monthly updates are enough. This should be augmented by communications from practice leaders, key client leaders and C-level staff. It can be helpful in the early days to create a schedule for communications (eg, leadership messages on Monday, practice messages on Tuesday etc).

#### (b)    *Content*

In keeping with the simple and direct idea above, it can be useful to build messages around a few key themes. These might be client successes, practice successes and a people update. If you provide too many details, the key message can get lost.

#### (c)    *Tone*

The tone of messages can make a difference. This is not just about highlighting positive messages, but also making sure that there is no 'us' versus 'them' language that slips into the messages. Emphasise the new firm that has been created. Some firms, for example, have specifically banned the use of terms like 'legacy firm', as that perpetuates a two-firm mentality longer than need be. At some point it is useful to move on from merger integration to simply firm management and planning to emphasise the future rather than the past. This point is typically after 18 to 24 months, but could be shorter in smaller combinations. When doing cross-border combinations it is also important to be culturally aware in your tone.

#### (d)    *Medium*

The appropriate vehicles for communication will depend a bit on the culture of the two firms. Typically, there is no substitute for face-to-face contact, and moving management meetings around the offices, having in-person practice group meetings, having partner retreats, and visiting other offices whenever possible provides the best forum for communication and interaction. Regular video conferences, telephone conferences, emails, or more creative things like video messages, can be effective supplements to the in-person meetings. If you are adding several time zones as part of a combination, be sensitive to that in scheduling. Do not have 'lunch time' calls if it is only lunch time in New York, as it makes people feel out of the loop.

7.    **Conclusion**

We expect merger to continue to play a significant role as the legal industry consolidates globally. In order to increase the percentage of 'Home Run' mergers (see Figure 1), leadership must increase the focus on ensuring that there is a strong business case for the merger, and that the post-merger integration is well planned and effectively executed. Too few mergers historically have succeeded on both of these dimensions and the market is less forgiving today than it was a decade or two ago.

# What can your firm do to win and keep clients today?

**E Leigh Dance**
ELD International LLC

I would not be here writing at my laptop if I could convey in a short chapter a foolproof way for your firm to win and keep more clients today. Law firm leaders think a lot about how to develop new business and may easily spot problem areas in the firm. But rarely do they proceed and shepherd sustained efforts to win and maintain successful client relationships. Training in selling services and communicating understanding of needs is important and should be a part of any firm's continuing professional development, but it is far from enough.

There is plenty of basic information available on business development fundamentals, and so this chapter will focus on some approaches your firm should be considering in today's environment.

Winning and keeping clients today is hard work – harder than a few years ago. There are more competitors, and the competitors tend to look very similar from the client's seat. Clients are far more demanding, requesting broader service capabilities and expertise at the same or lower cost. It is what it is, and if you want to gain market share and thrive in the future, your hard work will pay off.

To keep clients today, a firm and every person in it needs to communicate clearly and listen carefully to deliver what you and your clients have agreed, and do so in such a way that clients take the view that your value is well worth the cost. This chapter will expand on those core concepts and discuss a few factors important to winning and keeping clients today.

## 1. Flexibility and adaptation

There are many factors at play that affect how your firm wins and keeps clients. One of the aspects that makes your efforts a challenge is that clients are increasingly diverse, with a wide range of cultural backgrounds, ages, legal education, business needs and priorities, and often widely differing ways of working with outside counsel. All of those factors affect their approach to selecting and instructing you and your firm. You must be able quickly to understand their style and adapt, and then be ready to switch your approach for the next client you meet.

Law firms must also make careful decisions about what types of clients they really want to target. You cannot likely be all things to all people without having fees that are too high for your clients to bear. Therefore, you may need to narrow the areas where you can best compete to win the clients. Is it your global outlook, the contacts your lawyers have worldwide in every practice? Or is it certain industry or geographic expertise? Are you a short-list firm for renewable energy or the hospitality industry, or the go-to firm for expanding in Africa or southeast Asia? These are decisions firm leadership must make and lawyers in the firm must communicate in their daily interactions with clients and others in their networks.

Clients are in the driver's seat at the moment, and some are fully leveraging that position. Globalisation and information technology play a major role in law firm competition today, because they respond to changing client needs. Both of these mega trends alter the investment cost of effectively advising in certain legal practices and geographic markets. This is another reason to make tough decisions about what your firm wants to be and where firm leadership should focus its energy. The firms that have made the investment in being more globally focused – through direct presence in certain countries or through effective liaisons with lawyers elsewhere – can demonstrate how they are responding to client needs and differentiate themselves from competitors for matters with international aspects.

The firms that have invested in information technology and process management to improve how they produce and deliver legal services (not just how they manage their own finances) are immediately visible to clients. For example, a firm with client-focused reporting, budgeting and billing systems makes it easier for its client to see how various matters are progressing. Clients see that as a competitive advantage.

Some firms use IT and process tools to streamline their handling of due diligence so that a multi-country due diligence effort will be consistent and easier for the client to review and digest. Some firms gather and provide historic data to help their clients map time and cost-saving strategies for disputes and litigation. It is the IT tools and knowledge management that the firm has chosen to invest in that then enables them to differentiate their services to clients.

## 2. Creativity, discipline and persistence

In addition to your lawyer credentials, to win clients today you will need to be creative, disciplined and persistent. These credentials are increasingly expected of you. It has nothing to do with being a lawyer, except that practising these three attributes will enable you to do more of the kind of work that you love to do.

Law firm leadership can support creative problem-solving and client-focused solutions by encouraging and enabling firm disciplines such as human resources, marketing, finance and IT to work together with the legal team to deliver client-tailored services. How often does this happen in your firm? How can you make it happen? You can start by selecting a dozen of the firm's most important strategic client relationships and providing the multi-disciplinary input that can lead to excellent legal work and superb delivery.

Clients demand more transparency and predictability on timing and costs of the legal services that they hire law firms to provide. Many law firms may be roughly even in their technical legal capability for certain matters, but the differentiator lies in the firm's ability to deliver what was agreed on time and within budget. Delivering transparency and predictability is essential today, and it requires a joint and coordinated effort across many areas of the firm. Firm leadership must determine and ensure consistent delivery of a few practices, which provides the clients with the transparency and predictability they want. For this reason, project management skills have become increasingly important for lawyers.

### 3. Continual improvement in targeting and pitching

A lot of business development comes down to playing the odds. Many lawyers are dissatisfied with their ability to win clients, but in fact their error is that they do not have enough targeted prospects in the pipeline. To be successful at client development it is a requirement, not an option, for lawyers to schedule time every week, month after month, to make calls, have lunch appointments, visit clients' offices, attend social and professional events where lawyers will meet your target clients, send emails, and whatever methods work best for the fee earners to strengthen professional relationships and rapport with those prospects.

Law firms do not consistently manage practice and industry groups to do this sort of consistent development and maintain a good pipeline of prospects. Too often, business development is a hit-and-miss process where the marketing or business development staff rush to keep up with one-off requests for support (often neither strategic nor targeted) from individual lawyers. Firm management must clarify the expectations, set standards and manage them.

Developing and constantly adding to and maintaining a contacts database is an important discipline in winning clients, and is all too often neglected. I have often been shocked to find that firms with underperforming international offices have poor to non-existent contacts databases or consistent business development practices. It does not need to be costly or complicated, but it does need to happen, week to week and month to month.

It may take a few days, weeks, or even years eventually to win an instruction from a prospect. Along the way, your firm's key practices will want continuously to improve in the targeting of clients and in presenting credentials in a way that leads individuals to see the firm as a 'short list' choice for their work.

Monitoring and revising approaches is essential. Does firm leadership put enough emphasis on this area? If a particular practice or industry area leaves every meeting confident that the client was truly impressed and will give the firm some work immediately – and then nothing comes through week after week – it is time to revise the approach. More analysis of the pitch process and messages, and more business development skills training may be called for. In a small firm, invite lawyers with good business development experience to share tips, and bring along other lawyers to observe them in action. In a larger firm, the resources of the marketing and business development team must be aligned with the key growth areas so that they can provide the support needed to deliver wins.

### 4. The importance of follow through

Many lawyers make the mistake of losing touch with a client after a matter or case is finished. The firm must ensure that lawyers create regular opportunities to reach out to clients. Otherwise, your clients will lose track of your firm, think your lawyers are busy or uninterested, and you will slip from their mind. Your competitors that are better at keeping in touch will receive the next instruction.

Follow through does not have to be grandiose, and in fact it is better when it is simple enough to be carried out consistently. For example, lawyers can regularly attach a note to articles or firm newsletters of interest, for a number of clients and prospects. The firm can organise and host a simple biannual event with a group of clients and prospects, creating a tradition over time. Lawyers can keep a practice of two breakfast meetings a week, with a client, a prospect, or someone who will provide an introduction to a target client. By following through systematically, a portion of those that lawyers meet with will eventually become clients, and those that do not will likely recommend you to others.

A foundation of winning clients is to understand and effectively respond to the client's situation. Understanding the business fully is essential; perhaps more hard to grasp is understanding the environment in which your clients and prospects work – their fears, concerns and priorities. My general summary of that environment follows, taken from my extensive work with global corporate counsel.

**5.  Understand the impact of an uncertain economy**

Whether in mature or young and growing markets, when thinking about your clients' situation and how your firm can help, it is important to remember how profoundly many are affected by the uncertain economy.

Financial performance often seems to shift from one location to the next; a leading company is going through massive lay-offs one day and restructuring the next. The past instability in the global economy has led to great uncertainty among executives and employees. Employees at all levels worry about keeping their jobs. In many parts of the world, company leadership is less open to risk. Business people tend to be slower in making decisions.

In more mature markets, leaders tend to be focused on controlling the company's activities to avoid losses and distractions, as a priority over navigating growth. In emerging markets, companies are likely to have a far more opportunistic approach to growth, and research confirms there is far greater focus on transactions. Skilled in-house and outside lawyers can be in short supply and tend to be very expensive. Economic uncertainty is still present, often triggered by other uncertainties, such as political unrest or issues relating to monetary policy or infrastructure. For private practice lawyers hired by corporate counsel, it is important to understand each company's perspective and risk appetite – it is usually safe to assume that the mindset of in-house counsel will mirror that of their business leaders.

The good news is that in this uncertain environment, everyone wants a lawyer in the room. Managers at every level want to avoid mistakes that could derail the company, send the share price plummeting, or end in disputes that could slow down corporate growth for years. Since in-house lawyer demand exceeds supply and budgets are increasingly limited, there is a necessity for triage – determining what is most urgent to address. This is an opportunity for law firms, if you can convince the client that your firm can assist with responding to demand in ways that are cost effective for the client.

6. **Downward pressure on costs**

Around the world, law firms that are aiming to win new business are colliding with companies that are trying to reduce what they spend on outside counsel and other legal expenses. Legal is not the only area under the spotlight – in many companies today, the budget for all service areas is stagnant or shrinking. Finance, HR, IT support all face reductions. They are under pressure to spend less unless they can convince corporate executives that there is a viable business strategy for spending more. Entire companies are distributing more complex products and services across a far broader geography, and in many cases profit margins are shrinking since competition is fierce. As a result, all functions in the company that provide internal services are being asked to do more with less.

Given that outside counsel fees represent a large proportion of their company's legal services spend, a straightforward way for clients to respond to budget cuts is to reduce outside counsel costs. Many companies are doing this by consolidating the number of law firms that serve them, and asking each of their selected firms to provide special offers through discounts, fixed rates for certain services, valuable offerings at no cost, and other benefits. Companies talk among each other about outside counsel costs, and many in-house counsel receive higher performance evaluations and bonuses that reward their skill at lowering costs.

Since this situation will not change in the foreseeable future, everything that your firm and your lawyers work on must translate to value for your client. You may know exactly why what you do is valuable, but unless you can communicate your value in ways the client will appreciate, the client often will not recognise it on his own.

7. **Global complexity and how it affects your clients**

Doing business across borders has become increasingly complex, and that makes your client's job far more demanding than even just a few years ago. For companies large enough to have organised law departments, the individuals that run them today often focus mostly on reducing legal risk, complying with the enormous range of laws and regulations, monitoring and controlling operations to ensure compliance (often alongside a compliance function), and interacting with regulatory authorities when there are inquiries.

It is likely that most of your clients are international, in that they source components of their products outside of their headquarters (HQ) country and they distribute their products and services wider than outside of HQ country. As globally connected as the business world is, laws are still primarily local. Then there are some regional laws (European Union, for example) and some global legal bodies to complicate matters further. Your clients must make sense of all this, and if you choose to be a firm that serves international clients, your firm should position itself to help them.

In the thick of the economic downturn, a 2009 survey of senior corporate counsel in FTSE 200 companies found that in-house legal functions had more frequently changed or reduced external advisers, that the majority of senior counsel had a far more senior commercial advisory role in their companies post-crisis, and that they were under internal pressure to reduce compliance risks while providing greater coverage, better value and cost reductions.

A major study of law department leaders in multinationals in more than 30 countries worldwide (World Law Group, LexisNexis and ELD International) found that clients are juggling multiple concerns. The top four exemplify the complexity of their challenges:

- meet legal services demand given resource constraints;
- effectively cover legal risks in high-growth markets;
- manage so many compliance challenges;
- keep up with constant change in our business.

The same study found that these concerns translated to the following top priorities for 2013 and beyond: to improve their compliance capability, reduce external costs, improve their knowledge management capability (presumably to use IT in managing legal services more efficiently), and reorganise the legal function for higher performance. That is a lot of priorities to be juggling at once. Is your firm aware of your clients' priorities and actively helping address them?

When you roll together the demands on today's client to cover multiple emerging and high-growth markets, increasingly aggressive regulatory enforcement practices in many jurisdictions, the range of corporate structures they cover and the flow of new products and technologies, it all adds up to: complexity.

## 8.     Building trust

Out of this complexity, each law firm needs to build trust that your lawyers and staff will be part of the solution, rather than add to their dilemma. Outside counsel that provide legal advice that is full of legal jargon are increasingly viewed as a problem for clients. Clients are frustrated with outside lawyer advice that is lengthy and provides 101 ways of viewing a situation, yet avoids suggesting a course of action. When lawyers in your firm provide a memo or opinion that requires translation for business executives to understand, you have added to the client's problem, since it will be left to them to provide the translation.

If lawyers in your firm consistently take the time to understand what each client sees as his biggest priority and greatest concerns (is it a country? a newly acquired subsidiary? a pending regulatory inquiry? an aggressive new procurement executive?), you will have made a huge step in the right direction. But understanding is only the first step – to keep a client the firm needs to find ways to make the client's life easier and to reduce their concerns. Firms can help do this by gathering and sharing experiences and best practices, and suggesting structures that will help clients deal with various challenges.

## 9.     The increasing importance of service

Unfortunately, the comments above have relatively little to do with actual legal technical work and individual lawyering skills. The client typically has a hard time differentiating legal skill between providers that he has not worked with, and after working with your firm will then evaluate your technical legal expertise. What makes the difference in both winning clients and keeping them is the way your firm serves its clients. Most clients will differentiate the ways that your firm provides legal advice, and often it can be a tipping point in selecting a lawyer or law firm.

In my view, lawyers must earn the client's trust by demonstrating an ability to work with them to define, scope, budget and report on a matter or case. This will not be pleasant territory for many lawyers that are accustomed to receiving an instruction, doing the work as they wish, and sending an invoice. Those lawyers expect the client to have chosen them because they understand their expertise and value, and trust them to charge what is fair.

But the situation today is different, and firm leadership must set the example for lawyers to accept and take part in transformation. Too many factors combine to make it the client's responsibility to carefully monitor outside legal costs. More and more buyers of legal services today want to understand what they are buying, what it will cost, and when it will be delivered. It is that simple. Lawyers need to convince the client to spend time to answer questions that will enable your firm to define and scope a potential project or instruction. Then your firm and the legal team for the client must be able to respond with clear information, a timeline and a reasonable estimate of costs.

## 10.  Key performance indicators and the like

Law department leaders around the world will tell you that the key element – far above all others – to help them perform better is to integrate with the business. Integration with the business is facilitated by talking and acting like other parts of the business. This is the main driver of law departments' interests to use metrics and measurement to evaluate and communicate performance. It is also why in-house lawyers have accepted the necessity of cost controls, and why they have adopted project management tools and approaches sometimes far in advance of outside counsel.

While your firm is handling the define-scope-budget aspects, an important factor in winning the client is how well you can demonstrate the other ways that your lawyers and staff will meet their efficiency and productivity requirements. You will want to be able to demonstrate your firm's ability to answer questions such as the following, before the client even has to ask.

- Can you grasp and respond to my issue in context of the diverse markets in which we operate?
- Can you answer the question in more than one jurisdiction?
- Can you make your services transparent and the cost predictable?
- Can you let our team do some of the work?
- Can you provide reporting across borders that makes my job easier?

## 11.  Conclusion

To conclude this chapter on winning and keeping clients, here is a simple outline of what we have discussed. Consider using this outline as a construct for your firm's business development planning. For each of the following themes, identify what actions you will take. Then review and prioritise; gain input and revise; and finalise your plan, with a timeline and calendar.

- Core concepts of winning and keeping clients include:
  - flexibility and adaptation to diverse clients;
  - globalisation and IT mega trends;
  - creativity, discipline and persistence;
  - continual improvement in targeting and pitching;
  - consistent follow through.
- To determine the right approach to win and keep a client requires understanding:
  - the impact of our uncertain economy;
  - reasons for downward pressure on costs;
  - global complexity and how it affects your clients;
  - fundamentals of earning the client's trust.
- Today's legal services provider focuses more on service to win clients:
  - why service delivery aspects have become nearly as important to clients as technical legal skill;
  - demonstrating your ability to define, scope, budget and report;
  - incorporating key performance indicators into the legal service.

We have covered a lot of territory. Particular elements of the advice provided here on winning and keeping clients today will resonate with some; other elements will be more meaningful to others. What is important is to map out a plan for your practice, get input from peers and business development professionals, and get started.

# Corporate reputation: definitions and dimensions

**Will Harvey**
University of Exeter Business School; Centre for Corporate Reputation,
Saïd Business School, University of Oxford
**Tim Morris**
Centre for Corporate Reputation, Saïd Business School, University of Oxford
**Michael Smets**
Novak Druce Centre for Professional Service Firms, Saïd Business School,
University of Oxford

## 1.  Introduction

Research in the field of management on the concept of reputation has drawn on several disciplines including economics, sociology and psychology. Each discipline has contributed to the definitions of the concept that exist in management. For example, economics focuses on the relationship of reputation and firm performance and sociology focuses on status and legitimacy of organisations in particular fields. The management literature has built upon these core disciplines to develop the concept of reputation in terms of quality, prominence (or familiarity) and in terms of esteem (or favourability) among a set of organisational stakeholders. Recent theoretical and empirical work has acknowledged that while the concepts derive from different disciplines, there are connections and overlaps between them (eg, D Lange, PM Lee, and Y Dai (2011) "Organizational Reputation: A Review", *Journal of Management*, 37(1): 153–84).

## 2.  Reputation: definitions and dimensions

There have been a number of attempts at defining reputation that suggest that the concept has three important attributes. First, reputation is based on the perception of stakeholders towards organisations; secondly, it is based on the perception of internal and external stakeholders; and thirdly, it is a comparative measurement made in relation to competitors or the relevant peer group (CJ Fombrun (1996) *Reputation: Realizing Value from the Corporate Image*, Cambridge, MA: Harvard Business School Press). Reputations can be positive or negative, but are generally stable and enduring rather than changing with each event or new piece of information. Others have argued that it is not feasible to talk of an aggregate reputation among a diverse set of stakeholders, because each stakeholder may have different concerns and ways of interpreting the focal firm's behaviour. For instance, the firm could be highly profitable and viewed favourably by investors but have a reputation as a tough employer and be viewed less favourably in the labour market. Therefore, reputation must be stakeholder-specific (M Jensen, H Kim, and BK Kim (2012) "Meeting Expectations: A Role-theoretic Perspective on Reputation", in ML Barnett, and TG

Pollock (Eds), *The Oxford Handbook of Corporate Reputation*: 140–59, Oxford: Oxford University Press). Fombrun recently proposed a definition of reputation which aims to address these points:

> *A corporate reputation is a collective assessment of a company's attractiveness to a specific group of stakeholders relative to a reference group of companies with which the company competes for resources* (CJ Fombrun (2012) "The Building Blocks of Corporate Reputation: Definitions, Antecedents, Consequences", in ML Barnett and TG Pollock (Eds), *The Oxford Handbook of Corporate Reputation*: 100, Oxford: Oxford University Press).

Thus, reputation focuses on the distinctiveness of a focal organisation from others in its peer group and its attractiveness to external stakeholders (A Bitektine (2011) "Toward a Theory of Social Judgments of Organizations: The Case of Legitimacy, Reputation, and Status", *Academy of Management Review*, 36(1): 151–79). Further, by focusing on attractiveness to stakeholders, this definition proposes that reputation is something which organisations project from within, but which is judged from the outside. It is a socio-cognitive concept based on peer group perceptions, or what is called a social fact (VP Rindova, IO Williamson, and AP Petkova (2010) "Reputation as an Intangible Asset: Reflections on Theory and Methods in Two Empirical Studies of Business School Reputations, *Journal of Management*, 36(3): 610–19) and the signals that an organisation sends are important for building reputation among external stakeholders (DD Bergh, DJ Ketchen, BK Boyd,, and J Bergh (2010) "New Frontiers of the Reputation–Performance Relationship: Insights from Multiple Theories", *Journal of Management*, 36(3): 620–32). Reputation develops over time, reflecting past behaviours or outcomes that are salient to stakeholders. In other words, in judging a firm's reputation, stakeholders are selective in the information they use and the inferences they make about that information. Underlying this process of judgement, stakeholders assume that the present and future behaviour of a firm can be assessed by looking at its past performance (however defined). The notion that under conditions of imperfect information the past is a guide to the future explains why reputation is important.

Other work has noted that the concept of reputation incorporates different dimensions (see Table 1) and unfortunately there has been something of a proliferation of terms in defining these dimensions. Barnett *et al.* (M Barnett, J Jermier and B Lafferty (2006) "Corporate Reputation: The Definitional Landscape", *Corporate Reputation Review*, 9(1): 26–38: 32) summarise the different ways in which reputation is defined by suggesting that stakeholders have three levels of engagement with reputation: reputation as a state of awareness, reputation as an assessment and reputation as an asset. Awareness is when actors know of a focal organisation's name or logo, but make no judgement about its activities. Assessment implies more than awareness, as stakeholders judge the attributes or quality of the focal organisation. Asset refers to the proposition that a corporate reputation holds a particular value for the focal firm. Lange *et al.* (2011) summarise the definitional landscape in a way that substantially overlaps with the above typology, suggesting that being 'known', being 'known for something' and 'generalised favourability' are three significant dimensions for building reputation. Being known is when different stakeholders are familiar with the activities, products and services of an organisation, and the reputation of the organisation tends to be stronger when different stakeholders have a broad awareness as well as a distinct understanding of its activities. This form of reputation is also referred to as prominence. Being known for something is when a particular aspect of the organisation is of interest to or holds value for a stakeholder, and an organisation holds a reputation for something such as producing high-quality products. This form of reputation is referred to as quality. Generalised favourability is a broad assessment of the organisation based on multiple as opposed to specific attributes. These multiple attributes are aggregated into a single judgement, which varies depending on the stakeholder.

Rindova *et al.* (VP Rindova, IO Williamson, AP Petkova, and JM Sever (2005) Being Good or Being Known: An Empirical Examination of the Dimensions, Antecedents, and Consequences of Organizational Reputation", *Academy of Management Journal*, 48(6): 1033–49) compress the definition of reputation somewhat, proposing that there are essentially two dimensions that they call quality and prominence. Perceived quality is defined as how stakeholders evaluate the particular attributes of organisations (similar to Lange *et al*'s concept of being known for something) and prominence is defined as a collective awareness and recognition that an organisation has accumulated in its field (similar to Lange et al.'s concept of being known) (see also Rindova *et al.* 2010).

One issue which is pertinent to professional service firms is the level at which reputation is judged. It is clear that much of the work on reputation discusses corporate reputation, or the reputation of the overall organisation, such as Ford or Coca Cola, or Enron. However, given the breadth and diversity of many large organisations and the multiple brands and different environments in which they operate, it makes sense to disaggregate reputation under certain circumstances, notably where the core operating organisation is not closely associated with its parent, or where its brands are run autonomously from other parts of the organisation. GE or Coke's multiple businesses might be a case in point. (Furthermore it is worth noting that brand represents the internal efforts to project a statement about the value or benefits of a product or service but this is not the same as reputation, which is based on external perceptions.)

For professional service firms, which are often a relatively loose confederation of different practices and driven by the expertise, efforts and connections of individual partners, the notion of a unitary corporate reputation may therefore make little sense. Indeed, it can be argued that professional service firms are essentially built by the interaction of individual and corporate reputations. Partners win business based on their own market reputations but are aided by the reputation of their firm; in turn, the firm's reputation is sustained by the actions of its individual partners. The dynamics of this interaction will depend on how far the firm is internally integrated, shares work and projects a unified image.

Finally, it is worth noting that reputation is closely linked to the concept of status. Status is based on possession of desirable or socially approved attributes and the status of an organisation is defined by how closely it can demonstrate those appropriate attributes. Such attributes might include where a corporation is listed or with whom it is associated. Indeed, status is frequently generated by association with others who already have some form of status, such as by doing business with high-status partners, by having high-status advisors or bankers and by hiring high-status directors. Status is somewhat different from the concept of reputation insofar as it is based on similarity or convergence around a set of attributes rather than positive difference, which is at the heart of a strong reputation. However, the concept of status is extremely useful because it emphasises how reputation is not simply built on the actions of the focal organisation, but is influenced by the way in which intermediaries, recommenders or connectors provide information about it to external parties. Again, incomplete information is key here: in such circumstances, these third parties are filling in the gaps by summarising relevant information and offering judgements to others about the reputation of the organisation.

### 3.     Reputation in professional service firms (PSFs)

'Reputation' and 'quality' are often assumed to be one and the same in relation to professional service firms. We set out to test this assumption by exploring how far reputation was matched by the quality of projects in a leading international management consultancy and found that the reputation of the firm by no means necessarily aligns with the quality and success of its projects. Not only is the relationship between reputation and quality uncertain in management consultancies, the process of building and sustaining reputation is complex and various. It is a process of overriding importance to both consultancies and clients and demands to be better understood and carefully managed.

### 4.     The relationship between reputation and quality in PSFs

#### 4.1     Reputation matters to firm and client alike

To date, most of the evidence used to analyse issues of reputation and quality has focused on consumer products where reputation is strongly aligned with the actual physical quality of the product. However, the role of reputation in the professional service sector, where judgements of quality are far harder to make, is much more complicated. The 'products' in PSFs consist of complex, customised solutions devised for clients who themselves are often required to play a key collaborative role in helping create them.

Beyond this there are other uncertainties. One is the lack of institutional standards in the profession such as legal regulation, fee rates and necessary qualifications. Another is 'transactional uncertainty'. This refers to the way in which 'experience goods' cannot be inspected, compared or controlled for quality by the client in advance. In choosing between competing professional service organisations, therefore, the client often has to fall back on other signals, notably reputation.

Reputation is important in other ways for PSFs, in that it helps guarantee a continuing flow of business. Professional service clients experience a high degree of risk at the point of purchase. They will be tempted to repeat purchases with a highly regarded professional service organisation because this reduces the uncertainty of switching to an untried and untested firm.

## Table 1: Summarising the reputation terminology

| *Lange* et al. (2011) | *Being known for something* | *Being known* | *Generalised favourability* |
|---|---|---|---|
| | When different stakeholders are familiar with the activities, products and services of an organisation. | When a certain organisational attribute holds particular interest or value for different stakeholders. | A broad comparative assessment of an organisation based on multiple attributes which are aggregated into one single judgement. |
| *Rindova* et al (2005) | *Perceived quality* | *Prominence* | *Favourability not defined* |
| | How stakeholders evaluate a particular organisational attribute. | Collective awareness and recognition that an organisation has accumulated in its organisational field. | Not defined. |
| Rindova *et al.* (2007) (VP Rindova, AP, Petkova and S Kotha (2007) "Standing Out: How New Firms in Emerging Markets Build Reputation", Strategic Organization, 5(1): 31–70) | *Quality not defined*<br><br>Not defined. | *Prominence not defined*<br><br>Not defined. | *Favourability*<br><br>More difficult to build than visibility and therefore potentially more valuable (see also Greenwood *et al.*, 2005). |
| *Definition* | *Quality* | *Prominence* | *Favourability* |
| | When a firm is known in the client universe (potential, existing and former clients) for having expertise in certain areas. | When a firm achieves high attention among a broader group of stakeholders and they understand who the firm is and what work it does as well as its claimed competencies. | When a firm is generally well regarded by particular clients, in relation to its competitors, in specific industries. |

In addition, reputation plays an important role in PSFs' own labour market. The work of PSFs involves delivering knowledge-intensive services, whose knowledge is embedded in professional staff and delivered through individuals and teams of employees interacting with clients. Hiring and retaining professional staff of the appropriate quality is therefore critical to the competitiveness of PSFs, especially as such staff are relatively mobile.

In short, reputation matters a great deal for both PSFs and their clients. This is broadly accepted, but how reputation is formed and what specific aspects of reputation are particularly critical in choosing PSFs are little understood. The received view rests on two untested assumptions, both of which merit challenge: first, that that reputation and service quality are identical and, secondly, that a PSF's reputation is the same for all its stakeholders.

## 4.2    Quality is an uncertain quantity

There have been few attempts to link the quality of project delivery of professional service firms to their reputation, but the general assumption seems to be that reputation is built through consistently delivering high-quality services. Once a firm's reputation is established, so the thinking goes, there are spillover effects that it can exploit in new practice areas that, if successfully developed, can further generate or consolidate its reputation. The process can be illustrated as follows:

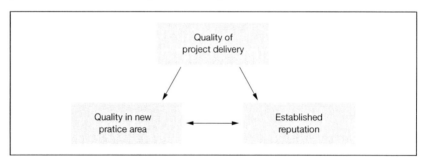

However, before accepting this model at face value a number of qualifications need to be made. Reputation is most strictly applicable in situations when transactions of the same kind are repeated. Even then, reputation is only strictly relevant if processes are the same across all transactions, and in the case of professional service firms no project is ever exactly the same as another in aims, content, delivery or personnel.

Overall, there are two main dimensions to service quality. The first is 'technical quality', which refers to the core service being delivered. The second is 'functional quality', namely how the service is delivered. The quality of what is delivered may be very different from how it is delivered. The two dimensions are not mutually exclusive and each affects how clients perceive the quality of the other.

The distinction between the two dimensions matters, however, because they demand different skills. Technical competency depends on firms applying their core knowledge and skills to deliver tangible results to clients. Functional competency depends far more on interpersonal skills, style of delivery and expectation management. In both cases, however, managing relationships is critical and effective, and regular communication between the service provider and the client is important for instilling trust and reducing the risk of failure in the relationship.

In transactions with PSFs, clients are exposed to considerable risks in terms of the confidentiality, integrity and commitment of a consultant. Keeping promises has therefore been singled out as the most important aspect of engagement success. Relationships between PSFs and clients demand empathy, responsiveness and reliability – with reliability often cited as the most important dimension.

### 5.    Choosing a consultancy: the interplay of networks, trust and knowledge

Three factors are of overriding importance in helping build reputation among PSF stakeholders: networks, trust and knowledge.

### 5.1    Networks are key

Client and employee alumni networks can result in significant financial returns. According to one recent survey of management consultancy firms across three different countries, some 80 to 85% of their fees resulted from such networks. Networks not only generate positive word of mouth, but are even more important when one takes into account clients' tendency to repeat purchases and their resistance to competitive offers. However, while the importance of networks is generally accepted, the interaction between reputation and trust is less well-understood.

### 5.2    Two types of trust

As noted, projects within the professional service sector are particularly difficult for clients to evaluate. How do consumers not trained in law, for instance, know whether they actually received the best legal advice? As a result, clients have to rely heavily on their trust in the service provider. There are two important types of trust that management consultancies need to nurture: 'competence trust', which rests on the service provider possessing the necessary qualifications, skills and capabilities to fulfil a particular task, and 'goodwill trust', which turns on the moral and ethical commitment of service providers not to behave opportunistically.

Competence trust is more one-sided and easier to signal and recognise, whereas goodwill trust is more reciprocal and therefore involves the motives and actions of both parties. Clients may trust a firm to deliver a high-quality project, but not necessarily that it will treat its information confidentially. Moreover, different projects demand different types of trust. Clients may be more interested in competence trust in short-term strategy projects than long-term cost-cutting projects, where they may be more interested in goodwill trust.

The relationship between trust and reputation is problematic in other ways. A client may be well satisfied with how a management consultancy has used their confidential information on a particular strategy project, and this will help to instil trust. However, this is only the first step. The firm needs to exhibit consistent behaviour over time in different projects to build this form of reputation on a solid basis.

## 5.3    Knowledge trade-offs

Clients' choice of management consultancies is not only influenced by networks and the types of trust they inspire, but also the type of knowledge involved in the project. Projects which demand a greater degree of client-specific and client-intensive knowledge tend to be placed with existing consultants. This is not to say that clients are not open to working with new management consultants, but there is a strong preference towards using consultants with whom they have established business relationships when the project involves sensitive information. In contrast, in projects that are more functional and industry-specific, clients often prefer to use external consultants with whom they hold looser business relationships. In short, the type of knowledge that a particular project entails has important implications.

When clients are reaching decisions about which management consultants to use, they often have to make trade-off choices between the type of knowledge and the level of confidentiality. If they are less concerned about innovative knowledge, but confidentiality is a key factor, they will err on the side of using established consultants and prefer 'goodwill trust'. In contrast, when clients are more concerned about innovative knowledge and confidentiality is not so important, they will err on the side of using new consultants and prefer 'competency trust'. The process can be summarised as follows:

**Table 2: Client criteria for choosing a consulting firm**

| Choice of management consultants | Established management consultants | New management consultants |
|---|---|---|
| Type of knowledge | Less innovative knowledge | More innovative knowledge |
| Level of confidentiality | High | Low |
| Form of trust | Goodwill trust | Competency trust |

To an extent, therefore, clients could be said to act rationally in their choices of management consultancies. But in other ways they appear to be driven more at random. This is one of the reasons why clients typically rely on other criteria, in particular reputation, as a signal of quality, even though reputation is not necessarily synonymous with quality.

In order to study the significance of reputation and the process of reputation formation across different competencies and stakeholder groups we looked at a global management consultancy, examining offices in various countries and markets and interviewing clients, key 'gate-keepers' and other employees and alumni.

## 6.    Findings

### 6.1    Reputation helps get firms through the door but does not guarantee quality

A strong reputation undoubtedly helps consultancies get to the starting line in the race to win a project. Both internal and external stakeholders frequently referred to the tendering process as a 'beauty contest' implying that invited participants need a minimum reputation simply to be considered. However, once a certain level of reputation is reached, the quality of particular projects is not taken into account because it is assumed that if a firm has an excellent reputation then it must be delivering high-quality projects. Consequently, firms with strong reputations do not need to exceed the expectations of clients and can afford occasionally to get away with lower quality.

## 6.2 Quality and reputation are not a two-way street

Reputation affects how quality is perceived and judged; and client expectations are driven by a firm's reputation, and influence clients' views of the quality and success of a project. But the converse is not necessarily true.

## 6.3 Reputation is not a monolith

Consultancies have multiple reputations. Firms' reputations not only vary widely among clients and potential clients but even, we found, within the consultancy itself. Even its own employees' assessments of functional expertise, quality and reputation varied significantly, and they identified a wide variety of different reputations based on factors such as office location, the respondents' area of expertise or their positions in the company.

## 6.4 Networks are key transmitters

The relationship between consultant and client may transcend the purely commercial and become a strong personal relationship. This is important not only in generating repeat work from the client but in referrals. Consultants and clients both agreed that strong referral networks are important for securing projects, and some even felt that reputation built through networks is a more decisive factor than quality when clients are deciding which firm to choose for a project. Networks can help overcome a lack of information and experience in selecting a competent supplier. In this regard, the reputation of the network connecting the client and the consulting firm acts as a critical factor in selection.

## 6.5 Reputation 'stickiness' is an issue

One problem with transferring reputation from the firm to a specific project team is 'reputation stickiness', whereby clients are unable or unwilling to transfer reputation from one type of work to another until they are clear that the firm holds an established position in that service line. In cases of uncertainty, clients will tend to opt for firms who have established reputations in those areas to minimise risk.

## 6.6 Project 'match' also counts

Reputation is important, but during the tendering process potential clients become more interested in the potential quality of the project. At this stage the focus of the firm's reputation shifts significantly from the firm to the project team. Clients not only focus on how their project needs tally with what the consultancy is proposing in terms of the process of addressing the project goals, but also whether the experience and skills of the firm's proposed project team fits with the needs of the project.

The seniority of the consulting team is an important proxy for skill and experience. Consulting firms with weaker reputations often have to allocate more senior and expensive consultants than those consulting firms with stronger reputations. In turn, this affects the relative profitability of the consultancies, with the more reputable firms able to generate greater profits per assignment on average. Higher profitability in turn also attracts higher quality staff who see the opportunity for greater earnings from higher profits, thus setting in motion a virtuous circle arising from reputation in both labour and client markets.

### 6.7 Consistency in delivery is key

The consistency of project delivery is an important bridge between quality and reputation. The view of the quality of project delivery by the firm, particularly in its core markets, was not always consistent in all its international offices. Although the firm's reputation for particular projects was very strong across a range of clients, this was not the case among all clients and for all competencies. Consequently, clients often received mixed signals about what to expect from the firm, and to resolve these differences consistency in delivery is essential.

### 6.8 Clients use consultancies' reputations as signals about themselves

Some clients seem more interested in which management consultancy delivers the project rather than what they deliver, because they want to signal to external stakeholders such as board members and the media that they are taking a particular issue seriously by hiring a market leader. Often clients also need to validate their own policies or proposals or obtain an insurance stamp in case problems crop up later.

### 6.9 Client expectations are on the rise

Both clients and consultancy employees agreed on this point. Many clients had previously worked in the management consultancy sector and therefore had an intimate understanding of the industry and what they can realistically expect in terms of price, consultancy team and quality. However, firms who had extensive alumni networks had an advantage because they had established strong ties with clients and potential clients.

### 7. The lessons

- In practice, quality and reputation are by no means aligned. For instance, one consequence is that firms with strong reputations, can get away with poorer quality service, and a strong reputation can buffer firms against mistakes. In contrast, firms with weaker reputations not only have to work harder but often over-deliver on the quality of projects. That said, quality and reputation can also diverge due to the conflicting interests of clients (who are looking for both high quality and low costs from consultancy firms) and consultancies (who are looking for high returns from their clients and clients who are simply satisfied with adequate quality).

- There can be damaging repercussions for consultancies whose reputation does not keep pace with their quality of service. Our subject firm experienced great difficulties winning bids against competitors, even though the client considered them in certain contexts as delivering the best quality, because other competitors had a stronger reputation. Firms with strong reputations are able to expand into practice areas in which they are not necessarily strong, while firms with less strong reputations cannot diversify so successfully. One consequence is that firms with less strong reputations may lose the opportunity to bid for larger projects in which several practices are involved.

- Building and sustaining reputation is a many-sided, open-ended activity and demands continuous sophisticated management. Consultancies need to decide exactly what reputation and, more specifically, what aspects of reputation they wish to communicate and then clearly project these to both their internal and external stakeholders through the three interrelated channels of signalling, networks and client relationships. Consultancies also need to focus on the functional as well as the technical aspects of their projects – the 'how' as well as the 'why' and the 'what'. Trust and knowledge are key. So, in parallel with this they need to develop trust of two different kinds: 'competence' trust and 'goodwill' trust. And, on an individual basis, project by project, they must ensure they apply the types and levels of knowledge demanded.

# Reputation and relationship capital of law firms

**Philip Rodney**
Burness Paull

## 1. Introduction

According to Benjamin Franklin:

*Glass, china and reputation are easily cracked and never well mended.*

But what does 'reputation' mean in the context of a law firm? In their paper "Reputation and Performance in Large Law Firms", Michael Smets, William Morris and Tim Morris suggest that it is:

*... a signalling device that serves as a proxy for the quality of a firm's products, strategies and employees relative to its competitors, when communicating with clients and other stakeholders.*

This is as elegant a definition as one can find for a quality which is quite ephemeral in nature. The reality is that when applied to the supply of legal services, reputation is difficult to measure objectively. Like the proverbial elephant, it is something that you know when you see it. In the context of a law firm, reputation is a multi-faceted quality. Some elements can be benchmarked, whereas others are subjective. Some elements can be built up; others are there as a default but can be lost. Reputation is arguably the most important factor that a potential client takes into account in selecting and appointing a law firm. It is generally more important than price. No matter how low a firm's fees are, if it has a poor reputation, in practice it will not be considered by a general counsel. Likewise, it is an extremely important facet for a potential employee when selecting the firm that they want to invest in for their career.

Reputation is not marketing; but reputation can be marketed either overtly or passively.

Nor is reputation a synonym for branding. Brand is a physical manifestation of a firm's identity. It focuses on what the firm wants to project to its audience. Reputation, on the other hand, is about how the world sees the firm. Ed Wesemann writes in his article in the *Edge International Review* about what reputation really means. He says:

*"In short, brand is what the firm says about itself and reputation is what others say about the firm ... both are intangibles that are based on perceptions. And both therefore, can be created, changed and damaged."*

Because they are based on perceptions, reputations do not always have to be based on actual client experience. We have all heard comments about businesses that we have never worked with. Notwithstanding that we have not actually engaged with them, they will have a reputation in our eyes. Once we have heard something about a business, it is difficult to distance ourselves from it. While it may not be a personal experience for us, it becomes part of the framework within which we operate. It is also difficult to shift people from their perceptions, particularly if the perception is a negative one. That is the power and the danger of reputation.

Advertising is also not reputation. It may, however, be a way of communicating reputation.

Early in my career, I worked in a small law firm which would nowadays be termed a 'boutique'. The senior partner was very disdainful of marketing, to the extent that partners were forbidden to have business cards. But reputation was of key importance to him. Reputation for him and the firm was grounded in ethics and the quality of advice and delivery.

Reputation is also reflective in nature. If the reputation is exceptionally high, then clients can see it is a signal that relates to themselves. If the firm they instruct has a strong reputation, that in turn builds on the client's reputation. The reflective nature of reputation can therefore lead to a stronger connection with the client.

In this chapter, we look at the constituent parts of reputation, and why it is important.

The constituent parts of reputation for a law firm are disparate and unlimited. Some of the elements that would appear to be important are as follows:

- ethics;
- authenticity;
- uniqueness;
- quality and consistency of advice;
- quality and consistency of service delivery;
- quality and consistency of teams;
- relationship with staff;
- engagement with the community.

One has to distinguish between the componentry of reputation and the ways in which you build it. Later we look at the ways in which you can do this. Again, the list is not exclusive. Some elements are:

- directories;
- relationships with the media;
- seminars/awards;
- corporate social responsibility (CSR) programmes;
- staff advocacy;
- client advocacy.

We also look at how one can set up systems to ensure that reputation is improved and preserved.

Finally, we examine ways in which reputation can be lost and the strategies for dealing with reputational crises.

2.      **What is reputation?**

Before embarking on an examination of reputation, it is very important to examine a dynamic that is at play. When looking at reputation in the context of legal advisers, it comprises two elements. There is that part of reputation that relates to the firm and that part which connects with the individual lawyer who is delivering the service.

Which is the 'lead' and which is the 'lag' element will depend on the actual circumstances. So, for instance in relation to a specialist area of practice such as pensions or defamation, the individual lawyer supported by a strong firm is likely to attract a client. Where the service being provided is more generic, the reputation of the firm itself is more likely to be the determining factor.

Of course, one cannot over-generalise, but it is important to recognise the two elements.

In the best situation, the mixture of the reputations of the individual and the law firm create an alchemy. So, a pensions lawyer with strong market recognition in a firm with a developed profile in the financial services market is likely to build a better reputation than if they were in a firm with perceived expertise in, say, insurance.

Law firms are likely to build their reputation on their core competencies. The expression that 'one has to be famous for something' resonates here. Where one has recognised expertise in an area, it is easier to build a reputation there, rather than try to establish it in another field.

It is also easier to build a reputation in an area that is consistent with the established expertise that the firm has established already.

While it was an iconic destination in New York, Maya Schaper's cheese and antiques shop could not make enough money and closed its doors in 2008. Likewise, it will inevitably be much harder building a reputation in two areas of legal practice that do not have a natural connection.

Where a firm has built up a reputation in one area, can this be transferred to other legal practices? It does not automatically follow that because a law firm has a positive reputation in one area that this will transfer to another. Where there is uncertainty that a firm has a strong reputation in a second area of law, it is much more likely that a client will look for a firm with specialist expertise in that specific field.

3.      **Why is reputation important?**

This might sound like a trite question, but it is worth stopping to take stock.

While reputation is important when one is buying a physical object, it is much more so when it comes to sourcing professional services. One cannot touch or examine them. A lot is taken on trust. Reputation is therefore an extremely important analog which is used when deciding which law firm to instruct or at least shortlist. Why would one include Firm X on the short list, but not Firm Y? The most likely reason is that one has a better reputation than the other. Reputation is therefore a way of making the market aware of the firm without advertising.

In their article, "Reputation, Diversification and Organizational Explanations of Performance in Professional Service Firms", Greenwood, Li, Prakash and Deephouse say that reputation offers professional service firms three benefits:

- The ability to hire the very best candidates: firms with the best reputations will have the pick of those in the job market. They will also be able to recruit at lower cost.
- Lower marketing costs: clients actively seek higher status firms rather than those firms having to look for the business.
- The ability to charge premiums because of their brand.

In many instances, it will be hard for clients to differentiate law brands. The differentiator that reputation provides can translate into the firm's competitive advantage.

What is interesting is that in their paper, Smets *et al* conclude from their research that there is a stronger relationship between reputation and profit than reputation and fee income. Why is this the case? Their view is that reputation may be an important source of competitive advantage for leading firms, but it seems to offer little leverage for others. Why would this be so? It seems logical that when one is buying vanilla services or is driven by price, reputation will be of less importance than in situations where general counsel first focus on quality for complex, high-value transactions.

Reputation also assists in cross-selling.

The brand effectively provides a security blanket which the client is prepared to pay for. ('Nobody ever got fired for hiring IBM.') It may therefore provide an opportunity to sell other services.

However, 'stickiness' of reputation is a complex topic for the increasingly more sophisticated buyer of legal services. The reputation is more likely to translate into services with some connection – whether by reference to skill or sector.

## 4.     The components of reputation

Reputation is undoubtedly a part of brand. However, reputation does not equal brand. One only has to remember the demise of Arthur Andersen to understand this. Arguably, Arthur Andersen was the strongest brand among the 'Big Five' global accountancy firms. However, the Enron scandal and its impact on Arthur Andersen's reputation effectively put the firm out of business. What we learn from that episode is that no matter how much one might spend on promoting a brand, if its ethics are perceived as materially tarnished, so is its reputation. In an extreme situation such as Arthur Anderson, the firm will not survive. Ethics therefore are a fundamental element of reputation.

Ensuring that the ethics of a firm are never compromised is something that will be core to its reputation. Ethics are not an adjunct to the firm, but its very cornerstone.

Supporting the ethics of the firm requires policies and practices that are robust and cannot be compromised. This necessitates systems that are rooted in every aspect of the firm, and cannot be overlooked or bypassed. There must be a regime where identifying potential problems that could impact on the ethics of the firm is in the forefront of the minds of everyone in the organisation. This requires dedicated and constant training on conflicts of interest, anti-money laundering etc. It is important to have a dedicated, independent and respected team within the firm that can be scrambled at any time to examine conflicts of interest or any other issue that could impinge on the reputation of the firm. When it comes to dealing with these issues, there can be no compromises. Bending the rules to allow the firm to accept an instruction is not only ethically wrong, it is something that could irreparably damage the firm's reputation. The decision of that team therefore has to be final.

It is not only important to identify and deal with issues that arise, but also to learn from them. Having a system in place whereby learning is shared with the firm at large is more likely to ensure that the problem will not be encountered again.

Creating a culture where any errors identified are immediately and transparently addressed is also an important element of the firm's ethical reputation. Again, having a culture where the focus is not on blaming people for errors, but rather on supporting them is more likely to create a system where ethical issues are resolved constructively and swiftly. Where an error is identified, it is good practice to bring in another lawyer to manage the issue. That ensures objectivity and also provides support for the lawyer who may be compromised.

The reputation of a law firm must be authentic. That means not projecting what will go down well in the market, but rather the firm's true values. This ties into the next element – uniqueness. To distinguish the firm in the market and establish distinctiveness in its reputation, one has to identify what it is that defines the firm. This is likely to be a combination of a number of factors – its sector focus, its service lines, its client base, its people, its successes. The list is not closed.

In developing its distinctiveness, it may also be as important to identify what the firm does not do, as much as what it does. If a firm pretends that it is operating in an area where it does not have expertise, this will detract from its reputation in other areas where its performance is renowned.

Quality in advice, service delivery and the teams are all obviously very important components of reputation. But, of equal importance is consistency. The market will always have a tendency to look at the lowest common denominator. So, for example, if one office or one service line is perceived not to be of the same quality as provided elsewhere in the firm, it is by that lower standard that the firm will be judged.

The raison d'etre of a law firm is to sell legal services. It is therefore fundamental to its reputation that both the substantive advice provided and the service delivery are better than those of its peers.

The reputation that a firm has with its clients, is obviously of key importance. However, while all firms talk about being client facing, that is not the only important relationship that reinforces the reputation of a firm.

The reputation that the firm has in engaging with its team members is of enormous importance. To be a successful law firm, we have to be able not only to attract, but also retain the very best staff. So, reputation among them is of equal importance. That reputation may be about certain abstract concepts, such as being supportive, fair-minded, having a stimulating place to work. It is also about the more tangible elements such as pay, benefits, physical environment etc.

It is one thing to read about the deals that a firm is involved with, the PEP its partners are enjoying, its clients' wins etc. The firm's reputation will not be sustainable if at the same time posts on Roll on Friday demonstrate that morale is low, there is a loss of faith in management or that staff are poorly treated.

Nowadays, it is also not sufficient that there is a satisfactory relationship between a law firm, its clients and its staff. The reputation has to be one that is recognised by the community at large. A successful law firm must also be regarded as a good citizen. This means that a firm has to be seen to be putting something back into society. This can be done in a number of ways. But the essential point is that as part of its reputation, a firm has to be able to show that it is not just taking from the community, but is also giving. Engaging with the community is what our clients do. We have to be measured by the same standard.

## 5. How does one build reputation?

In the previous section, we looked at the behaviours that comprise reputation. Now we look at some of the processes that can be followed to build and maintain reputation. Again, the list is not exclusive.

### 5.1 Directories

Law directories provide some form of benchmarking of the profile of firms. While not scientific, they do depend on client and peer analysis of individual firms in different practice areas. These assessments, by their very nature, will be subjective. However, if one steps back and considers the results, they do provide a surprisingly accurate measurement of the skills and standing of individual law firms.

Directories are clearly indicators of reputation which are of importance in the eyes of existing and potential clients and team members.

There can be some time lag between the development of expertise and market position in a law firm, and that then being picked up by the legal directories. To climb the directory rankings can therefore be a slow process. It is necessary to make a case for the firm and to be able to vouch for this by client feedback. Again, a firm is much more likely to climb the directory rankings if it can demonstrate expertise in a limited number of fields rather than attempt to do so in all.

### 5.2 The media

Reputations can be strengthened through engagement with the media in a number of ways.

First of all, a firm can be identified as being thought leaders in particular areas of practice. Being recognised as the leaders in a particular area and providing commentary will support reputation.

Engagement with the media is important in another way. If there is a situation where something negative impacts on a law firm, it is imperative that the media gives you a platform to explain your position and provides a fair hearing. You can achieve this by building up relations with the media beforehand.

There is a temptation to focus only on the legal media. These journals are read by some general counsel. However, most of our clients are as likely to be influenced by coverage in the business pages of newspapers and magazines.

It is important therefore to identify the business pages of newspapers and sector magazines that your stakeholders read and then develop your reputation through engaging with them. This can be through communicating news about the firm, or articles demonstrating that you are regarded as leading commentators in areas that are relevant to your audience.

### 5.3 Seminars

Likewise, speaking at seminars can assist in developing a profile and reputation. These can help an individual or a firm to demonstrate that they are leaders in a particular field. However, presentations should be focused on your target audience and relevant seminars must themselves have credibility. If the platform is correct, seminars can be an effective way of building reputation in specialist fields.

### 5.4 Awards

Awards have become an industry in the legal sector. Many organisations generate substantial profit through the collateral of these awards – dinners, advertising, and the sale of trophies or plaques are examples. Some awards are genuinely extremely prestigious. Winning them can demonstrably improve your reputation both externally and internally. However, for these to have any benefit in improving reputation, they have to be credible. On occasions, we have seen awards being received from publications we have not even been aware of and for awards categories we have certainly not entered! Some awards panels appear to have a real understanding of the category and their awards are genuinely based on merit. In others, being cynical, there can be a sense of giving every firm a turn of winning.

A lot more benefit will be generated if awards can consistently be won in a particular category, demonstrating that the firm has genuine specialist or sectoral expertise. Winning awards in random categories is less likely to add to the firm's reputation.

In entering for legal awards, it is important therefore to ensure that the publication has credibility and that you are targeting areas that are relevant to the strategy of the firm. And an award is only as good as those you compete with.

### 5.5 CSR programme

Increasingly, building a relationship with the community at large is an important part of a firm's reputation. Our clients see corporate responsibility as an important facet of their business and expect professional service firms to adopt a similar approach. Engaging with the community demonstrates that a firm, more than being simply a business looking at its bottom line, has a sense of depth and commitment. It is also a good way of developing a sense of pride within a firm which can be translated into staff advocacy.

Building relationships with the community at large can be achieved with a CSR policy. The firm must identify projects which are perceived as relevant and worthwhile. Fundraising is not of itself CSR. In addition, the impact on reputation is likely to be deeper and spread more widely if it involves a larger number of the team rather than focusing on an individual or a small group.

5.6    **Staff and client advocacy**

The reputation of a law firm is much more likely to be broadcast effectively by those who have a real engagement with it.

Obviously the client experience is one that is likely to have a major impact. If a client indicates that they have worked with a law firm and have had a positive (or negative) experience, that is likely to have a considerable effect on a firm's reputation. No matter how strong its brand is, how many awards have been won and the view of the media, the comments of clients will materially benefit or detract from the reputation of a firm. If clients have enjoyed the experience and are actually prepared to advocate the firm to their peers, this can have significant positive impact on the firm's reputation.

Similarly, team members will have an intimate understanding of the firm. They will know its technical strengths and weaknesses. They will be aware of whether it is well run or not and if it is a good place to work.

With social media, views can be expressed by the team members constantly. Their comments will aid or detract from the firm's reputation in recruiting and retraining team members. Staff advocacy is accordingly an important element in developing reputation.

In order to develop staff advocacy, it is important to have clear internal communications and transparency. One must continually engage with the team, keeping them up to date with the firm's strategy and its performance. It is important that team members learn about developments internally and not second-hand or from external sources.

All too often, one sees a reputation being built by a firm, only to be diluted or damaged by adverse client or staff comment.

6.    **Reputational crises**

Unfortunately, the unexpected sometimes comes from left field. Events such as negligence claims, client dissatisfaction, partner behaviour, accident or poor financial performance are all examples of the problems that a law firm can experience.

Each one can have a negative impact on the reputation of a firm.

Episodes which relate to the ethics and integrity of a firm will be the most damaging. As noted above, Arthur Andersen's involvement in the Enron scandal serves to illustrate how catastrophic a challenge that relates to the fundamentals of a professional service firm can be.

At some stage, all law firms will face challenges of some sort which will have the potential to affect their reputation. For those who handle such challenges badly, the effects can be lasting and will be very difficult to recover from. For those that deal with the challenges effectively and openly, there can sometimes be the potential to turn badwill into goodwill.

If an event occurs that is likely to impact on the firm's reputation, it must be treated as being serious and it must be confronted immediately. Forming a crisis team can be a good idea. This should involve those who are not directly affected and who can provide some objectivity. The firm should involve its internal communications team and preferably also external advisors.

Identifying a strategy at the outset is crucial. What is it that you wish to achieve? Only once you have identified what your objective is can you start to develop the methodology for dealing with a reputational crisis.

It is always better to confront situations. If you try to obfuscate, this will inevitably be picked up.

Often the event may relate to an individual within a law firm. Distancing the firm from the individual can create an impression that the firm is not joined up or collegiate. On the other hand, being supportive can demonstrate that the firm does actually live its values.

Generally speaking, it is better to deal with all the issues at the outset. This can be less damaging reputationally than a drip feed of bad news.

It is also important that the firm should speak with one voice. The spokesperson should be someone who has credibility with the media, having built up a relationship over a period of time rather than being a face that is just parachuted in to deal with the crisis.

It should go without saying that more will be achieved by being honest rather than putting a spin on the facts. For example, if a firm is imposing redundancies, it is better to explain why than to suggest that in some way it represents part of a positive strategic move.

It is essential to be serious when speaking to the media; trying to be flippant will backfire. Always be humble and respectful. If possible, it is good to be able to present a solution that will resolve the problem, or to project when there is likely to be a positive outcome.

When law firms do not deal with reputational crises effectively, the effects can be devastating. If, on the other hand, you confront the issues and demonstrate that the firm is sufficiently robust and sensitive to deal with these issues, it is possible to secure empathy and in some cases admiration from your stakeholders.

## 7. Conclusion

Frank Zappa said "In a fight between yourself and the world, always side with the world." What the world thinks of a law firm is what signifies reputation. That will always be more important than what we think of ourselves.

# About the authors

**Mats Anderson**

Senior counsel, Linklaters

Chief executive officer, clear blue water

mats.anderson@linklaters.com

mats.anderson@clearbluewater.se

Mats Anderson is a senior counsel and head of Linklaters Nordic tax team. He also runs the consultancy, clear blue water AB, which focuses on the strategic development of larger law firms in the Nordic Region, continental Europe and the United Kingdom.

Mr Anderson had his initial management-to-change experiences in the mid-1990s in his then Swedish law firm. Since then, he has been involved as a partner in relevant firms or as a consultant in a number of projects, such as mergers, the opening up of greenfield offices in new markets and general strategy projects.

Mr Anderson started with Swedish law firm Lagerlöf & Leman in 1991. This firm merged with the international firm Linklaters in 2001, in which Mr Anderson was a partner to 2007 when he left to start his consultancy. Today he divides his time between Linklaters and clear blue water.

**Ashley Balls**

Principal, LegalBestPractice

co-jones.pmf@clear.net.nz

Ashley Balls was a founding director of a UK-based international consulting business. He specialises in optimising performance in legal practices and corporate legal departments working for clients in the United Kingdom, the European Union, Southeast Asia and Australasia. He is currently principal of LBP Ltd (LegalBestPractice), an international business well known for facilitating partnership disputes, carrying out market analysis, developing business strategies, re-structuring remuneration and reward systems, improving working capital controls, mergers and acquisitions, re-structuring partnerships and partnership constitutions and introducing disruptive technologies and systems.

A non-practising lawyer and statistician, Mr Balls is passionate about modernising legal services delivery. He is widely published, having written *Law Firms – Managing for Profit* (Federation Press, Sydney), co-authored the *Business of Law* (Thomson Reuters, Wellington) and written numerous articles for journals in England, Australia, Hong Kong and New Zealand. He is a founding member of the Law Management Group, which is affiliated to the Law Consultancy Network.

**David Barnard**

Partner, Blaqwell

david.barnard@blaqwell.com

Blaqwell's founding partner David Barnard advises leading law firms across the globe including many of the largest US, Canadian, and international law firms – leveraging his more than 10 years in legal consulting and his more than 20 years as a leader and partner at Linklaters.

At Blaqwell Mr Barnard focuses on law firm strategy, structure and operations. He has also advised on some of the largest recent law firm mergers.

Mr Barnard is an experienced former managing partner and international attorney, having led Linklaters' North American operations for 15 years and worked in the areas of corporate law and international finance. He was one of the co-founders of Linklaters' international finance practice and has worked on financial transactions around the world. He is a frequent speaker on the evolution of the legal industry and for 10 years was a lecturer at Columbia Law School, where he taught "The Anatomy of Large Law Firms".

**Robert C Bata**

Principal, WarwickPlace Legal, LLC
rbata@warwickplace.com

Robert C Bata is the founder and principal of WarwickPlace Legal, LLC, a law firm management consultancy. A prominent international M&A lawyer, he has been the managing partner of the international offices and regional practices of several major US and UK law firms throughout Central and Eastern Europe and China, and in London.

WarwickPlace Legal is exclusively focused on providing international strategic advice, and its clientele are law firms based in, or seeking to establish a presence in, the United States, the United Kingdom, Eastern and Southeastern Europe, Asia, Latin America and Northern Africa. Mr Bata is development officer for the Senior Lawyers Committee of the International Bar Association and is a member of the International Legal Practice Committee of the Association of the Bar of the City of New York. He is a graduate of Yale University (BA in Russian and East European Studies) and the University of Texas School of Law.

**Máximo Bomchil**

Senior partner, M & M Bomchil
maximo.bomchil@bomchil.com

Máximo Bomchil is a senior partner in M & M Bomchil in Buenos Aires, Argentina. He was formerly head of the firm's tax department and is presently a member of the corporate and M&A departments.

He has represented clients in large M&A and privatisation transactions, particularly in the telecommunications, power generation, water and sewage and airports management sectors.

He is a board member of important commercial, industrial and utility companies in Argentina, co-chair of the Law Firm Management Committee of the International Bar Association, member of the International Court of Arbitration of the International Chamber of Commerce and president of the Alliance Française of Buenos Aires.

Mr Bomchil holds law degrees from the Catholic University of Buenos Aires, the Ludwig Maximilian University of Munich, and University College London.

**E Leigh Dance**

President, ELD International LLC
eldance@eldinternational.com

E Leigh Dance helps law firms execute strategies for business development in over 30 countries on all continents. She has helped firms such as Eversheds win Tyco's legal work across 37 jurisdictions. ELD is a legal services management consultancy based in New York and Brussels.

Ms Dance's global network of in-house and external lawyers gives her a rare perspective. She works with many large global legal services buyers and advises their corporate legal teams on panel competitions, law firm management, alternative sourcing, emerging markets and compliance. She also leads the Global Counsel Leaders Circle.

In March 2013, the *Value Challenge in Europe* guide she compiled for ACC was published. Ms Dance's articles on legal issues facing corporate leaders can be found in leading business and legal media. Her acclaimed book *Bright Ideas: Insights from Legal Luminaries Worldwide* presents 26 essays by legal industry leaders.

**Richard Given**
Deputy general counsel and head of legal, HSBC
richard.given@hsbc.com

Richard Given is deputy general counsel and head of legal for the operations of HSBC worldwide, overseeing legal support for the critical infrastructure of all the global businesses. Previously, he was director of legal at Cisco managing the legal team across Latin America, Europe, Middle East and Africa, and Russia.

Mr Given drives effective and timely decision making as a key business partner. He is a natural disrupter, regularly re-working the provision of legal services, challenging pre-conceptions and constantly striving to find better ways to use technology and drive operational excellence.

Mr Given is an alumnus of Freshfields and Cambridge University.

**Dina Gracheva**
Marketing leader, Russia and Central Europe/North, Dow Chemical
dina.gracheva@mba2012.imd.ch

Dina Gracheva is a business development and strategy professional in the legal industry. She has extensive experience in emerging markets and has managed marketing and business development for a leading Russian law firm. She currently specialises in innovation and strategy researches for the legal arena.

Ms Gracheva holds degrees in law and marketing, and an MBA from Switzerland's IMD business school.

**Will Harvey**
University of Exeter Business School;
Centre for Corporate Reputation,
Saïd Business School, University of Oxford
william.harvey@exeter.ac.uk

Will Harvey is a senior lecturer at the University of Exeter Business School and an associate fellow in the Centre for Corporate Reputation at the Said

Business School, University of Oxford. He received his PhD from the University of Cambridge, where he was a millennium scholar. His current work focuses on how companies can build, sustain and rehabilitate their reputations and leadership among different stakeholders, with a particular focus on professional service firms. He has also conducted extensive work on the movement and economic impact of foreign talent in the United States, Canada, Australia and the United Kingdom.

Dr Harvey has published in the fields of business and management, sociology, industrial relations and geography, and has also conducted research, case studies and consultancy work for Rio Tinto in Madagascar, Mercer in the United States, Eni in the Republic of Congo and China Radio International and the Shanghai Government in China.

**Miriam Herman**
Partner, Blaqwell
miriam.herman@blaqwell.com

Blaqwell partner Miriam Herman has been advising leading US law firms and general counsel since the 1990s when she founded McKinsey & Company's law firm practice. A graduate of Yale Law School and business consultant for 20 years, she brings a deep understanding of best practices in the professional service and the corporate sectors and a highly analytical approach to her engagements which span issues of strategy, mergers, talent, governance, and profitability improvement.

Ms Herman joined Blaqwell in 2003. Based in Washington, DC, she has counselled a broad range of national, international, and global law firms. Prior to joining Blaqwell, Ms Herman was an associate principal at McKinsey & Company, where she worked from 1994 to 2003, leading consulting engagements in the professional service, consumer, health care, financial, and government sectors.

Ms Herman received her JD from the Yale Law School (1993), where she received the John Fletcher Caskey Prize.

## Silvia Hodges Silverstein

Lecturer in law at Columbia Law School
Adjunct professor at Fordham Law School
Director of research services of TyMetrix Legal
Analytics
hodges@silviahodges.com

Silvia Hodges Silverstein helps law firms and legal departments become more efficient and effective. She focuses on client purchasing decisions, in particular the influence of procurement on the purchasing of legal services. She is also a lecturer in law at Columbia Law School, as well as an adjunct professor at Fordham Law School in New York, where she pioneered courses in law firm management and law firm marketing.

Dr Hodges Silverstein co-authored the Harvard Business School case *GlaxoSmithKline: Sourcing Complex Professional Services* on legal services procurement with Professor Heidi Gardner of Harvard Business School and is the author of *Buying Legal: Procurement Insights and Practice and Winning Legal Business from Medium-Sized Companies*. Her book *Legal Spend Management* will be published shortly. She regularly researches, speaks and publishes internationally.

She earned her PhD at Nottingham Law School. She also holds a master's degree in business from Universität Bayreuth and Warwick Business School, and an undergraduate degree in economics.

## Mark Jones

Partner, Addleshaw Goddard LLP
mark.jones@addleshawgoddard.com

Mark Jones is the leader of Addleshaw Goddard's innovative professional practices consultancy and advises on strategy, management and organisational development work for professional services firms. Prior to launching the consultancy in 2009, Mr Jones was, for 17 years, the managing partner of the firm and was the longest serving managing partner of any top 20 UK law firm.

In over 20 years of involvement in professional services firm leadership and management, Mr Jones has dealt extensively with strategic and business planning, mergers, acquisitions, performance management, change management, the entire spectrum of partnership issues and the development and operation of a large professional practice in a continually changing business environment.

## Peter Kurer

Partner, BLR & Partners AG
peter@kurer.com

Peter Kurer is a former business executive and lawyer. He now works as a partner of the private equity firm BLR & Partners AG and as an independent advisor. He is also a non-executive member of the steering committee of Schönherr, a leading Central European law firm.

Mr Kurer has obtained law degrees from the University of Zurich and the University of Chicago. He was a law clerk at the Zurich District Court (1977 to 1979), a lawyer with Baker & McKenzie (1980 to 1990) and a partner of the Zurich law firm Homburger (1991 to 2001). He specialised in M&A and corporate law and also served on a number of boards of public and private companies. In 2001, Mr Kurer joined UBS as its general counsel and member of the group executive board. As from April 2008, he has served as chairman of UBS for a one-year term.

Mr Kurer has regularly published articles on M&A topics, corporate governance issues, financial regulation and legal management.

## Paul Lippe

Chief executive officer, OnRamp Systems
paullippe@legalonramp.com

Paul Lippe is chief executive officer of OnRamp Systems, the leader in legal department operational platforms to improve quality and efficiency and reduce costs of legal work. Legal OnRamp was first developed at a legal department productivity and collaboration platform for Cisco Systems.

Mr Lippe was at various times general counsel and senior vice president, business development and corporate marketing at Synopsys, an electronic design automation company. He was also chief executive officer of Stanford SKOLAR, a medical digital library and e-learning company sponsored by Stanford Medical School.

A graduate of Yale College and Harvard Law School, Mr Lippe speaks and writes regularly about the 'new normal' in law, including at the *ABA Journal* (www.abajournal.com/legalrebels/new_normal/).

## Bente R Løwendahl

Professor, BI Norwegian Business School
bente.lowendahl@bi.no

Bente R Løwendahl is professor of strategic management at BI Norwegian Business School, Department of Strategy and Logistics. Her research interests are the strategic management of knowledge-intensive firms, with a particular focus on professional service firms (PSFs). Her book *Strategic Management of Professional Service Firms* (1997, third edition, CBS Press, 2005) is widely cited by researchers as well as practitioners in this field. Her research has also appeared in academic journals such as *Strategic Management Journal, Human Relations, Organisation Studies, Scandinavian Journal of Management*, and *California Management Review*. She has also contributed to a number of books, including, but not limited to, a Norwegian textbook on strategy for Bachelor-level students (third edition, Cappelen Damm, 2010) and the recent *Handbook of Research on Entrepreneurship in Professional Services*, edited by Markus Reihlen and Andreas Werr (E Elgar, 2012).

Ms Løwendahl holds degrees in economics and business administration (MSc), as well as strategy/applied economics (PhD – The Wharton School, University of Pennsylvania).

## Jaime Fernández Madero

Founder, Fernández Madero Consulting
jfm@fmaderoconsulting.com

Jaime Fernández Madero is a lawyer and consultant in strategy and management of professional service firms. He was a founder of Bruchou, Fernández Madero & Lombardi, an Argentine law firm, and acted as its managing partner for 10 years until 2009, when he left the firm to concentrate full-time in the field of management of professional service firms.

He founded Fernández Madero Consulting (FMC), a strategy and management consultancy firm focusing on law firms and legal departments in Latin America (www.fmaderoconsulting.com). FMC is associated with Hildebrandt Consulting.

Mr Fernández Madero has a master's in organisational studies (2011) from the Universidad de San Andrés (Argentina). He has written a thesis entitled "Identification Process in Professional Service Firms" and a book, *Organising Professional Service Firms. The Case of the Lawyers*, published by Thomson Reuters La Ley (2011). He has a master's in comparative law from Southern Methodist University, Dallas, Texas (1982).

## Patrick J McKenna

Principal, McKenna & Associates Inc
patrick@patrickmckenna.com

For more than 30 years, Patrick McKenna has constructed and designed competitive strategies for law firm transformation and growth. He has worked with at least one of the top 10 largest law firms in each of over a dozen different countries.

Mr McKenna is widely credited with being one of the profession's foremost authorities on practice group leadership and the author or co-author of seven books including international business bestseller *First Among Equals: How To Manage A Group of Professionals* with David Maister (Free Press) and *Serving At The Pleasure of My Partners* (Thomson Reuters). He co-leads *First 100 Days: MasterClass For The New Firm Leader*, an annual programme held at the University of Chicago.

Mr McKenna's expertise was acknowledged when he was identified by Lawdragon as one of "the most trusted names in legal consulting" and he is the subject of a Harvard Law case study entitled "Innovations in Legal Consulting" (2011).

### Rob Millard

Partner, Venturis Consulting Group LLP

rob.millard@venturisconsulting.com

Rob Millard has practised as a law firm strategy consultant since 2001. Prior to co-founding Venturis Consulting Group, he was senior strategy manager at Linklaters. He holds an MBA degree from Henley. In 1998, he was among the first participants in Harvard Business School's 'Leadership in Professional Service Firms' programme.

Mr Millard has two specialisations. He advises global and regional firms on entry and growth strategies in emerging markets (especially in Africa) and he advises law firms on developing systems and structures to develop better strategies and execute more successfully. Mr Millard's other experience ranges from developing partner compensation systems to advising on a major transatlantic law firm merger to strategic reviews to facilitating strategy retreats.

Mr Millard serves on the IBA Law Firm Management Committee's advisory board. He previously served on the committee of the Law Practice Management Section of the American Bar Association.

### Tim Morris

Centre for Corporate Reputation,
Saïd Business School, University of Oxford

tim.morris@sbs.ox.ac.uk

Timothy Morris was appointed professor of management studies at the University of Oxford in 2002. After graduating from Cambridge University, he studied for a master's degree and doctorate from the London School of Economics.

Professor Morris regularly engages with practitioner audiences through his consulting work, executive education and writing. His recent practitioner-oriented work has been concerned with three themes: leadership issues, particularly the challenges of strategic decision-making and change; innovation capacity and new career models in professional service firms; and the development of models of competitive strategy relevant to knowledge-based organisations. Professor Morris's research interests include the nature and patterns of change and processes of innovation in organisations of professionals where he has studied firms in a range of sectors including law, architecture, executive search, accounting and management consulting. His publications include several books, contributions to numerous edited collections and papers in leading US and European management journals.

### Peter Oberlechner

Partner, Wolf Theiss

peter.oberlechner@wolftheiss.com

Peter Oberlechner is partner and head of real estate and construction at Wolf Theiss, the largest Austrian law firm, and a leading law firm in the Central Eastern Europe/Southeast Europe region with offices in 15 countries. Mr Oberlechner is consistently ranked as one of the leading lawyers in Austria and in the CEE/SEE region, and is regularly involved in large-scale developments and transactions. Mr Oberlechner has served in the firm's partner evaluation committee for more than 10 years, and has significantly contributed to the firm's system of partner evaluation.

Prior to joining Wolf Theiss, Mr Oberlechner worked with the corporate international department of the New York firm Curtis, Mallet-Prevost, Colt & Mosle. He is the co-chair of the European chapter of the Chicago-based Counselors of Real Estate, an association of elite real estate advisors, and member of the Royal Institute of Chartered Surveyors. In addition to Austrian law degrees, Mr Oberlechner holds an LLM degree from the London School of Economics and Political Science. He is admitted to the Austrian bar, and to the Czech bar as an international attorney.

**Irina Paliashvili**
Managing partner, RULG-Ukrainian Legal Group, PA
Founder and co-chair of the CIS Local Counsel Forum
irinap@rulg.com

Irina Paliashvili began her private practice in 1992 by founding one of the first private law firms in Kiev. In 1995, she founded the Washington-based RULG-Ukrainian Legal Group, PA, where she is the managing partner.

Dr Paliashvili frequently speaks at international conferences and publishes on the legal and business climates in Ukraine and other countries of the CIS economic region. She is the founder and co-chair of the CIS Local Counsel Forum, the informal network of managing and senior partners of leading business law firms from the CIS economic region.

Dr Paliashvili graduated with high honours from the Kiev State University School of International Law and received a PhD in private international law from the same school. She also holds an LLM in international and comparative law from George Washington University.

**Philip Rodney**
Chairman, Burness Paull
Philip.Rodney@burnesspaull.com

Philip Rodney is a partner in the dispute resolution team at Burness Paull and was appointed chairman of the firm in 2005.

He was responsible for developing the strategy of the firm, including its merger in December 2012 with Paull & Williamsons when he became chairman of the merged firm.

He has written and spoken extensively on law firm management.

**Michael Smets**
Novak Druce Centre for Professional Service Firms, Saïd Business School, University of Oxford
michael.smets@sbs.ox.ac.uk

Michael Smets is a university lecturer in management and organisation studies at Saïd Business School, Oxford, where he is also a fellow of the Novak Druce Centre for Professional Service Firms. His research focuses on the management of professional services in general and of global law firms in particular. His recent work in the legal sector examined internationalisation and inter-professional collaboration, changing career structures and capacity for innovation, as well as reputation management. His work has been published in high-profile academic journals, such as the *Academy of Management Journal, Human Relations* and the *International Journal of Human Resource Management*, as well as in various handbooks on the management of professional services.

**Lisa R Smith**
Principal, Fairfax Associates
Lisa.smith@fairfaxassociates.com

Lisa Smith is based in Washington, DC and consults to leading professional firms worldwide. She focuses on advising law firms on strategy development, mergers, management and governance, partner issues and financial and operational performance and management.

Prior to establishing Fairfax in the United States, Ms Smith was head of the law firm strategy and structure practice group and founded the Washington office of Hildebrandt Baker Robbins (a subsidiary of Thomson Reuters). Before joining Hildebrandt, she was a consultant in Price Waterhouse's Law Firm Services Group.

Ms Smith has written white papers, articles and blogs on the strategic and management issues facing law firms. In addition to this chapter on merger, she has also co-authored *Anatomy of a Law Firm Merger* (2004) published by the American Bar Association.

Ms Smith holds an MBA from Dartmouth College and a BA from Carleton College.

**Christoph H Vaagt**
Managing partner, Law Firm Change Consultants
chv@vaagtundpartner.de

Chris Vaagt has specialised in consulting to law firms, after working as a strategy consultant in general industry and then as a lawyer in Munich.

Having worked with leading UK and US law firm consultants, he has acquired detailed knowledge of management styles and law firm strategies in different markets. Since 2005, he has been working for leading mainland European law firms, advising in the area of strategy and organisational development in order to help them become sustainable businesses.

In particular, he focuses on changes of behaviour and cultures so that law firms can align to their strategies. He is a specialist in law firm strategy processes which include deep changes in the governance of law firms. This is particularly important for nationally independent law firms trying to cope with increasing competition from international firms.

He is also the author of the only publication in the law firm industry worldwide benchmarking the leading firms of a jurisdiction (Germany). He is a frequent speaker for the International Bar Association, he was chairman for nine years of the law firm management section of the German Bar Association, and speaks and publishes widely.

Mr Vaagt holds a degree in law from Munich University.

**Tomasz Wardyński CBE**
Partner, Wardyński & Partners
tomasz.wardynski@wardynski.com.pl

Tomasz Wardyński is a founding partner of Wardyński & Partners, an independent Polish law firm operating since 1988. He specialises in arbitration and is also an expert in civil, commercial and competition law with widely recognised experience in negotiations on large public projects. He was one of the first lawyers in Poland to develop specialisations in EU and competition law.

Mr Wardyński is a graduate of the Law Faculty at the University of Warsaw and the College of Europe, Bruges. He was a visiting scholar at the American Bar Foundation (1985). From 1991 to 1996, he was a member of the Advisory Council on Privatisation to the prime minister of Poland. He is an honorary legal adviser to Her Britannic Majesty's Ambassador in Poland. He is the author of numerous articles in the field of arbitration and co-author of *Competition Law* published by Lexis Nexis in 2012.

Globe Law
and Business

# Also in this series

for further details and a free sample chapter go to
**www.globelawandbusiness.com**